W9-CIG-572

Gramley Library
Salem College
Winston-Salem, NC 27108

SILENCE

IN THE NOVELS OF

ELIE WIESEL

SILENCE
IN THE NOVELS OF
ELIE WIESEL

■

Simon P. Sibelman

WITHDRAWN

St. Martin's Press
New York

Gramley Library
Salem College
Winston-Salem, NC 27108

© Simon P. Sibelman 1995

All rights reserved. For information, write:

Scholarly and Reference Division,
St. Martin's Press, Inc., 175 Fifth Avenue,
New York, N.Y. 10010

First published in the United States of America in 1995

Printed in the United States of America

ISBN 0-312-12214-4

Library of Congress Cataloging-in-Publication Data

Sibelman, Simon P.
    Silence in the novels of Elie Wiesel / Simon P. Sibelman.
        p.   cm.
    Includes bibliographical references and index.
    ISBN 0-312-12214-4
    1. Wiesel, Elie, 1928-   —Criticism and interpretation.
    2. Holocaust, Jewish (1939-1945) in literature. 3. Silence in
    literature. 4. Jews in literature.   I. Title.
    PQ2683.I32z874 1995
    843'.914—dc20   94-27525
                                               CIP

Interior design by Digital Type & Design

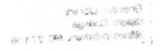

CREDITS

I wish to acknowledge with deep thanks the invaluable assistance offered by Elie Wiesel and his literary agent, The George Borchardt Agency, Inc. of New York in securing the various permissions required to reprint from original materials.

For permission to reprint from textual materials, I acknowledge gratefully:

A Beggar in Jerusalem by Elie Wiesel, © 1973 by Elie Wiesel. Reprinted by permission of Schocken Books, published by Pantheon Books, a division of Random House, Inc.

The Fifth Son by Elie Wiesel, © 1986 by Elirion Associates, Inc. Reprinted by permission of Summit Books, a division of Paramount Publishing.

Five Biblical Portraits by Elie Wiesel, © 1981 by Elie Wiesel. Reprinted by permission of the University of Notre-Dame Press.

The Forgotten by Elie Wiesel, © 1992 by Elirion Associates, Inc. Reprinted by permission of Summit Books, a division of Paramount Publishing.

From the Kingdom of Memory: Reminiscences by Elie Wiesel, © 1991 by Elirion Associates, Inc. Reprinted by permissions of Summit Books, a division of Paramount Publishing.

The Gates of the Forest by Elie Wiesel, © 1966 by Holt, Rinehart and Winston, Inc. and re-published in 1982 by Schocken Books, distributed by Pantheon Books, a division of Random House. Reprinted here by permission of Henry Holt and Company.

A Jew Today by Elie Wiesel, © 1978 by Elirion Associates, Inc. Reprinted by permission of Random House, Inc.

Legends of Our Time by Elie Wiesel, © 1968 by Elie Wiesel. Reprinted by permission of Henry Holt and Company.

Messengers of God by Elie Wiesel, © 1976 by Elirion Associates, Inc. Reprinted by permission of Summit Books, a division of Paramount Publishing.

The Night Trilogy: Night, Dawn, The Accident by Elie Wiesel, © 1985 by Elie Wiesel. Reprinted with permission of Hill and Wang, a division of Farrar, Straus & Giroux, Inc.

The Oath by Elie Wiesel, © 1973 by Elie Wiesel. Reprinted by permission of Schocken Books, published by Pantheon Books, a division of Random House, Inc.

One Generation After by Elie Wiesel, © 1970 by Elie Wiesel. Reprinted by permission of Random House, Inc.

Sages and Dreamers by Elie Wiesel, © 1991 by Elirion Associates, Inc. Reprinted by permission of Summit Books, a division of Paramount Publishing.

Souls on Fire by Elie Wiesel, © 1972 by Elie Wiesel. Reprinted by permission of Simon & Schuster, a division of Paramount Publishing.

Somewhere A Master by Elie Wiesel, © 1982 by Elirion Associates, Inc. Reprinted by permission of Summit Books, a division of Paramount Publishing.

The Testament by Elie Wiesel, © 1981 by Elirion Associates, Inc. Reprinted by permission of Summit Books, a division of Paramount Publishing.

The Town Beyond the Wall by Elie Wiesel, © 1964 by Elie Wiesel. Reprinted by permission Henry Holt and Company.

Twilight by Elie Wiesel, © by Elirion Associates, Inc. Reprinted by permission of Summit Books, a division of Paramount Publishing.

Special thanks is also expressed to Marcie Bates of University of Notre-Dame Press, Michelle Dennehy of Farrar, Straus & Giroux, Elizabeth Lipp of Pantheon Books and Kevin J. Sullivan of Paramount Publishing, as well as to Jennifer Farthing, my editor at St. Martin's Press.

I *dedicate this work to my parents*

ROSE AND MORRIS SIBELMAN
of blessed memory

*for the love, truth, and faith they
instilled in me*

*and
to my godson*

HYMIE GENDERSON

for his commitment to our future.

CONTENTS

Note to Readers ix

List of Abbreviations xi

Acknowledgments xiii

Introduction 1

CHAPTER 1: Silence: Definitions and Degrees 9

CHAPTER 2: Victims to Victors: The Trilogy 31

CHAPTER 3: Images of *Teshuva:* The Beginning of the Return 59

CHAPTER 4: The Dialogue of Peniel 85

CHAPTER 5: The Mystical Union 103

CHAPTER 6: Apocalypse and Life 117

CHAPTER 7: The Mute Son, The Missing One 133

CHAPTER 8: Madness and Memory 153

CHAPTER 9: Conclusion 173

Appendices 177

Notes 185

Bibliography 193

Index 199

A time for silence and a time for speaking.

— Ecclesiastes 3:7

*Son of Man, keep not silent, forget not the deeds of Tyranny,
Cry out at the disaster of a people.*

— Yehuda L. Bialer

*Ça va être moi, ca va être le silence, là où je suis, je ne sais
pas, je ne saurai jamais, dans le silence on ne sait pas, il
faut continuer, je ne peux pas continuer, je vais continuer.*

— Samuel Beckett

*He may well slay me; I may have no hope;
Yet will I argue my case before Him.*

— Job 13:15

NOTE TO READERS

Language and silence stand as paradoxical partners in the creation of a text. As such, any consideration of silence as a literary tool or theme must likewise examine language and the means by which silence is elicited on the printed page. This fundamental reality poses obstacles enough without the compounded burden of dealing with translation. Each language possesses unique linguistic characteristics, subtleties, rhythms—*la petite musique,* according to Céline. Such elements elude even the best translators. Translation can inevitably impoverish a text and deaden the original intent and impact of silence as a literary tool.

Translation stands as a formidable impediment when analyzing the oeuvre of Elie Wiesel. Like Samuel Beckett, Wiesel is a polyglot whose chosen means of literary expression is the French language. Although most of his works have been rendered admirably into English (the vast majority translated by his wife, Marion), they still lose something of their distinction in translation. Wiesel's poetic power lies in the unusual blend of traditional Eastern European Jewish storytelling and Hasidic* mysticism with the severity and disciplined purity of the French language.

This study seeks to view Wiesel's work and the theme of silence in his novels within the context of the French language and its literary traditions. The analysis, while based on examinations of the primary texts, has been conceived in English in order to reach a wider audience of Wiesel scholars and admirers for whom the French texts may remain closed. As such, I shall cite from the published French editions of Wiesel's novels, following all such quotes with the accepted English translation. Several quotations from the original French texts have been rendered in my own English translations.

Finally, owing to the nature of Wiesel's oeuvre, numerous quotations from biblical, talmudic, rabbinic and cabalistic sources appear in this study. All citations will be made in English, taken from the Soncino Press series of Jewish holy texts. It should be noted that talmudic and cabalistic commentary make reference by citing argument portions, such as *Ta'anit 14b*. This form of notation has been retained throughout.

---

* Hasidism: based upon the Hebrew word *hesed,* meaning *pious,* the term today refers to that mystical movement born in eighteenth-century Eastern Europe, founded by Israel Baal Shem Tov. Its principle innovation resided in its injunction to its adherents (Hasidim) to enter into full communion with God in joy and ecstasy by means of song, dance, and prayer.

In referring to prayers from the Jewish liturgy, I have used the English translations in the following editions:

> *The Authorized Prayer Book*. Edited and translated by Rev. S. Singer. London: Eyre and Spottiswoode, 1962.
>
> *High Holiday Prayer Book*. Translated and annotated with an introduction by Philip Birnbaum. New York: The Hebrew Publishing Company, 1951.
>
> *Prayer Book for the Three Festivals: Pesach, Shavuoth, Sukkoth*. Translated and annotated with an introduction by Philip Birnbaum. New York: The Hebrew Publishing Company, 1971.

Any words or expressions not likely to be familiar to the reader will be marked with an asterisk and defined on the first appearance in the text.

It should also be mentioned that the reader will find variations in the transliterations of Hebrew and Yiddish words (e.g., cheder/heder). When quoting from other sources, I have retained their spellings.

Certain portions of this text have appeared in other forms in various periodicals. Portions of the Introduction were published as "Language and Silence: A Case for Elie Wiesel" in *The Jewish Quarterly* 33.4 (1986). Significant portions of Chapter Five have been printed under the title "The Mystical Union: A Re-examination of Elie Wiesel's *Le Mendiant de Jérusalem*" in *Literature and Theology* 7:2 (1993), while the central argument in Chapter Six appeared under the title "Tremendum to Apocalypse: An Examination of Elie Wiesel's *Le Serment de Kolvillàg*" in *Romance Studies* 10 (1987). Elements of Chapter Four were printed as "The Dialogue of Peniel: An Examination of Elie Wiesel's *Les Portes de la forêt* and Genesis 32:23-33" in *The French Review* 61 (1988). Finally, one significant portion of Chapter Seven has been published as "Phylacteries as Metaphor in Elie Wiesel's *Le Testament d'un poète juif assassiné*" in *Studies in Twentieth Century Literature* 18:2 (Summer 1994).

LIST OF ABBREVIATIONS

The following abbreviations are used to represent Elie Wiesel's work in this study.

AS   *Against the Silence: The Voice and Vision of Elie Wiesel*, three volumes. Selected and edited by Irving Abrahamson. New York: Holocaust Library, 1985.

BJ   *A Beggar in Jerusalem (Le Mendiant de Jérusalem)*. Translated by Lily Edelman and the author. New York: Random House, 1970.

CAL   *Le Crépuscule, au loin*. Paris: Bernard Grasset, 1987.

CB   *Célébration biblique: Portraits et légendes*. Paris: Editions du Seuil, 1975.

CF   *Le Cinquième fils*. Paris: Bernard Grasset, 1983.

CH   *Célébration hassidique: Portraits et légendes*. Paris: Editions du Seuil, 1972.

CM   *Le Chant des morts*. Paris: Editions du Seuil, 1966.

CM-CH   *Contre la mélancolie: Célébration hassidique, II*. Paris: Editions du Seuil, 1981.

CT   *Célébration talmudique: Portraits et légendes*. Paris: Editions du Seuil, 1991.

D   "The Holocaust as Literary Inspiration" in *Dimensions of the Holocaust: Lectures at Northwestern University*. Evanston, Illinois: Northwestern University Press, 1977.

EDS   *Entre deux soleils*. Paris: Editions du Seuil, 1970.

F   *The Forgotten (L'Oublié)*. Translated by Stephen Becker. New York: Summit, 1992.

FBP   *Five Biblical Portraits*. Notre Dame, Indiana: University of Notre Dame Press, 1981.

FS   *The Fifth Son (Le Cinquième fils)*. Translated by Marion Wiesel. London: Viking, 1986.

GF   *The Gates of the Forest (Les Portes de la forêt)*. Translated by Frances Frenaye. New York: Avon, 1967.

JT   *A Jew Today (Un Juif aujourd'hui)*. Translated by Marion Wiesel. New York: Random House, 1979.

K   *From the Kingdom of Memory: Reminiscences*. Various translators. New York: Summit, 1991.

LT   *Legends of Our Time (Le Chant des morts)*. Translated by Steven Donadio. New York: Schocken, 1982.

MG   *Messengers of God (Célébration biblique)*. Translated by Marion Wiesel. New York: Summit, 1976.

MJ   *Le Mendiant de Jérusalem*. Paris: Editions du Seuil, 1968.

N   *The Night Trilogy: Night, Dawn, the Accident (La Nuit, L'Aube, Le Jour)*. Translated by Stella Rodway, Frances Frenaye, and Anne Borchardt. New York: Hill and Wang, 1987.

NAJ   *La Nuit, L'Aube, Le Jour*. Paris: Editions du Seuil, 1969.

O   *The Oath* (*Le Serment de Kolvillàg*). Translated by Marion Wiesel. New York: Random House, 1973.

OGA   *One Generation After* (*Entre deux soleils*). Translated by Lily Edelman and the author. New York: Pocket Books, 1979.

OU   *L'Oublié*. Paris: Editions du Seuil, 1989.

PE   *Paroles d'étranger.* Paris: Editions du Seuil, 1982.

PF   *Les Portes de la forêt.* Paris: Editions du Seuil, 1964.

SD   *Sages and Dreamers* (Portions appeared in French as *Célébration Talmudique: Portraits et légendes*). Translated by Marion Wiesel. New York: Summit, 1991.

SE   *Signes d'exode.* Paris: Bernard Grasset, 1985.

SF   *Souls on Fire: Portraits and Legends* (*Célébration hassidique*). Translated by Marion Wiesel. New York: Random House, 1972.

SK   *Le Serment de Kolvillàg.* Paris: Editions du Seuil, 1973.

SM   *Somewhere A Master* (*Contre la mélancolie: Célébration hassidique, II*). Translated by Marion Wiesel. New York: Summit, 1982.

SMH   *Silences et mémoires d'hommes.* Paris: Editions du Seuil, 1989.

T   *The Testament* (*Le Testament d'un poète juif assassiné*). Translated by Marion Wiesel. New York: Summit, 1981.

TBW   *The Town Beyond the Wall* (*La Ville de la chance*). Translated by Stephen Becker. New York: Schocken, 1982.

TP   *Le Testament d'un poète juif assassiné.* Paris: Editions du Seuil, 1980.

TW   *Twilight* (*Le Crépuscule, au loin*). Translated by Marion Wiesel. New York: Summit, 1988.

UJA   *Un Juif aujourd'hui.* Paris: Editions du Seuil, 1978.

VC   *La Ville de la chance.* Paris: Editions du Seuil, 1962.

Full reference to all other writings by Wiesel will be made in the endnotes.

Acknowledgments

No academic endeavor comes into existence without the assistance and guidance of numerous hands serving as midwives. I have been fortunate to encounter many such people without whose help I could never have completed my research. To the staff of the King's College-London Library, the University of London Library, the Taylor Institution of Oxford University, the Library of the University of Cambridge, the British Library, London, the Bibliothèque Nationale, Paris, Le Centre de documentation juive contemporaine, Paris, les Editions du Seuil, Paris, les Editions Bernard Grasset, Paris, and the libraries of the Hebrew University of Jerusalem, I offer my appreciation for the assistance and tolerance shown to me. A special note of thankful recognition must also go to Miron Grindea, founder and editor of *ADAM,* to the Office of the Chief Rabbi of Great Britain, to the late Professor Philip Ouston of King's College-London, and to Hadassah Modlinger of Yad Vashem. My gratitude is also extended to Edward J. Hughes and Madelaine Renouard of Birkbeck College, University of London, for their keen interest and academic stimulation during the early stages of my work.

Scholarly research cannot progress without financial support. I have happily encountered individuals and institutions who found merit in my study and offered some of the necessary funding. To the late Montague Bloch and his wife, Ray Bloch, I express profound thanks for their years of support, encouragement and love. To my cousins Si and Rochelle Pollack, I can only offer my love for the comfort and shelter they have always provided to me in good times and bad. To Rabbi Charles Lipschitz and to Eve and Reuben Friedlander I offer my profound thanks for their belief in me when all avenues appeared closed. Special thanks must likewise be given to Eileen Walker and Peggy Crosland for their trust and assistance. I would likewise thank Mr. C. N. Nathan and the Anglo-Jewish Association for their philanthropy. Special thanks is reserved for the Central Research Committee of Senate House, University of London, for their very generous grant that enabled me to pursue research in Israel.

I would also like to thank Professors Carol Bedwell, Laurie Fitzgerald, Andrew O'Shaughnessy and William Urbrock for their assistance and suggestions in the final stages of the preparation of this manuscript. Thanks must also be given to Sean Kern for his tireless proof-reading and to Philip Wegner for his stylistic recommendations. I also wish to acknowledge the skillful wordprocessing skills of Mary Hepola.

A special loving token of thanks is due to two individuals who have served as mentors not only in my present pursuit, but also in my personal quest for knowledge and truth. First, to Isaac Waldman, himself a survivor, I offer my thanks and faithful devotion. Religious teacher and spiritual guide for more than a quarter of a century, he has made me aware of my role in the chain of tradition, for through him as well as through works of Elie Wiesel, I am inexorably linked to Zeide the Melamed. Second, to Professor Norma Rinsler I extend my humble thanks and profound admiration. Her firm methodical manner has not merely guided me through my research, but has also provided a living example of the humanist tradition functioning in a world bent on abandoning it.

And, to Elie Wiesel: for his words and silences.

SIMON P. SIBELMAN
Paris/Oshkosh
August 1994/Elul 5754

SILENCE
IN THE NOVELS OF
ELIE WIESEL

Introduction

> *A chaque effondrement des*
> *preuves le poète répond par*
> *une salve d'avenir.*
> R. CHAR

Catastrophe impresses us with man's relative insignificance before the uncaring potency of the cosmos. The myth of Orpheus and the biblical story of Lot's wife instruct us that humans are incapable of looking into the face of night, into the naked reality of catastrophe. Both stress humanity's impotence in gaining significant insight. Historical facts and figures cannot unveil the profundity concealed beneath the painful surface of tragedy. Catastrophe would therefore remain meaningless and menacingly silent without human efforts to impose meaning and order on chaos. Only then does humankind demonstrate its superiority over those human or natural forces that seek destruction.

In our century of tragedies, the Holocaust has provided us with perhaps its unique demanding challenge: To uncover significance in the inhuman carnage and in the reality of absolute evil. Since the liberation of the Nazi concentration camps, countless men and women have sought not simply to remember and implant those events in the common human consciousness, but likewise to evolve systems of thought that might conceivably assist us in comprehending the depth of the ontological significance of the *anus mundi*[*][1] and its implications for the future of humanity.

From the philosophical and pseudoscientific origins of the Hitlerian policies that resulted in the *Endlösung*[†], the Final Solution of the "Jewish problem" in Europe, rose another menacing shadow: silence. With reference to the *Endlösung* one can speak of the silence of God, the silence of mankind, and the very silence of the victims. In addition, silence became a tool expropriated by the Nazis themselves as evidenced in a speech delivered by Heinrich Himmler on October 4, 1943:

---

[*]*anus mundi:* a term whose usage was coined during the aftermath of the Second World War. It appears to have been in common usage among those soldiers who were stationed in the concentration camps, though its first "official" usage was at the time of the Nuremberg Trials. The obvious medieval shading of the term would seem intentional, as the concentration camp world approximated to the worst notions of hell.

[†]*Endlösung:* the German euphemism adopted with reference to the mass murders of the "Final Solution" to the Jewish Question in Europe.

Most of you know what it means to look at 100 corpses, 500 corpses, 1,000 corpses. Having borne that and nevertheless...having remained decent has hardened us. This is a glorious, *unwritten page of our history, one that will never be written.*[2] [my emphasis]

This imposed silence signified death and stands as an antithesis to the traditions of Judeo-Hellenic civilization. If the Holocaust were to teach anything, it would be that such an insidious use of silence can and must be combatted by the innate positive ontology that the phenomenon normally possesses. In order to confront this negative silence, to cause silence to reveal its hidden significance and thus enable it to speak for the survivors as well as the dead, it is imperative to effect a union between two divergent places on specific dates.

What power, what formidable events might link Sighet, Romania, September 30, 1928 to Berlin, Germany, May 10, 1933? The first event: Simchat Torah, the Jewish festival of rejoicing in the Torah, a celebration of the gift of the Word. The second, the "Burning of the Books" by the National Socialists, a ritual marking the abolition of the Word. These two events stand in frightening opposition to one another, an absolute antithesis that threatens the very foundations of occidental civilization. How can these two dates and venues appearing so paradoxically oxymoronic be coupled in some freakishly unharmonious union? How might they produce a glimmer of hope out of the ashes of the Holocaust? The bond uncomfortably joining them is Elie Wiesel. He has been referred to as "the poet of the Holocaust," "the voice of contemporary Jewry," and "an eloquent spokesman for humanity." All these appellations are apt. Yet I believe he represents more.

Elie Wiesel is a modern day *navi,* a prophet. I do not mean to suggest he offers humanity prophecies that serve as windows to the future. He is a *navi* in the true sense of its meaning: Someone who forcefully speaks out in an attempt to move others to review the course of life, to probe deeply into the consciousness in an attempt to redefine the human condition, and to pursue some method for rendering the human experience more godly. As such, Wiesel represents a continuation of the Jewish prophetic tradition. His voice cries aloud from the wilderness created by the Holocaust to all humanity, imploring us to become more cognizant of the past before humanity's future is forfeit. One of the intentions of this study, therefore, will be to clarify—even marginally—this message.

Born on September 30, 1928, Wiesel eventually suffered the full destructive power that was unleashed by the Nazis in that spring of 1933. Wiesel becomes our bridge to that annihilated past, a voice for the silenced millions and a spokesman for the evolution of the human condition. He has sought and still strives to put the bloodied and burnt fragments of the past together.

The life Wiesel had known, life as perceived and conceived in the warmth of the shtetl*, was cruelly and tragically wrenched from him. All notions of the purely human or divine were cast into the void of Auschwitz. Wiesel's entire opus to date represents a lengthy attempt to resurrect both the Jewishness and the humanism which perished in the muck and flames of the *anus mundi* and to reconcile the eternal truths of the universe with the banality of evil. His work exemplifies the tension between the Word and the Nazi initiative to eradicate and prostitute it, between the silence of the "Kingdom of Night" and the painful need to bear witness to that depravity. This is the delicate point on which Wiesel's literary opus balances.

Wiesel emerged from the world of Eastern European Ashkenazic Jewry, the world of the shtetl, one of several continuations of the ancient traditions of Israel. Here he was initiated into the timeless joys of being Jewish and leading a Jewish existence. His father represented the light of reason and humanism; his mother imparted to him the essence of Judaism, and his maternal grandfather, Doyde Feig, a Hasid attached to the court of the Wizsnitzer Rebbe†, taught him the pious joys and astounding legends of the Hasidim.

In the calm of Sighet, Wiesel began his education in a heder‡ where the importance of language and books—especially of the Book, the Torah—was instilled.

> La Torah, mes enfants—c'est quoi? Un trésor rempli d'or et de pierres précieuses. Pour y pénétrer, il vous faut une clef. Je vous la confierai, faites-en bon usage. La clef, mes enfants, c'est quoi? L'alphabet. Donc, répétez après moi, à voix haute, plus haute: Aleph, beit, guimel. (CM, 17-18)

> The Torah, my children, what is it? A treasure chest filled with gold and precious stones. To open it you need a key. I will give it to you, make good use of it. The key, my children, what is it? The alphabet. So repeat after me, with me, aloud, louder: Aleph, bet, gimmell. (LT, 10)

---

*shtetl: those towns and rural communities of Central and Eastern Europe whose populations were predominantly Jewish. The shtetls exerted a formidable influence on the formation of the Jewish character (communally and individually) from the fifteenth century until the Holocaust, serving as backdrop in the literature of several authors, notably Sholom Aleichem, I. L. Peretz, S. Y. Agnon, and I. B. Singer.

†rebbe: the Yiddish appelation for the rabbi or leader of a Hasidic sect, community or dynasty.

‡heder: based upon a Hebrew word for *room*, the Yiddish term referred to a Jewish school, often one room, for younger children where the basics of Jewish learning were taught.

The mystery of the letters and the power of the words with their accompanying silences transmitted a message. His teachers and his contacts with various Hasidim and their rebbes imparted a profoundly reverential respect for language and a love for the past. Likewise, he inherited through his father an enlightened humanism that professed a belief in the goodness and perfectibility of humanity.

The humanist and Judaic ideals so cherished by the young Wiesel were negated when he was metamorphosed into an abject object within Hitler's "Kingdom of Night." For Wiesel, the Second World War remained remote until the spring of 1944, when Adolf Eichmann established his deadly SS apparatus in Budapest. In April 1944, the tense serenity that had protected the enclave of Hungary's 750,000 Jews was shattered as deportations began. Sighet proved no exception. The pale of Nazi horror engulfed the Jews, leaving behind only silence: "le silence parfait du dernier acte. Les Juifs sortaient de scène. Pour toujours." (CM, 154); "Silence: the perfect setting for the last scene of the last scene of the last act. The Jews were retiring from the scene. Forever" (LT, 116). The young Wiesel was forced to recognize the existence of evil and of God's complicity in its perpetration. In extremis, the Jew had come to symbolize alienated humanity and the burden of the human condition.

Wiesel witnessed as never before the painfully absurd reality of Jewish alienation, of the Jew as outcast. "To be man is a drama; to be a Jew is another," proposes E. M. Cioran. "The Jew, therefore, has the privilege of living our condition *twice over.* He represents the alienated existence par excellence" (70) [my translation]. This factor has remained one of the central elements of Wiesel's literary creation. The Jew who had endured slavery, oppression, exile, prejudice, and persecution became his paradigm of humanity. And, in the twentieth century, the Jew witnessed the absolute depravity lurking within humanity's collective soul and verified the utterly bankrupt nature of Western civilization. The young student who had such fervent belief in God and in his fellow beings discovered his own soul barren and silent in the face of the *univers concentrationnaire.* The community through which he had traditionally drawn strength and life had perished, leaving him alone.

As a survivor, Wiesel faced the monumental task of returning to life. More important, he undertook a search for truth, a quest to understand the events that had so completely altered his existence. A bitter existential conflict arose between the Jewish tradition that demanded bearing witness and what appeared to be the inevitability of saying nothing. This struggle resulted in a solemn vow of silence.

A ten-year mute gestative period wrought numerous changes in Wiesel. The shtetl and a majority of his family had been consigned to the flames of

Auschwitz. As one of millions of displaced persons, he eventually came to France with other child survivors where at Taverny, near Paris, Wiesel began to learn French, an act described as a "new beginning, a new possibility, a new world" (Cargas, 1976, 65). This acquisition of a new language likewise opened literary doors. As a student in postwar Paris, he was caught up in the flood of writing and philosophizing that gripped the capital. He was exposed to the literary and intellectual movements that shaped the coming course of French literary history, as well as helping to chart Wiesel's own direction as a French writer.

The philosophical probings of André Malraux, Albert Camus, François Wahl, Jean-Paul Sartre, and Simone de Beauvoir greatly affected the scope of Wiesel's oeuvre. Having witnessed the reality of evil and absurdity, he discovered a degree of brotherhood and inspiration in the company of these men and women who offered the possibility and hope that a response to the depravity of the Holocaust might be uncovered in literature. Rather than rejecting life, Wiesel came to recognize his duty to face it through art. The absurdity that Wiesel had witnessed had to be encountered in order to make some sense of it, and in order to determine what course humanity should follow.

Wiesel's recourse to literature not only permitted him to combat his own despair, but it allowed him to cast off the mantle of indifference and become involved in life, thus reflecting Sartre's notions in *Qu'est-ce que la littérature?*:

> The engaged writer knows that speech is action: he knows that to reveal, to unveil is to change, and that one can only unveil by planning to change. He has abandoned the impossible dream of creating an impartial painting of society and of the human condition. (73) [my translation]

Wiesel's literary debut resulted from an event that happened in 1954 while he was serving as foreign correspondent for the Israeli newspaper *Yediot Aharonot*. He had secured an interview with François Mauriac as part of a larger journalistic assignment to interview Pierre Mendès-France, then the Jewish premier of France. The conversation between the Nobel laureate and the young journalist led to a discussion of the suffering of Christ, which in turn precipitated an unanticipated and acrimonious outburst from Wiesel concerning mankind's silence to Jewish suffering and death in the *anus mundi*. That moment of anger nonetheless evolved into a warm, rewarding friendship. It was Mauriac who insisted Wiesel commit to words his experiences in the *univers concentrationnaire*. "Vous avez tort de ne pas parler. . . . Il faut parler— il faut parler aussi" (UJA, 31); "I think that you are wrong. You are wrong not to speak out—one must also speak out" (JT, 19). One year later, Mauriac held the manuscript of Wiesel's first novel *La Nuit* (*Night*), "écrit sous le signe du

Silence et de la fidélité" (UJA, 31); "Written under the seal of memory and silence" (JT, 19).[3]

The decision to break down the sworn vow of silence and to write undoubtedly weighed heavily on Wiesel. The very notion of reading, much less writing, novels was foreign to his cultural heritage. And once he had begun his literary career, an element of guilt has always persisted for his having resorted primarily to fiction and secular literature.

With the appearance of *La Nuit* in 1958, prefaced by François Mauriac, Wiesel's life had entered a new phase. The imposed mutism was transformed into a language that was founded upon and articulated within silence. Wiesel's fiction is "haunted by echoes or premonitions of the cataclysm even though the center of dramatic action may be far removed from the actual scenes of massacre" (Ezrahi, 1980, 116). Even as he distances himself from the historical events, the residual effects never cease to plague his work. As will be demonstrated, silence metamorphoses into a regenerative power that offers the author the means to heal himself and others, the insights to challenge God and Humankind, and the desire to seek out the silent God of the *anus mundi*. Moreover, silence expedites the formation of questions that for Wiesel are paramount if humanity is to survive in a universe that has apparently gone mad. Questions are raised from the silent void in "an effort to articulate a meaningful way to live after the Holocaust" (Estess, 1980, 14).

The single most common element in Wiesel's fiction and nonfiction is silence. More than any other element, silence is elevated to the status of a theme, a *canto fermo* in the contrapuntal fugue of Wiesel's work. From silent, chaotic origins came the Logos on which his literary universe is constructed. But—and here my thesis differs significantly from that of Ellen Fine and several other scholars—I view silence as the central, primary theme in Wiesel's work. I would not argue against Fine's excellent analysis of the theme of the witness and its urgent, substantive prominence and significance in the scope of Wiesel's work, nor would I dispute the existence of a tense dialectic between silence and language as being at the core of Wiesel's work, and the aforementioned theme of the witness. Prima facie evidence would seem to point to the witness as being a central Wieselian theme. I believe, however, that the theme of silence in Wiesel's oeuvre establishes the basic matrix from which all other thematic material develops.

Its specter rises from the ashes of the Holocaust to shock and to jolt us with its powerful, subterranean forces drawing us into the void. "Ploughed, sown and reaped within the Kingdom of Silence, the work of Elie Wiesel is permeated with silence as a fruit is imbued with the soil which nurtured it" (Neher, 1970, 228) [my translation].

Silence is, of course, more than mere tension between a muted state and the vitally pressing necessity to bear witness. Silence stands as a monolithic thematic and structural tool that assists in the crystallization and sharpening of Wiesel's thought and action. Silence represents the medium through which and by which the witnesses' testimonies are transmitted. As André Neher has noted:

> It [silence] is certainly the theme, and even the word, which appears most often in the text—nearly a thousand times—and a computer would doubtless inform us that no literary creation of the twentieth century evokes silence with such variety, intensity and diversity as that of Elie Wiesel. (Exil, 228) [my translation]

Without its existence at the center of Wiesel's work, his literary accomplishment would not possess the potent force and poetic artistry it does demonstrate. Within the Wieselian context, silence represents more than a mere absence of the word.

> Pour le poète, l'artiste, le mystique et le survivant, le silence comporte plusieurs aspects, divers zones qui ne se recouvrent pas. Le silence possède sa propre ossature, ses propres labyrinthes—et ses propres contradictions. (CM-CH, 210)

> For the poet, the artist, the mystic and the survivor, silence has many facets, zones and shades. Silence has its own textures, its own spheres, its own archeology. It has its own contradictions as well. (SM, 200–201)

Thus, silence must first be defined and examined in its various degrees before one traces its thematic evolution chronologically through the novels. This study will seek to analyze silence first by an exposition of its linguistic properties and possibilities before probing its rhetorical development in Wiesel's work. The theme will then be investigated from its origins in a purely negative stance toward a more positive, mystical, and regenerative pole of reference. I shall endeavor to indicate the manner in which its application serves both as scenic decor and phenomenological impetus for the bearing of testimonial witness. I shall likewise attempt to demonstrate how Wiesel integrates silence into that particular challenge he offers the world, a clarion call to scrutinize and to reevaluate society's decayed, inadequate values, and civilization's corrupted morality, which had not merely resulted in the reality of an Auschwitz—with its accompanying physical and spiritual murder of millions of souls—but through our continued indifference perpetuates genocide, terrorism, torture, and the wholesale prostitution of language.

CHAPTER **1**

Silence:
Definitions and Degrees

Wovon man nicht sprechen
kann, darüber muss man
schweigen.
      L. WITTGENSTEIN

Le procédé qui consiste à
chercher derrière le discours
les peines secrètes de
l'auteur et la maladie sociale
qui le ronge, à son insu,
conduit, lui aussi au silence.
      E. LÉVINAS

INTRODUCTION

Following a miraculous series of earth-shattering pyrotechnic marvels in which the Divine Presence could not be discerned, the prophet Elijah unanticipatedly perceives the Almighty in a "still small voice" (1 Kings 19:12), in a dynamic, communicative silence permeated with profound mystery and meaning. In the Bible, silence represents an invincible inner strength, a source of inspired, creative energy at whose core stands God. And, just as Elijah heard the voice of God in the silence encountered in the wilderness, so too have other biblical figures discerned the Divine Silence calling. Their response: *Hinenni* (הנני), "Here I am," a response that similarly requires a reading of "I hear."

Abraham, Moses, Samuel: each humbly evokes this simple yet potent reply to the Silent Eternal Voice. Through their subsequent actions, they initiate a dialogue with God that consequently alters humanity. In his book *Ethics and Infinity,* Emmanuel Lévinas stresses: "When in the presence of the Other I say *'Here I am!,'* this *'Here I am!'* is the place through which the Infinite enters into language. . . . The glory of the Infinite reveals itself through what it is capable of doing in the witness" (106;109). Silence, frequently considered void of any dialogic essence, becomes both lieu and milieu: a place where silence propounds purpose as well as a means for transmitting that message. Elie Wiesel has noted that "if I use words, it is not to change silence but to complete it" (AS, 3:267). Silence in his novels communicates that which is transcendently ineffable. Silence stands as a significant presence drawing from the reader the same unadorned responses articulated by Abraham, Moses and Samuel: *Hinenni,* "Here I am."

Before entering upon any detailed analysis of the theme of silence in the novels of Elie Wiesel, however, certain preliminaries must, of necessity, be settled in order to provide a foundation and framework for that which will follow. An exploration of silence, which must likewise examine the phenomenon of language, could easily become a lengthy treatise. Therefore, I shall judiciously attempt to limit my discussion to those points most valid for pursuing a study of silence in Wiesel's work. As such, the following methodology would appear best to serve that goal.

First, I shall investigate the phenomenon of silence and its ontological significance in the broadest sense. My analysis will strive to prove that silence, far from being negative, represents a positive phenomenon with a myriad of applications. My inquiry will similarly probe the weakness and inherent negative qualities of language in an attempt to uncover those sources that have assisted in the creation of a facade of ontologically negative silence. Once defined, silence will be examined as a literary technique in the novel.

The second task must be an attempted reconciliation of such positive meanings of silence with the seemingly negative silences offered in response to the near-ineffable nature of the Holocaust. I shall cite examples from the writings of various survivors as well as critical and scholarly studies before I continue to examine those views espoused by Wiesel himself.

Finally, I shall explore the rhetoric of silence as evidenced in Wiesel's novels and the transformation of silence into a theme. It should be noted that only general references will be made to the novels at this time, as a more detailed analysis is undertaken elsewhere in this study.

DEFINITIONS AND DEGREES

Silence represents a rich and complex phenomenon easily detected in all facets of human existence. It is not merely the absence of something else,[1] a notion that would impart a highly negative ontological significance to the phenomenon, but rather is an adjunct to speech and sound, for as Bernard Daubenhauer postulates, "silence is a necessary condition for utterance and is somehow coordinate with utterance" (5).

In "Pleine eau," Julien Gracq presents the following image of silence: "*Le silence profond comme un grenier à blé abandonné, gorgé de chaleur et de poussière*" (24). His metaphor alternates between plenitude contained within silence and its negative, often stifling features. And yet the overwhelming sense of Gracq's image reflects the positive, active, and creative natures to be discovered within silence. Silence is the creative matrix from which *l'énonciation,* or speech, arises and into which it ultimately dissolves. Accepting Merleau-Ponty's view that "the conclusion of a speech or of a text represents the end of a magic spell" (209) [my translation], we must likewise propose that the beginning of *l'énonciation* out of silence casts the spell. Silence never ceases to imply its opposite and to depend on its presence. It launches *l'énonciation,* then echoes it when the articulation has ended. The two phenomena are linked in a temporal and an ontological interdependence despite their being incompatible elements. "The word is the sacrifice of silence," states Raimundo Panikkar, speaking of this paradox:.

> The self-immolation of silence brings about the word. Silence no longer exists when the word appears—but the word is there, and carries all that silence can express; the word is all that silence is—but silence is then no more; there is only word. (156)

In spite of the apparent supremacy of the word over silence, there is no beginning nor end to the latter. The word that appears and, as Panikkar suggests, "carries all that silence can express," is soon consumed by the silence that is within the word and that frames it.

Silence creates a tension, a magnetism that sets *l'énonciation* vibrating, thus creating sound out of zones of silence. The creation of such zones is incumbent upon the poet/writer. As Mallarmé notes: "The intellectual armor of the poem dissimulates itself and is found in that space which isolates the stanzas and is amidst the white spaces on the paper: meaningful silence" (872) [my translation]. Silence stands as the common denominator of *l'énonciation.*

Silence cannot be isolated from the word. The two are joined in a positive, symbiotic relationship. Both represent choice: One can choose to remain silent

Gramley Library
Salem College
Winston-Salem, NC 27108

or one can opt to speak. The choices are "distinguishable only in the quality of noesis, for that which is uttered or kept concealed in silence is the same," and thus one might state along with Daubenhauer that "silence . . . would be the positive abstinence from employing some determined expression" (55).

Silence similarly signifies power. Thomas Carlyle's assessment of the silent elements in Shakespeare's works highlights this point: "his sorrows, his silent struggles known to himself; much that was not known at all, not speakable at all: like roots, like sap and forces working underground. Speech is great, but silence is greater" (247–48). In L'Espace littéraire, Maurice Blanchot expresses the notion that the most admirable element in any literary work is not its style, nor its subject, nor the quality of the chosen language:

> but precisely that silence, that virile force by which a writer . . . main-tains a power of authority, that decision to be silent, so that in that silence there takes coherent form and understanding that which speaks without beginning or end: (18) [my translation]

Not only does silence signify power, it also imposes a sense of superiority within a text. Silent characters are frequently those who wield power over others, especially within a dramatic context. Thus, the silent character in Nathalie Sarraute's play Le Silence is a source of speculation and anxiety; the killer in Eugène Ionesco's play Tueur sans gages appears all the more threatening simply because he is silent; and, similarly, in many of Racine's plays the action revolves around silent characters or those who silently guard some truth. "Silence is the artist's ultimate other-worldly gesture: by silence, he frees himself from servile bondage to the world." (Sontag, 1976, 6) This power of silence, this choice, leads to freedom.

These positive features—choice, freedom, and the underlying sense of power—provided sufficient reason for both ancient Greeks and Romans to elevate gods of silence in their pantheons,[2] for the Bible to see silence as one of the abodes of God,[3] and for various schools of Renaissance thought to follow the advice of Erasmus against too much talk and his plea for more silence.[4] Nevertheless, these views have not deterred critics from continuing to impart negative values to silence. Brice Parain has suggested in his Essai sur la misère humaine that by reducing oneself to a state of silence, one abandoned all links to other human beings (217). Silence would seem to exile humanity. As indicated earlier, however, silence also represents a positive phenomenon. One must, therefore, seek to comprehend how certain critics, such as Parain, could arrive at such a negative ontological perspective.

For these critics, negative degrees of silence are perceived as a direct result of particular aspects inherent in language itself. When such fundamental elements of language are isolated and act upon a message, they can, in fact, induce a silence whose ontology would appear negative. Thus, in order to understand such a view of silence, one must review those features tending to provoke a negative reading of the phenomenon.

Language, according to Martin Buber in his *Ekstatische Konfessionen,* represents communion, communication, and community. He concludes that perceptual knowledge of singular or group experience demands transmission via language. Such knowledge (*Erfahrung*) can be conceptualized and hence expressed. Buber did not believe, as did Wittgenstein in the *Tractatus,* that factual language possessed limits. For Buber, perceptual knowledge could be made manifest. Intuitive or ecstatic experiences (*Erlebnis*), however, lie beyond the human capacity for adequate retelling, beyond words and language, a point Buber shares with Wittgenstein. Yet despite such apparent linguistic limitations, human beings possess an overriding desire to utter the unspeakable, fully cognizant that such an attempt may well be perceived as nonsense. Men and women plunge into the depths of their being to contemplate the *Erlebnis* desperately seeking to articulate it. "The natural conclusion of contemplation would be silence" (20) [my translation] states Brice Parain in *Petite métaphysique de la parole.* His use of the conditional mood conveys a sense that the result of meditation on such matters (*i.e., Erlebnis*) ought to lead to a noncommunicative state, *viz.* silence. The sense of community that Buber envisions cannot exist.

Language's inability to express a particular experience can lead to a degree of negative silence that would be incompatible with life itself. Elsewhere, George Steiner has postulated about life, death, and silence in connection with Herman Broch's *The Death of Virgil,* "that which is wholly outside language is outside life" (*Language,* 29). Language possesses limits, and this reality can lead to a frustrating and isolating silence. It must therefore be demonstrated that one of the negative degrees of silence finds its origin in the existence of a state stemming from the failure of human language to express either a situation or an experience.

Parain views language as an imperfect mode of communication harboring various limitations, rendering precise expression of thought or experience near impossible. That which we sense, or that which we perceive, can never be fully and faithfully transmitted by language. Language possesses an exceedingly finite ability to serve objective and emotional needs. Even when an utterance is articulated, one must acknowledge the existence of language's persistent requirement for interpretation owing to the impotence and inaccuracy inherent in words. According to Parain, language and communication are imperfect, never able to express anything without the imposition of interpretation.

This unavoidable need for interpretation leads to the discovery of another degree of silence: that resulting from the "impurity" of language and words.

Language is, as Roland Barthes states, "a body of prescriptives and habits, common to all writers of a given era" (*Zéro,* 10) [my translation]. Not being static, language develops and evolves, but certain residual elements or significations persist in lurking behind words and in the structures of language itself. These silent "hangers-on" often succeed in clouding or corrupting meaning. In Barthes's view "language is never innocent: words possess a secondary memory that mysteriously persist amidst new significations" (*Zéro,* 16) [my translation]. This secondary memory represents a degree of silence that can communicate. When it does, implications are made that can confuse, and perhaps contradict, the meaning intended by the originator of the transmission. One example should suffice here to illustrate this point.

Wiesel has been referred to as the "poet of the Holocaust." The term *holocaust* is derived from the Greek *holokautoma,* meaning "burnt whole," which was originally used in the Septuagint as a translation for the Hebrew term *olah* (עלה), literally, "that which is brought up." The intended reference was to the sacrifices offered in the Jewish Tabernacle and later in the Temples at Jerusalem. The use of the word *holocaust* to designate the destruction of European Jewry naturally connotes a burnt sacrifice. While this interpretation might be "consistent with a prevailing Christian reading of Jewish history," as Sidrah DeKoven Ezrahi indicates in her study of Holocaust literature (2), it nevertheless conveys an unpalatable and altogether unacceptable significance to the Jewish community, which is openly critical of such a usage.[5] Thus, for the so-called poet of the event, the term with its secondary memory imparts a silent meaning that is far removed from that actually desired by Wiesel himself. The silent element within the word represents an impure or corrupting factor that frustrates and drives the writer/speaker toward apparently negative silence, or even to its extreme degree, which I shall call *mutism.*

Before I examine this concept of mutism, I believe I ought to highlight a specific feature that represents a positive corollary to Barthes's notion of language not being innocent, and to Parain's remarks concerning interpretation. The elements intrinsically hidden in language and that frequently render it corrupt or impure, require active reading and thought, or as Parain has noted, investigation, interpretation, and commentary. These silent contents form keys that assist the receiver in decoding the message that has been transmitted. "Commentary is the legitimate form through which truth is approached" (Scholem, 1971, 289).[6] Such inquiries permit us to pick through these silent codes and arrive at a meaning that appears in accordance with the originator's intent. Though language possesses the weaknesses ascribed to it by Parain and

Barthes and is thus in need of interpretation or clarification, the silence within and without generates those activities that might lead to a fuller and more truthful meaning.

Emmanuel Lévinas in his study *Noms propres* suggests that modern civilization has robbed man and language of significance. Words have lost their virility and, in turn, are haunted by invisible entities that refract authentic meaning. Such problems can induce the negative state of mutism. I use the term *mutism* to signify that state in which a speaker or a writer, for whatever reason, retreats from *l'énonciation* into that realm of absolute silence. It is that state that Lévinas believes represents "textual holes at the level of the act of speech" (10) [my translation]. Within a purely literary context, this mutism frequently manifests itself in *la page blanche* (the white page), a page devoid of any sign, symbol or language. This state of mutism is akin to that condition experienced by the French Symbolist poets. The vision of the *au-delà* (the beyond) they strove to describe was an ecstatic *Erlebnis,* beyond the scope of human language. Their desire to transcend and eventually to transform reality was severely hampered by words. They sought to harness the magic of language and silence to serve them. But, as writing came from the intuitive *Erlebnis* noted by Buber, the experience remained nearly untransmittable as they had been affected by it. The conflict between language and experience, between *la parole* (speech) and *le mot* (the word), frequently resulted in a void of literary mutism, or *la page blanche.*

I stress the fact that mutism as I have here defined it would appear to elicit a purely negative ontology. The Symbolists, however, sought to deny the supremacy of any such negative meaning. In *"Le Mystère dans les lettres,"* Mallarmé states:

> Reading—
> Is an exercise—
> We must bend our independent minds, page by page, to the blank space which begins each one; we must forget the title, for it is too resounding. Then, in the tiniest and most scattered stopping—points upon the page, when the lines of chance have been vanquished word by word, the blanks unfailingly return; before they were gratuitous; now they are essential; and now at last it is clear that nothing lies beyond; now silence is genuine and just. (386–87) [my translation]

For Mallarmé, there exists the possibility of using such silences in tandem with language. By choosing the words and the *blancs,* or white spaces on the page, he insures that white is no longer gratuitous but becomes certain, the silence gaining authenticity and meaning. Mallarmé's ideas continue: "Thus the invisible air, or song, beneath the words leads our diving eye from word to music; and thus, like a motif, it invariably inscribes its fleuron and pendant there" (387) [my translation]. Even the white space that is used to fill a page, such as that at the end of a chapter, propounds meaning. Silence, though perhaps demonstrating the impotence of language to express fully and faithfully a given experience, nevertheless can convey a significant message. It has been employed as a *res poetica,* a positive, communicative feature. That incommunicable reality impossible to attain with language is therefore enshrined by visible silence.

Within the context of contemporary literature, one finds numerous examples of the aforementioned concepts of mutism and of the significance exercised by the *blancs* in a given text. Dramatic literature, for example, insists on silence, often requiring it in the stage directions. The theater of Samuel Beckett effectively employs silence in order to heighten dramatic effect. Poetry similarly employs visible silence via the space between stanzas, the broadly marked margins and other features of its traditional *mise-en-page.* But, within the contemporary context, it is in the novel that this white space has been uniquely exploited.

Such *blancs,* or as I shall refer to them, *le grand silence typographique-respiratoire,*[7] extend beyond the common usage of white spaces at the end of chapters or the occasional recourse to a gap within the text. I am referring to an author's deliberate imposition of numerous and significant silences that repeatedly break the flow of the printed page. *Le grand silence typographique-respiratoire* represents, as the term implies, a function of textual respiration. It punctuates a text; it can express musical or mystical values. The technique also stresses the temporal nature of the word as it becomes visibly delineated between such white spaces. It frequently serves as metaphor to emphasize the hidden meaning that has dissolved into this silence. Within such typographical silence, the significance of the articulation echoes and is frequently intensified. Words and statements appear more alive, more vibrant, more important when framed in such silence. The novels of Robert Pinget, Nathalie Sarraute, Renaud Camus, Marguerite Duras, Samuel Beckett, and, as will be demonstrated, those of Elie Wiesel have served to elevate this device to one of immense significance. The visible silence becomes an additional instrument for transmitting the message. Though words and language may not adequately suffice to convey a particular meaning, such a textual lacuna imposes itself and requires the reader to consider more closely that which is or is not being said.

In general, the use of silence, especially as evidenced in these white spaces, jolts a reader from complacent attitudes of reading as a purely mechanical operation. Forms of silence construct their own synthetic metastructure beyond the bounds of the textual realm of the printed page. The total narrative value of such a given text is only partially contained in its organic typographical elements that become significant referents, catalysts propelling the reader into the existing silence framing the reader into the existing silence framing the text. Meaning is therefore not solely conveyed *in* language but likewise *through* it. Silence demonstrates a principle of rhetoric that conditions our response to *l'énonciation* as well as to character, landscape, and plot within a text. According to Sartre, meaning evolves from what a particular author does not say, and this is emphasized by the *milieu lacunaire* within a given text. Though apparently gratuitous as *la page blanche,* it constitutes a meaningful phenomenon demonstrating a positive ontology.

Having uncovered a positive foundation to the more negative elements of silence, we must examine one final element: the temporal mode of silence. Barthes has suggested that the temporal mode of the past as represented in French by the *passé simple* is fixed. The verb forms an implicit link in a causal chain. The past, having been established, can be interpreted or even questioned, but it cannot be silenced. The present is transpiring. It is known and as such is being set in the firm concrete of language and thought. The present, though alive with words, is rapidly set into rigid molds that fashion it into the past. The future temporal mode alone alarms man because it is silent. André Neher proposes that the future tense "alone is completely identified with silence, in its plenitude but also in its remarkable ambivalence." He insists:

> Only the future is silent. Like silence, the future tells us nothing about itself, first because it is completely incapable of the word. Not having experienced or absorbed anything, how could it express the nothingness that dwells within it? (*Exil,* 183–84) [my translation]

Silence, like human beings, is continually in the process of becoming. Both represent possibility, hope, creation, or re-creation through some future orientation. I concur with Max Picard when he declares that being and silence belong together (77).

Thus I conclude that silence serves a positive function. The phenomenon produces an articulation that then points again to its own transcendence in silence. Even when the problematics of language appear to evoke a negative veil of silence, the essence of the resulting silence can and often does demonstrate an underlying positive ontology. Silence notably stresses power, choice, and freedom as it certifies the absence, renunciation, or completion of a thought. It provides a period of respiration in which the significance of an articulation can be considered. Silence likewise furnishes speech with an additional path for the transmission of a message. It aids *l'énonciation* to attain its maximum integrity and seriousness.

These definitions of silence provide a basis for examining its use as a technique in the novel. As a text rises from silence, novels can be viewed as a way of speaking in the absence of the writer. The text constructs a means of silent discourse in which words and silences interact to project a particular message. This silent discourse and the very use of silence as a tool within the novel demand acts of active reading and interpretation.

Silent elements abound in novels. An author uses certain words or phrases to the exclusion of others. Excessive emphasis upon those chosen terms can literally evoke the unsaid, thus creating a pervasive atmosphere of that which has been left mute. Even the use of negation imposes a level of silence, since negativity, far from being anti-vital, expresses notions that are not present. By insisting upon negation, the author illuminates other ideas and attitudes. Having chosen to include such rhetoric as part of the narrative, one must assume the author has done so in order to silence one element *in favor of another* that remains veiled but vaguely perceived through the negation. That which is declared to be "not present" makes itself known by its conspicuous absence.

Narrative technique can likewise extend pauses between words and phrases. In the guise of the elements of punctuation—end points, commas, dashes, ellipses—an author can heighten or prolong silence in a text, thus imparting a dimension of the phenomenon to all that is said or unsaid. Narrative also seeks to maintain a balance between that which is said and that which is left unsaid, an effect often achieved through indirect discourse. Employing this technique, an author permits more than one narrative voice to be perceived. This multiplicity of voices establishes moments of uncertainty from which silence can emerge. John Preston stresses that such scenes:

> encourage us to abandon the idea of a recognizable personalized narrator, and to understand the narration as a form of language whose function is to make palpable the silence which divides us from the scene. (262)

At times, novel narrative will present episodes where all speech and action are suspended, plunging the reader into a silent abyss. Gerard Genette asserts that "this interruption of dialogue and action suspends the speech itself of the novel and absorbs it, for a moment, in a sort of voiceless interrogation" (237) [my translation]. Each of these recourses to silence in the novel has traditionally been a means for writers to halt the progress of language, to highlight a scene, and to cause the active reader to examine—or reexamine—the text.

Contemporary narrative technique has likewise established a degree of meaningful silence that underlies a text. In her essay *"Conversation et sous-conversation,"* Nathalie Sarraute refers to this silent level of language as "Proustian sub-conversation" (*sous-conversation proustienne*) in which reality or highly personal reflections are willfully retained in silence. A character artic- ·
ulates other thoughts which, while possessing roots in the unsaid, are more often free of any evidence of it. Sarraute herself skillfully uses this technique to great advantage in several of her works, notably *Les Fruits d'or* and *Pour un oui ou pour un non*. Moreover, an author's recourse to this tool can lead to interior monologue. Such silent considerations frequently produce a more powerful impact than articulated dialogue, as evidenced in the works of James Joyce, Marcel Proust, Virginia Woolf, or William Faulkner. The thoughts guarded by the silence of the interior monologue or within the *sous-conversation proustienne* demonstrate an active imposition of authorial silence in order to advance the plot and to engage the reader.

Silence additionally serves as metaphor. I do not mean to imply here metaphorical usage within a traditional framework, but would rather wish to view it as proposed by Heinz Werne, namely as metaphor suggesting taboo. The reality of some topics cannot be adequately expounded by human language or by art. Aesthetic pleasure signifies a mental state that is essentially little altered from ordinary behavior. If artistic forms are bent or disfigured so as to permit certain realities being expressed, then the artist or writer courts rejection. José Ortega y Gasset argues that "artistic forms proper are tolerated only if they do not interfere with the perception of human forms and faces" (9). People are frequently incapable of modifying their mental attitudes and perceptual apparatus to view particular subjects, or to accept art in a radically different or refracted light. Such reactions account for the rise of the symbol and metaphor in art. I would extend Werne's hypothesis in order to see omission itself, or the literary silences previously defined, as being purely metaphorical. Metaphor and silence are inexorably linked as one of man's most fruitful potentialities, a primordial tool that both precede verbal imagery and are prompted by a desire to circumvent an ineffable reality or cultural taboo.

The current discussion demonstrates the prominent position silence displays within the array of tools at the novelist's disposal. Silence represents a linguistic treasure chest from which an author can choose any number of degrees of the phenomenon to assist in the creation of a text. Once chosen, a particular rhetoric establishes silences of various sorts. The author can erect a decor, or background, which projects silence, a role frequently exerted by nature in a given work. One need merely consider the novels of Leo Tolstoy or Thomas Hardy in which the presence of nature silently stalks behind the action, subtly exerting a particular force upon the characters. Likewise, the author can permit the evolution of a silence of contiguity to exist between characters, a silence that is defined, grows, and then diminishes in the characters' interrelationships. The proximity of characters can often elicit a silence of secrecy as in Dickens's *Great Expectations* or François Mauriac's *Le Noeud des vipères*. The author himself/herself may more forcibly impose authorial silence, cutting off readers, or even the fictional characters, from vital information. This sort of silence is most commonly encountered in the murder mysteries of Georges Simenon, Agatha Christie, or P. D. James, as well as in many of the novels of the French *nouveaux romanciers*. Silence represents precisely the element that keeps the reader guessing and continually off guard. Finally, a fifth sort of silence deals with relations of a superior character toward an inferior one similar to those found in the relationship between Frédéric Moreau and Mme. Arnoux in Gustave Flaubert's *L'Education sentimentale*. Every author utilizes such silences to a greater or lesser degree, and through them can expand the work's message by engaging in tacit conversation with the active reader.

A sixth form of silence has evolved in postwar literature: Survival silence, that of the survivor who witnessed the inexpressible. A complex silence, it highlights the unparalleled dilemma of contemporary literature and the human condition. In *L'Ecriture du désastre,* Maurice Blanchot has described it as: "The unknown name, beyond all naming. The Holocaust, the absolute event of History, historically dated, that burning hole in which all History is consumed and where all meaning falls away" (80) [my translation]. The Holocaust opened a chasm in the human consciousness and in language, for as Elie Wiesel continues to stress: "Auschwitz negates all systems, destroys all doctrines. . . . Treblinka means death, absolute death, death of language and of hope, death of trust and of inspiration" (D, 7). The elements of language and all definitions of silence have no meaning before the "Kingdom of Night." Silence assumes a mantle of deathly proportions. Thus, we must seek to effect some degree of reconciliation between the positive results of the present investigation of silence, and the imposition of the *nihil* of Auschwitz.

SILENCE AS RESPONSE TO THE HOLOCAUST

Piotr Rawicz notes in his novel *Le Sang du ciel:*

> One after the other, words—all the words of human language—
> wither, lose their ability to transmit meaning. And then, they fall, like
> dead scales. All meaning evaporates. But that is their normal state.
> Man becomes mute (118) [my translation]

For the survivor and for the creative writer, events of the Holocaust stand in opposition to language. In the *Tractatus,* Wittgenstein states: "*Wovon man nicht sprechen kann, darüber muss man schweigen*" (151). Though Wittgenstein was referring to nonreal absolutes, I believe one can extend Wittgenstein's view to encompass a real absolute such as the Holocaust, a situation where words prove incapable of describing in toto the event. Furthermore, the events of the *anus mundi* deformed language. "Language has been corrupted to the point that it had to be invented anew and purified" (D, 8), stresses Wiesel, as he and other writers struggle with the onus of witnessing and responding to the *shoah.**

Sartre states in *Qu'est-ce que la littérature?* that "to save literature, it becomes necessary to take a position in literature as the essence of literature is taking a position" (300) [my translation]. Wiesel, however, would counter Sartre's argument with, "Auschwitz nie toute littérature. . . . Le remplacer par des mots, n'importe lesquels, c'est la dénaturer. La littérature de l'holocauste. Le terme même est un contresens" (UJA, 190); "Auschwitz negates all literature. . . . To substitute words, any words, for it is to distort it. A Holocaust literature? The very term is a contradiction" (JT, 197). The reality of the events evades description. The words that relate the experience do not seem real; they cannot possibly convey a message that could be true. Those traditional forms that literature had established to convey meaning and to project art had no validity. Thus, Sartre's call to take a position in literature possesses no apparent meaning or validity in a world where language, already saddled with those inadequacies earlier delineated, has no power to capture the truth of events in the *anus mundi.*

In *Mauvaises pensées et autres,* Paul Valéry contends that which resembles nothing does not exist (878). As the brutal reality that was Auschwitz would appear to lie beyond life and language, as it has no parallel in human history, according to Valéry's statement, it might well never have existed. In all honesty, the *univers concentrationnaire* has but one analogue: Christian images of Hell. These fantasies of Western iconography were realized in the Nazi creations where degradation and death were the ultimate goals.

The fundamental belief in the autonomy of the word made possible the whole movement of humanism. Yet the Holocaust persists in demonstrating the inadequacy of the word to transmit even marginally the scope and gravity of the event. Various elements linger in contemporary language as a cancerous secondary memory of that era which, "after the turn of civilization to mass murder," forces one to ask along with George Steiner "whether speech,

---

*Shoah: a Hebrew word of biblical origins (Job 30:3) adopted to refer to the Holocaust.

whether shapes of moral judgement and imagination which Judaic-Hellenic tradition founds on the authority of the Word, are viable in the face of the inhuman" (*Language*, 149).

I do not mean to imply here that the debauching of language has been confined to the National Socialist phenomenon, or even to the twentieth century. Such a proposal would be fatuous and would ignore the numerous antecedents from antiquity to the present day that concentrate on man's mistrust of language. As I suggested earlier in this argument, words distort, mislead, and hide the truth. It is not surprising then that various Enlightenment thinkers probing for meaning in the human condition likewise felt the necessity to appraise the problematics of language. John Locke in *General Terms* in the *Essay Concerning Human Understanding,* Etienne de Condillac in his *Essai sur l'origine des connaissances humaines* and his *Traîté des systèmes,* and Jean-Jacques Rousseau in *L'Essai sur l'origine des langages* represent but a mere handful of those philosophers who attempted to extract some degree of sense from language. In our own century, the Dada and Surrealist movements constitute an aesthetic and epistemological rebellion against language, and an attempt to dismantle it and that "fabric of impotent rationality which, every day in the First World War, planned, authorized, justified the deaths of tens of thousands" (Steiner, 1971, 32). Language had gone mad; words had lost their meaning.

Despite this "mistrust" of language, Sartre maintains that "the function of the writer is to call a spade a spade" (*Situations II,* 304) [my translation]. Though words may not exist by which a writer can relate the horrors of the Holocaust, he must nevertheless strive to find them and thereby impart some degree of the reality of Auschwitz. Language cannot constitute an ally for man in this task. It represents a menacing instrument of oppression or torment. This remains the painful dilemma of the creative writer who is also a survivor: How can the message be transmitted to future generations if the word has failed?

The Hebrew poet Uri Zvi Greenberg insists upon the uniqueness of the Holocaust when he writes:

> Are there other analogies for this, our
>   disaster, that came to us at their
>   hands?
> There are no other analogies (all words
>   are shades or shadow)—
> There lies the horrifying phrase: No
>   other analogies! (126)

The diaries of the ghetto historians and communal leaders struggled to discover words appropriate for expressing the unprecedented misery and suffering the Jew was forced to endure. The notes and journals buried in the concentration camps by the victims themselves cry out for witnesses to recount in detail the nightmares of the *anus mundi*. And yet, as Roy Eckardt points out: "no written word can equal the experience itself" (24).

According to Wiesel, the most logical choice would appear to be to remain silent: "Alors, apprenez à vous taire" (CM, 220); "So learn to be silent" (LT, 197). Silence would seem most efficacious. Yet, to write of the experience in any manner, to seek to create new literary and artistic forms was to press for life. To impose silence would grant Hitler a posthumous victory. The survivor alone became responsible for uncovering the method of transmitting the ineffable vision of Auschwitz. Alone, either silence or words, would betray the event, its countless victims, and the survivors. As Wiesel states: "La vérité ne sera jamais écrite" (EDS, 248); "The truth will never be written" (OGA, 10). Nevertheless, one had to try, and I believe Wiesel hints at a suggestion when he advises survivors:

> d'apporter un mutisme absolu. Et transmettre la vision de l'holo-
> causte, à la manière de certains mystiques, en la soustrayant au lan-
> gage. Si tous s'étaient tus, l'accumulation de leurs silences eût été
> insoutenable: le monde en serait devenu sourd. (EDS, 247)

> . . . to maintain absolute silence. So as to transmit a vision of the
> holocaust, in the manner of certain mystics, by withdrawing from
> words. Had all of them remained mute, their accumulated silences
> would have become unbearable: the impact would have deafened the
> world. (OGA, 8)

Though the underlying message appears little changed from the statement of *Le Chant des morts,* "Alors, apprenez à vous taire," I detect an evolution in his thought.

The first consideration is the fact that Wiesel is using words to propose his absolute mutism, and couples those words to the verb "to transmit." Like that of the mystics, the message is deemed significant and must be passed on in silence. Silence evolves as the unique *milieu conducteur* that conveys the desired information. The second evolutionary development lies in the fact that in *Le Chant des morts,* having stated his advice: "Apprenez à vous taire," the text stops abruptly, dissolving into *la page blanche.* The inference: The message lies beyond transmission, beyond human understanding, so why persist? He silences himself. In the present case, the text fades into *le grand silence typographique-respiratoire;* it breathes, then continues.

These important differences convey the notion that although the unique-ness of the Jewish *tremendum* cannot be sufficiently expressed in words and conventional forms, although silence about the event would grant the forces of evil their posthumous victory, the survivor must somehow fuse together these two essential elements, language and silence, to serve as a means for witnessing the destruction made manifest at Auschwitz. Wiesel is proposing silence's being employed in tandem with the word to present some image of the *anus mundi* and to represent the fragmented soul of the survivor.

Thus, with reference to silence as response to the Holocaust, several important issues have been raised. First, the unique nature of the *univers concentrationnaire* would apparently place it beyond the pale of human language. Language, which has already been demonstrated as possessing numerous limitations, has few reserves to describe the events of the "Kingdom of Night." This impotence in language likewise leads to the imposition of a void of negative silence. Secondly, the survivor as writer has been affected by this impotence, for if language has failed, the post-Holocaust position is as alone and abandoned as it was during it. From these issues a third consideration arises concerning the creation of a literary text.

Simone de Beauvoir postulates the view that the novel and creative literature in general must present readers with imaginary situations that are as complete, as unnerving, and as patently real as any given life situation (*"Littérature,"* 115–55). Beauvoir believed that literature can and must involve the reader directly in the experience of the characters. Like her, Sartre calls for a literature born of imagination in extremis. It was he who in *Qu'est-ce que la littérature?* readily asserted that certain of his contemporaries had accomplished just that. Camus, Malraux, Koestler, and others had employed an historical or political truth to launch the imagination into extreme situations which sought to engage the characters of those works and, by extension, the readers themselves in an existential decision making process. Yet with the Jewish *tremendum,* we are no longer dealing with imagination in extremis but with reality in extremis. The survivor had been plunged into a world in which existence was judged a crime punishable by death. No longer was one dealing with philosophical questions, but with the physical reality of annihilation based upon being. Literature as traditionally defined ceased to convey any meaning and merely reflects the impotence of language and its own redundancy as art.

Language and silence in relation to the Holocaust have appeared to weigh wholly upon the witness as transmitter. There is, however, another feature I have not discussed that now requires investigation: the condition of the receiver. In *"Art and Fortune,"* Lionel Trilling claims that with reference to the Holocaust "the activity of mind fails before the incommunicability of man's suffering" (265). Human suffering appears pointless. Suffering can elicit eloquent effusions of words to extract some degree of meaning, as evidenced in the biblical book of Job; but, it nevertheless remains for all humanity the most ancient and pressing question arising from mortal existence. With reference to the *univers concentrationnaire,* even when events are meticulously delineated, as in David Rousset's *L'Univers concentrationnaire,* Bruno Bettelheim's *The Informed Heart,* or Leon Well's *The Janowska Road,* the full pain and horror of suffering cannot be fathomed by the reader. The following excerpt has not been culled from the gothic fiction of Edgar Allan Poe, nor from one of Franz Kafka's nightmarish parables. It is, rather, the essence of the *anus mundi* confronting the reader: "One of the German SD's takes the child by its small feet, swings it, crushing its head against the nearest tree, then carries it over to the fire and tosses it in. This is done in front of the mother" (Wells, 1963, 206). The reader's reaction can only be one of shock, revulsion, followed by a numbing silence.

The human psyche simply remains incapable of grasping the enormity of the reality of Auschwitz. Our ability to comprehend the horror and chaos of natural disaster is limited enough; much less are we capable of assessing the brutality imposed by manmade ones. Such events as those described above are either repudiated, repressed or serve as a sadistic, vicarious stimulus. Deeper inferences about the state of the human condition and occidental culture are ultimately ignored. The poets of the First World War recognized how the public rejected their particular message; the survivors of the atomic blasts at Hiroshima and Nagasaki recognized the world would be unable to understand the frightening magnitude and reality of their disaster.

In the public view, the testimonies and stories of these groups of survivors were confounded by the opinion that such horrors had already been seen. Photographs and news film clips had impressed these images of hell into the human consciousness. For the general public, literary treatments seemed superfluous. Protesting to know too much, the receiver either refuses to comprehend the message by choosing to be deaf, or by opting to neglect the material being transmitted. A silence of self-preservation descends.

Silence becomes the universal response to the Holocaust. The inadequacies of language lead the survivor-as-writer to silence; the event itself imposes a deathly silence through its nearly ineffable nature. Transmitting the reality of the *anus mundi* appears to represent an act of betrayal, just as would the imposition of absolute silence. At all levels, silence represents the materials of the Holocaust experience. Within such silences, however, lies the key that might lead, as Sartre suggests to a literature, "that joins and reconciles the metaphysical Absolute to the relativity of historical fact" (*Situations II,* 251) [my translation], or as Wiesel has expressed: "Dis-leur que le silence, plus que la parole, demeure la substance et le signe de ce qui fut leur univers et que, comme la parole, il s'impose et demande à être transmis" (EDS, 252); "Tell them that silence, more than language, remains the substance and the seal of what was once their universe, and that, like language, it demands to be recognized and transmitted" (OGA, 198). It is my contention that the novels of Elie Wiesel represent just such a fusion of the metaphysical and historical in which all forms of silence constitute the matrix from which his testimony and message emerge. Therefore, as the final stage of defining silence and before engaging upon a closer analysis of the theme of silence in Wiesel's novels, we must attempt a review of the rhetoric of silence he establishes in his works.

A RHETORIC OF SILENCE: THE PHENOMENON OF SILENCE IN THE NOVELS OF ELIE WIESEL

André Neher suggests that "silence is the metaphysical form of the cosmos" (Exil, 13) [my translation].[8] Silence exists behind all we care to perceive in this world, and it offers humanity the challenge of uncovering and understanding it. With reference to Wiesel's novels, we must seek to determine the validity of Neher's assertion. To do that, we must outline how Wiesel himself employs silence; that is, what rhetoric does Wiesel use to evoke silence as tool and theme?

Wiesel's Jewish foundations in the Bible, talmudic literature, and the stories of the Hasidic masters have firmly rooted him in a tradition of silence, for as Neher believes "silence forms the landscape of the Bible" (Exil, 13) [my translation]. The problem remains to uncover the layers of silence within Wiesel's novels, and to view how he creates a matrix out of which might come l'énonciation.

I endeavor here to adapt a method pioneered by the late André Neher in his study L'Exil de la parole. I shall initially establish certain levels of silence under the terms morphological and syntacic. I shall be using these terms in the loosest sense: morphology for the forms; syntax for the shapes. The morphology of silence will not dwell upon the various words Wiesel uses for silence, but rather on those statements of silence that constitute the basic forms lying at the core of Wiesel's work. These morphological structures will then be used to construct a syntactic level. An examination of these elements will attempt to indicate the manner in which the basic forms become shapes and colorations of silence that Wiesel arranges in his novels to create a "grammar" of silence.[9] I shall then seek to demonstrate how silence emerges from the text and proceeds to produce a unique third tier, the semantic, where meaning is given to these more abstract forms and shapes. It is also at this semantic level that the theme of silence is fully voiced. This tier will receive extensive treatment in the remainder of this study.

Morphology

As noted in this study's *Introduction,* the word *silence* and its synonyms have a high frequency of usage in Wiesel's works. These words, in turn, serve to construct the morphological level of silence within Wiesel's novels. This level consists of three distinct sorts of pronouncements: the statement of the unsaid; the statement without a counterstatement; the absence of God's voice. The first presents a notion that houses those realities uttered with difficulty or that remain virtually ineffable. The statement becomes a repository for the silence that at the semantic level will form the backdrop of silence for Wiesel's literary universe. In a similar manner, the second aspect of this tier represents those statements that directly or indirectly pose a question that ought to solicit some response, but none is offered. The reply itself is silence. And finally, the third category is the absolute silence of God.

Statements of the unsaid have numerous applications. Often, they are quizzical expressions inviting the reader to pause and ponder. "Il avait changé Moché. Ses yeux ne réflétaient plus la joie" (NAJ, 20); "Moché had changed. There was no longer any joy in his eyes" (N, 17). The silent questions elicited by the morphologically unsaid element are what indeed happened to Moché, and why do his eyes no longer reflect joy? Something stands behind the words of this morphological block. Another, more clearly delineated example can be seen in the following: "Devant nous, ces flammes. Dans l'air, cette odeur de chair brûlée. Il devait être minuit. Nous étions arrivés à Birkenau" (NAJ, 40); "In front of us flames. In the air that smell of burning flesh. It must have been about midnight. We had arrived—at Birkenau, reception center for Auschwitz" (N, 37). These terse statements propound several images of the *anus mundi,* i.e., the flames, burning flesh, etc., all the while leaving the unsayable in the meta-silence behind a single word: Birkenau, the extermination center of Auschwitz. The horrors of the gas chambers, crematoria, and death remain in the silence surrounding this single word, which appears all the more stark in the original French as it stands alone, unmodified. In *L'Aube (Dawn),* the protagonist's friend states: "En tuant, . . . l'homme devient Dieu" (NAJ, 143); "Why has a man no right to commit murder? Because in so doing he takes upon himself the function of God" (N, 144). Here again, a significant silent implication lurks behind the articulated statement. If man is to attempt to usurp God's position, the silent suggestion then is the need to abandon the Jewish ethos of the sanctity of life, as in order for man to become God, he must kill with impunity. Once more, Wiesel's deceptively simple statement presents an image of the *anus mundi* that is insinuated behind the actual words, as it was in the "Kingdom of Death" that man assumed the role of God, and with merely a silent gesture condemned millions of human beings to annihilation.

The statement without a counterstatement serves an analogous function. It is most frequently found in the form of rhetorical questions and statements: "L'Eternel, Maître de l'univers, l'Eternel Tout-Puissant et Terrible se taisait, de quoi allais-je Le remercier?" (NAJ, 45); "The Eternal, Lord of the Universe, the All-Powerful and Terrible, was silent. What had I to thank Him for?" (N, 42). "Où est Gavriel? . . . Dans le vent, dans le feuillage, dans le silence?" (PF, 130); "Where is Gavriel? . . . In the wind, among the leaves, in the silence?" (GF, 120). "La Torah défend d'égorger la vache et son veau le même jour; et voici qu'elle ne s'applique pas à nous qui obéissons à sa loi. Voici que ce qui est accordé aux bêtes sera refusé aux enfants d'Israël!" (MJ, 70); "The Torah prohibits killing the cow and her calf on the same day; yet this law, which we have faithfully observed, does not apply to us. See that what is granted to animals is refused to the children of Israel" (BJ, 73). "Le plus beau discours est celui qu'on ne prononce pas" (CF, 43); "The most beautiful speech is the speech one does not pronounce" (FS, 45). Each of these morphological blocks demands a response or commentary, but none is forthcoming. A call is uttered, but no one stands prepared to answer. Silence alone is evoked; it becomes a refuge and a weapon for the speaker. Moreover, many of the elements of the statement without a counterstatement call upon God, who likewise does not reply. A pervasive, cosmic silence is the only response, and it is precisely this silence that stands as the foundation of Wiesel's literary universe.

It is necessary to stress that these basic morphological forms of silence can be viewed as sharing features with actual morphological elements of language. Like them, these basic units of Wiesel's structure of silence harbor hidden degrees, secondary memories, and they generally signify the inability of Wiesel to utter the unsayable.

Syntax

The syntax of silence in Wiesel's novels represents a more complex level, for it is here that Wiesel attempts to assemble the morphological elements into specific patterns, and thus to elicit another set of implications through silence. A notable feature at this level is the continual use of negation. Wiesel frequently accomplishes this by using negative particles, or by the use of adjectives with negative connotations and adverbial expressions. These elements accentuate the silence descending about the text. And, by imposing these negatives, Wiesel introduces other elements hidden in the meta-silence. Secondly, the continual use of negation distances positive elements. These syntactic silences that Wiesel consciously imposes stress those elements of chaos and destruction.

The *page blanche* and *le grand silence typographique-respiratoire* must likewise be viewed as other forms of negation. The morphological blocks and their silences evoke an atmosphere in which reality becomes too wearisome to bear. A need is thereby created to banish language temporarily so that writer and reader might gather their wits. This textual silence is a visible feature and an active force. Furthermore, it signifies a presence in the absence of language and, as I shall demonstrate later in this analysis of the various novels, this presence permits the evolution of a positive direction.

Wiesel heightens the effect of these various factors by a masterful implementation of punctuation. The natural use of punctuation underscores our awareness of these silences and causes the written word to approximate the spoken one. Punctuation assists in framing words, phrases, and sentences. The silence they evoke enhances the power and artistic effect of the text itself.

Silence is also discernible at this level via notions of testing and absence. Through his protagonists, Wiesel often calls into play certain characters or events whose actual existence is doubtful. Two examples should provide support for this point. In *Le Mendiant de Jérusalem (A Beggar in Jerusalem),* the protagonist persists in awaiting the return of his friend, Katriel. Katriel's presence permeates the novel, yet that very existence is continually called into question. Katriel inhabits the silence that frames the text. He is an absent presence who forces the protagonist, David, to tests of truth. Similarly, in *Le Cinquième fils (The Fifth Son)* we are presented with another such silent presence: Ariel. His shade appears in almost every episode of the novel, and forces the nameless protagonist into a bizarre act of *dédoublement,* or doubling. This element of absence (viz., silence) becomes a significant catalytic force in the story and intensifies the reader's awareness of a larger, omnipresent presence weaving itself into the entire Wieselian literary tapestry.

Semantics

The various layers of silence blend together to produce a semantic tier. The rhetoric of silence in Wiesel's novels allows the phenomenon to transmit vital messages and communicate truth. The silence within and behind words, the visible silences of *la page blanche* and *le grand silence typographique-respiratoire* combine in this final level to create a new *milieu conducteur:* A fusion of language and silence that serves Wiesel as the means to expose the realities of the *anus mundi* and to investigate the human condition in its wake.

In Wiesel's oeuvre, meaningful silence serves several principal functions. It operates at a phenomenological level assisting in explanation, criticism, and challenging God and humanity. It is here that silence submits human beings to tests of truth. Secondly, morphological elements of silence as the unsaid come to fruition at this stage as the phenomenon itself approximates to the scenic backdrop of silence against which all other actions in the novels are played out. Finally, silence is theological. Wiesel utilizes it to highlight God's absence, to demonstrate His guilt and to challenge His Creation. The ensemble of these functions on the semantic level establishes the generative material for Wiesel's oeuvre and all subsequent themes. Silence represents the gathering energy that will dispel the chaotic, negative silences of Auschwitz and those of linguistic impotence and produce *l'énonciation* that may eventually evolve into authentic dialogue.

If theme is the central subject or motif of a work, then surely silence stands at the core of Wiesel's. Silence presents itself at the linguistic level. Silence is both an intention and an interest in his novels as well as being a source of information. The novels demonstrate a label and aboutness of silence. It is a global sign in each work. The theme of silence is that feature of Wiesel's novels that correctly unites the divergent elements, and gives them cohesion while promoting the evolution of additional themes. To examine in detail the evolution and exercise of the theme of silence in Wiesel's novels, I shall now undertake a chronological examination of them, from *La Nuit* (*Night*) to the most recent, *L'Oublié* (*The Forgotten*).

CHAPTER 2

Victims to Victors: The Trilogy

La Nuit (1958), L'Aube (1960), Le Jour (1961)

Dire l'indicible est presque impossible.
E. WIESEL

The existence and significance of the *univers concentrationnaire* occupy a central position in the history of the twentieth century. Prior to the rise of Hitler and the creation of his unique hell on earth humanity had never faced such barbarity, depravity, or abject terror where existence was a crime punishable by death. Merely to remember those horrors is not sufficient. As Paul Thibaud believes, we must forge new modes of thought and art to assist in responding to the two most obsessive questions arising from the Holocaust: How did the event occur, and how shall we think and act after the fact? As in a crystal, Auschwitz stands as the focal point through which all facets of contemporary civilization and culture pass. It constitutes the delicate fulcrum on which human history currently shifts. Auschwitz is likewise to be viewed as central to Wiesel's attitudes toward life and philosophy. Moreover, in his earliest novels, Wiesel demonstrates an affinity for the nucleus of preoccupations to which he would subsequently gravitate throughout his career: Silence. Through *La Nuit* (*Night*), his first novel, this event, Auschwitz, encounters the phenomenon of silence, together forming the epicenter of his literary creation.

LA NUIT

The text of *La Nuit* represents the survivor's cautiously painful attempts to set down a record of the horror and incarnate evil that was the *univers*

concentrationnaire and about which David Rousset has proposed several interesting notions: "The camps were inspired by the world of Ubu. . . . Camp
inmates inhabited a world torn from the imagination of Céline with the haunting obsessions of Kafka" (13; 63) [my translation]. Rousset's proposal suggests
a most striking metaphor, for in relating to the reality of the camps, his language fails and he has been obliged to resort to literary references as if they
offer the only means by which he can properly hope to define the *univers concentrationnaire*. More explicitly, Rousset alludes to three writers—Jarry, Céline,
and Kafka—each of whom presents chilling, nightmarish visions of the world
and of humanity. Yet, even allusions to particular literary figures and their
deformed view of the world can only approximate the full reality.

Against this phantasmagorical decor, the sixteen-year-old Wiesel witnessed
the destruction of the world he had known, that peaceful existence of the
Jewish shtetl where the changing seasons had been celebrated by the pious joys
of the Jewish holy days and festivals. That unique pre-Holocaust world had
undeniably suffered the poverty and deprivation of two millennia of prejudice,
pitting against them the light of Jewish life and learning. This distinctive culture had nurtured in Wiesel "a respectful, almost reverential attitude toward
language" (Estess, 1980, 5). Neither the traditional strengths nor the word itself
could stave off the onslaught of this particular "Night." If one accepts part of
A. Alvarez's definition of Judaism "not as a narrow orthodoxy but as a force
working perennially on the side of sanity" (7), *La Nuit* would then appear to
announce the advent of ungodly insanity.

La Nuit is a *témoignage,* a *document vécu* that mercilessly projects the reader
into Hitler's inferno. Eugene Heimler suggests that "you can only create from
something which is negative" (6), and it does seem that Wiesel has used the
nihil of the Holocaust as the generative material for a work that recounts the
deportation and destruction of a single Hungarian Jewish community and
details the loss of the witness's identity, who is reduced to a physical and spiritual cadaver at the novel's denouement. As shall be demonstrated, this text is
written in ever more negative layers of silence.

In *La Nuit*, silence combines with sparse, tautly concise prose in which the
naked horrors of the *univers concentrationnaire* infrequently appear, and from
which hysteria and disingenuous sentimentality are banished. If the Holocaust
as macro- /micro-experience reflecting on the human condition cannot be
properly expressed, then one must shroud in silence those unspeakable elements. Wiesel has stated that uttering the ineffable is almost impossible (PE,
28). His idea elicits a paradox common to Holocaust literature. As noted in
the previous chapter, the survivor must bear witness to what has been; yet
aspects of that reality cannot be told. Despite this, the author/survivor must

strive to achieve what he or she can. Wiesel's acceptance of the need to speak, in spite of the imposed silence of Auschwitz and of the impotence of words to describe the event, highlights his personal quest for a sense of truth.

In *La Nuit,* one is faced with silence in its most negative forms. It exists firmly as the novel's core. In referring to silence, I am not alluding to the high frequency of the word silence itself, but to those other structural features previously described and employed by Wiesel to evoke silence, notably *la page blanche* and *le grand silence typographique-respiratoire.* Within the space of this slim volume, Wiesel interrupts the text with such *blancs* eighty-two times. Elsewhere, the author himself emphasizes the importance such bits of white space signify when he writes: ". . . in the universe Auschwitz, everything is mystery. . . . White spaces themselves have their importance."[1] Clear evidence of this abounds in this *document vécu.*

The theme of silence found in *La Nuit,* however, extends far beyond such textual elements of words and blanks. If this *témoignage* represents the absolute negative pole attainable by silence, we must undertake to seek out its cancerous growth within other elements as they are drawn into the vortex of the *nihil.* The primary level at which one discovers this negative silence is the utter destruction of the self. "Silence in its primal aspect, is a consequence of terror, of a dissolution of self and world that, once known, can never be fully dispelled" (Des Pres, 1977, 38). This loss of identity effectively silences the image that constitutes human essence. "One literally became a number: dead or alive—that was unimportant; the life of a "number" was completely irrelevant" (Frankl, 1964, 52).[2] This destruction extends beyond simple identity as it seeks to silence the unique world of childhood and innocence. One must therefore seek to trace the evolution of the antithesis of all human values, in general, and the Jewish ethos, in particular, an action that is achieved by a painful silencing of words by words as readers are conducted into the chaos of silent, destructive negativity. Proceeding a step beyond, one must subsequently seek the ultimate denial of God, humanity, and the word in order to arrive at the heart of the *nihil ani mundi.*

The first element of life that must be silenced is time. Time lies at the heart of existence, a principle particularly true in Jewish thought and teachings. Abraham Joshua Heschel notes that "Judaism is a religion of time aiming at the sanctification of time" (216-17). So it is that at the beginning of *La Nuit,* time meticulously and meaningfully guides the young protagonist through life, through his studies and prayers. Time is represented as a creative force, a bridge linking man to eternity.

The first incursion of night into the harmonious passage of time is the deportation and subsequent return of Moché-le-Bedeau. The destructive silence of the Jewish tragedy has taken its toll. "Il ferma ses yeux, comme pour fuir le temps" (NAJ, 21); "He closed his eyes, as though to escape time" (N, 17). More importantly, this silencing of time brings with it other startling transformations. "Il avait changé, Moché. Ses yeux ne reflétaient plus la joie. Il ne chantait plus. Il ne me parlait plus de Dieu ou de Kabbale. . . ." (NAJ, 20); "Moché had changed. There was no longer any joy in his eyes. He no longer sang. He no longer talked to me of God or the cabbala" (N, 17). As time is silenced, creativity ceases, and negative silence descends over life.

Moché's return not only marks the initial transformation of time, but it evokes a curious response from the Jewish community of Sighet. Moché (whose name is Moses), the prophet who has seen the advancing night, is viewed as being a madman. The Jews would prefer to purchase his silence, to erase his message. Ironically, Moché's purchased mutism only permits the Jews of Sighet to resume life behind a protective facade of silence that descends. But this brief contact with the night has unquestionably altered life. Though the Allied broadcasts offer a degree of hope, Wiesel underlines the text with a bitter irony: The utter silence of the Allies concerning the fate of Europe's Jewish population.[3]

Though metamorphosing, time persists in its existence. With its natural passage the Nazis arrive. The course which would lead to Birkenau has been set into motion. Ghettos were established where life sought to maintain a degree of normalcy. Stories, part of the fabric of Jewish life, continued to be told. But, in medias res, the good stories being told are silenced and will remain forever unfinished. Words have lost their positive creative powers. The only remaining significant communication becomes nonverbal. Whereas time had previously stimulated creativity, it now stifles the word/Word. Time comes to represent a negative force, and even the "ongoing tale" is tainted by it.

Religious traditions whose foundations rest on the positive nature of time are effectively altered."Nous avions fait . . . le repas traditionnel du vendredi soir. Nous avions dit les bénédictions d'usage sur le pain et le vin et avalé les mets sans dire mot" (NAJ, 34); "We had the traditional Friday evening meal. We said the customary grace for the bread and wine and swallowed our food without a word" (N, 31). The traditional Jewish Sabbath meal, which inaugurates the day of rest, is a time of joy and song. The table is literally considered an altar to God around which special Sabbath songs, *zmirot,* are sung. Family and friends join together in peace and speak of God, the Sabbath, and the joys of life. These elements are pointedly absent. Wiesel's use of the French verb *avaler* likewise imparts a sense of haste foreign to the Sabbath table, as well as presenting connotations of animal-like behavior, both notions sadly lost in the English translation.

Wiesel's use of the Sabbath in this context is essential, for if the silencing of time is to be absolute, the element of *kdusha* (holiness), which first appears in the Bible with reference to time—"And God blessed the seventh day and made it holy" (Genesis 2:3)—must be removed. Holiness is lodged in time, most notably on one particular day: the Sabbath. The Talmud explains that the Sabbath represents *m'en olam ha'ba,* something akin to the world to come. Heschel believes the Sabbath is:

> The microcosm of spirit. . . . The seventh day is a reminder that God is our father, that time is life and the spirit our mate. . . . For the Sabbath is the counterpart of living; the melody sustained throughout all agitations and vicissitudes which menace our conscience; our awareness of God's presence in the world. (225–26)

As the final blow, therefore, the Sabbath, replete with its holiness, is silenced. "Samedi, le jour de repos, était le jour choisi pour notre expulsion" (NAJ, 34); "Saturday, the day of rest, was chosen for our expulsion" (N, 31). The synagogue where Sabbath prayers had previously been offered is transformed into a scene of desecration.

> La synagogue ressemblait à une grande gare. . . . L'autel était brisé, les tapisseries arrachées, les murs dénudés. Nous étions si nombreux que nous pouvions à peine respirer. Epouvantables vingt-quatre heures passées là. Les hommes étaient en bas. Les femmes, au premier étage. C'était samedi: on aurait dit que nous étions venus assister à l'office. Ne pouvant sortir, les gens faisaient leurs besoins dans un coin. (NAJ, 34)

> The synagogue was like a huge station. . . . The altar was broken, the hangings torn down, the walls bare. There were so many of us that we could scarcely breathe. We spent a horrible twenty four-hours there. There were men downstairs; women on the first floor. It was Saturday; it was as though we had come to attend the service. Since no one could go out, people were relieving themselves in a corner. (N, 31)

Not only has the Sabbath been stilled, but with this act of unholiness, universal *menuhah* (rest; repose) has been destroyed.[4] In the ensuing timeless silent void, there is no place for the Jews of Sighet.

The final rupture of time occurs with the arrival of the deported Jews at Birkenau-Auschwitz. After a seemingly endless night in the stinking confines of the cattle cars, time ceases to exist as they enter the kingdom of night where all the imagined horrors of two millennia of Christian iconography become real.

> Non loin de nous, des flammes montaient d'une fosse, des flammes gigantesques. On y brûlait quelque chose. Un camion s'approcha du trou et y déversa sa charge: c'étaient des petits enfants. Des bébés! Des enfants dans les flammes. (NAJ, 44)

> Not far from us, flames were leaping up from the ditch, gigantic flames. They were burning something. A lorry drew up at the pit and delivered its load—little children. Babies! Yes, I saw it—saw it with my own eyes . . . those children in the flames. (N, 41)

Such a vision cannot be real; it cannot exist within a normal temporal framework. "Je me pinçai le visage: vivais-je encore? Etais-je éveillé?" (NAJ, 44); "I pinched my face. Was I still alive? Was I awake?" (N, 41). Moral time, creative time, that dimension in which humanity exists and in which it discovers traces of the living God has been abrogated. "J'avais complètement perdu la notion du temps. . . . C'était sûrement un rêve" (NAJ, 48); "I had lost all sense of time. . . . Surely it was a dream" (N, 46). The coup de grace is finally dealt by the camp code of hairlessness. All vestiges of age disappear as young and old are reduced to naked, hairless beings. With the erasure of time, little remains of the protagonist.

This argument has merely attempted to point to the silencing of time within the Wieselian universe. In *La Nuit,* time ceases to have a creative dimension and enters the realm of pure negativism. As Wiesel's work evolves, time will remain fragmented as he passes from the world of the living to the domain of the dead. This particular feature produces a unique literary structure that will facilitate the blending of the past, present, and future, and will reinforce the notion of the instantaneous multiplicity of various levels of perception and significance.

Wiesel's use of time and fragmented structure firmly entrench his oeuvre within the traditions of contemporary writers, most especially the *nouveaux romanciers.* The role of the writer has been radically altered. Beliefs in former literary dogmas, which had propounded a faith in the unshakable nature of civilization, can no longer be supported. As a result, chronological time as a traditional aspect of storytelling can no longer be viewed as an ally; it has become a menacing shadow. Time had been equated to man's perception of reality. Moreover, after Auschwitz, reality could no longer be viewed as before. For Jean Cayrol, this fact represents perhaps the most influential element in the creation of modern literature. He discerns aspects of the *univers concentrationnaire* within all men. The fragmentation of linear time permits the past inexorably to become part of the future. Thus one can view Wiesel's use of this technique as representing his adherence to current literary trends, as well as serving as a universal reminder of those events that produced the initial rupture. Moreover, one must also view Wiesel's perception of time as being reflective of his own Hasidic background. Hasidic stories do not adhere to occidental conventions of temporal exigencies, but create notions of time that are subordinated to the message of the tale. Metaphysics and mystery reign, and the storyteller manipulates past and present to enhance particular moral themes.

As time is closely related to our understanding of reality, its silencing must therefore effect the existence and perception of truth. As previously noted, when Moché-le-Bedeau returned from his deportation and sought to warn the Jews of Sighet about the existence of the *univers concentrationnaire,* no one would believe him. His vision of truth could not be accommodated within a traditional temporal framework. This attitude is strengthened when, during the journey to Auschwitz, Moché's words are echoed and even intensified in the frightening prophetic ravings of Mme. Schächter.

Within the timeless world of the sealed cattle cars that serve as the bridge between Sighet and Auschwitz, between life and death, the journey becomes a metonomy of existence in the *univers concentrationnaire.* In this environment, Mme. Schächter's voice painfully reiterates the horrific reality Moché's had announced earlier, and which their current journey represents. The others react to her much as they had to Moché: They attempt to silence her. Nothing, however, is capable of stifling her violent, prophetic outbursts.

This action possesses intense irony as Wiesel here expresses a particularly Jewish element: The desire of a community to silence or drive away any bad tidings. Such behavior can be traced to the manner in which many prophets of the Old Testament were treated when pronouncing their visions. Wiesel has stated that the people of Judah rejected the prophet Jeremiah in much the same way as the Jews of Sighet spurned Moché and Mme. Schächter:

> One feared his words, therefore one rejected the person. They called him false prophet, madman. They pushed him aside, tormented him in public, they threw him into the dungeon: in short they did everything possible to discredit him. (FBP, 109)[5]

Nevertheless, Mme. Schächter's prophecies, like those of Jeremiah, become unbearable reality as the sealed train arrives at Birkenau.

Eliezer has come to exist within a timeless void from which truth has been either exiled or deformed. In this silent wasteland, he will suffer the destruction of his own beliefs in a just and true God, as well as in the goodness of fellow human beings. Wiesel accomplishes this annihilation of Eliezer's essence within the space of seventeen pages as the devouring black flame of the *anus mundi* rapidly erases the being who had existed. Within the text, silence becomes the method by which Eliezer is reduced to a cipher. This silence is evoked by several techniques. Sparse dialogue couples with terse, journalistic language, and *le grand silence typographique-respiratoire* to create a taut, fearful atmosphere. The word *silence* and its synonyms do not recur frequently, a choice that saves them from becoming meaningless clichés. Wiesel does, however, strike upon another technique: Punctuation. The use of punctuation accentuates the rapid respiration of the text and creates a feeling of impending doom. The text progresses haltingly, tripping and falling on its descent to hell.

Another striking feature is the absolute lack of gruesome detail, or even the mention of death. For the reader, these elements exist, but only in the meta-silence that Wiesel imposes and which forms the background of the story. The language of the *univers concentrationnaire* is one which cannot be expressed in common terms. "Languages have great reserves of life," states George Steiner. "They can absorb masses of hysteria, illiteracy and cheapness. . . . But, there comes a breaking point" (*Language,* 101). Wiesel does relegate certain realities of the *anus mundi* to silence. And yet, unexpressed elements do eventually rise from the depths to extinguish the voices of the living.

Roland Barthes believes that the voice is the symbolic substance of human life (*Bruissement,* 212). As a symbol of life, the voice has no rightful place in the kingdom of death and is therefore methodically silenced. First, the protagonist's father's voice is stilled, then Eliezer's. Gradually, language itself is silenced. Life as it has been perceived ceases to exist.

With time and creative language silenced, the spirit of the *anus mundi* proceeds to invade Eliezer's soul and crushes his spiritual identity. One of the most painful acts is the demolition of the protagonist's view of God. The young talmudic student deeply believed in God, and had always nurtured the notion of the unique convenantal relationship between the Jews and God. Man would supplicate; God would respond. To those faced with the reality of Auschwitz, God reveals Himself as an impotent entity who has been robbed of His attributes of justice and mercy by the Angel of Death. For Wiesel, the God of the yeshiva* student has abdicated His Throne.

The pious Jew prays three times daily. During the morning prayers, psalms are chanted to the Creator of the Universe. Within the horrific kingdom of night such psalms would prove to be ironically blasphemous or utterly senseless. So it is that Wiesel composes a new psalm, one which reflects the negativity of Auschwitz and the eclipse of God. Its form and message offer the antithesis of Psalm 150, the culmination of the Psalter, a psalm which is an ecstatic exaltation in the Divinity. The French text alone is considered here:

---

*yeshiva: a Jewish school of higher education.

Jamais je n'oublierai cette nuit, la première
    nuit de camp qui a fait de ma vie une
    nuit longue et sept fois verrouillée.
Jamais je n'oublierai cette fumée.
Jamais je n'oublierai les petits visages des
    enfants dont j'avais vu les corps se
    transformer en volutes sous un azur muet.
Jamais je n'oublierai ces flammes qui
    consumèrent pour toujours ma Foi.
Jamais je n'oublierai ce silence nocturne qui
    m'a privé pour l'éternité du désir de
    vivre.
Jamais je n'oublierai ces instants qui
    assassinèrent mon Dieu et mon âme, et
    mes rêves qui prirent le visage du désert.
Jamais je n'oublierai cela, même si j'étais
    condamné à vivre aussi longtemps que Dieu
    lui-même.
Jamais. (NAJ, 45–46; N, 45–46)

Each line of Psalm 150 commences with the word: Hallelujah. The short flowing verses positively direct and enjoin humanity to exalt in God's presence. They resume the aspiration of Israel's mission. In contrast, Wiesel's lugubrious eight lines negate that message while openly accusing God of complicity in the creation of the *anus mundi* and in the murder of His "Chosen People." The Francophone reader would also hear in Wiesel's anti-psalm a more secular echo: the resounding *"J'accuse"* of Emile Zola. Stylistically akin to Zola's controversial piece of 1898, Wiesel hammers out the message of his inability to forget what he had witnessed. The driving rhythm accentuates that the author will force God to remember what He had permitted to occur. This striking text similarly signifies the protagonist's utter disillusionment with God. Former beliefs possess no validity. Eliezer has found that his God is lost amid the negative silence of the *univers concentrationnaire*. And God's own silence amid such incarnate evil indicts and condemns Him. Yet despite such a challenge to his beliefs, Eliezer never rejects the existence of God. The silence of Auschwitz has submitted the omnipotent God of Eliezer's youth to the test of truth, only to find Him wanting.

Not only is God called to the bar in this silence; the very notion of humanity, the enlightened being to which Mauriac makes reference in his Preface to the novel, is likewise examined and found to be wanting. The vision of the human race has radically altered. On "planet Auschwitz," human moral responsibilities are silenced and deformed into indifference. Humankind blindly and mutely accepts the events of the Holocaust. Human guilt is first evidenced while the Jews of Sighet are still in their ghetto. The "others" in the town indifferently accept matters, and eventually witness the deportation of their Jewish neighbors. Their silence condemns them and, by extension, all humanity. As Cynthia Haft concludes: "Non-activity, passivity, for Wiesel . . . is equated with negative activity; therefore the man (*i.e.*, the Other in *La Ville de la chance*) is guilty of collaboration" (36). The very fact that the Jewish population could so easily be deported destroys Eliezer's innocent illusions about human goodness and justice. Thus, for the protagonist, the corrosive, negative mentality of the concentration camp philosophy, that of every peron for himself/herself and every person being your enemy, evolves and assumes primacy. The view of humanity, created in the image of God, is shattered and banished. The last shreds of respectful human dignity fall away under the cries of camp guards. The ultimate silencing blow to human identity occurs when Eliezer is stripped of his name and thereafter becomes A–7713.

By the conclusion of this third episode, the silent backdrop of Auschwitz has annihilated the voices of the pre-Holocaust world. The remainder of the narrative merely serves to supplement this initial silencing. The voice that is bound up with life and in life is strangled and muted. Only the chaotic, destructive silence of the *nihil* remains.

Each of the various episodes comprising the story of *La Nuit* reflects the omnipresent scenic silence of Auschwitz. Wiesel's use of the morphological, syntactic, and semantic aspects of silence permit the novel to descend into the depths of depraved negativity. And the principal question raised by the theme of silence emerges as: Where was God? This becomes the central issue about which silence and all other themes come to revolve.

In the opening episodes, Eliezer had been transported from the light of learning and truth to the blackness of the void as experienced at Auschwitz. Prayer and praise were cut off before a silent God. The only force to which one could respond, the only source of potency, was the SS, whom David Rousset defines as: "In the high places of a merciless cult of punishment, the SS were the frenzied sacrificial priests dedicated to the service of an output-hungry Moloch and to a sinister, burlesque justice. Ubu was their god" (107) [my translation]. God no longer controls His creation. The SS decide who shall live and who shall die; it is they who direct the fate of the Jewish prisoners. Throughout the book, the fiery cloud created by the Nazis compels the Jews to move on. When the Jewish remnant is starving, sadistic workers—emanations of this *Ubu-Dieu*—cast stale bread into the open railway cars, a scene serving as the antithesis of God's gift of manna in the wilderness (Exodus 16: 13–17).[6] Each step, every example, emphasizes the absence of the divine and the presence of evil. Akiba Drumer, another character whose faith is shattered, poses this most serious question: "Where is God?" Those three words, like the four opening notes of Beethoven's Fifth Symphony, pound out the single most urgent question against which Eliezer and all humanity must struggle. Where was God? At the public hanging of a young boy that obsessive question arises from the meta-silence before uneasily dissolving again into it:

> —Où donc est Dieu?
> Et je sentais en moi une voix qui lui répondait:
> —Où il est? Le voici—il est pendu ici, à
> cette potence. . . . (NAJ, 74)

> "Where is God now?"
> And I heard a voice within me answer him:
> "Where is He? Here He is—He is hanging here on
> this gallows. . . ."[7] (N, 72)

According to André Neher, this scene echoes the Crucifixion:

> A strange evocation of the Passion, with the difference, deep as an abyss, that it was not, however, God who was hanging on the cross but an innocent little Jewish child, and that after three days he was not to rise again (Exil, 236) [my translation]

This particular scene reflects the final silencing of the young protagonist's faith and hopes in the God of his youth. The powerful God of his religious studies possesses no meaning in Auschwitz. How could one maintain belief in the majesty and justice of God in the face of such debasement and depravity? The overwhelming silence of God generates a spiritual revolt within Eliezer, so that on Rosh Hashana*, he refuses to pray or to bless God's Name. God stands in the dock, accused by Eliezer of silent indifference. This rebellion casts the protagonist into the depths of a void where he is painfully alone in a world whence God has been exiled. This bitter estrangement culminates ten days later on Yom Kippur† when Eliezer abandons the obligatory fast and stresses: "Je n'acceptais plus le silence de Dieu" (NAJ, 77); "I no longer accepted God's silence" (N, 76).

As Eliezer no longer possesses faith in God, he must seek strength and life elsewhere. In the context of traditional Jewish life, such a source of comfort and renewal can be found within the family. Yet the family unit Eliezer had known was forever ruptured upon his arrival in the *univers concentrationnaire*

---

*Rosh Hashanah: literally "head of the year," the Hebrew refers to the Jewish New Year.
†Yom Kippur: the Jewish Day of Atonement that occurs ten days after the Jewish New Year. It is the culmination of an intense period of introspection and repentance.

when his mother and sisters had been marched off to the gas chambers. His only hope lies in his father whose hand he tightly holds. The remainder of *La Nuit* reflects the relation of father and son within the *anus mundi.*

Wiesel demonstrates a particular fondness for introducing biblical stories and characters into his oeuvre. In *La Nuit,* the tale he evokes is that of the *Akeda,** the story of Abraham and Isaac and God's demand for sacrifice. *La Nuit* becomes a rewriting of this story; and, Eliezer's question "Where is God" stands as the antithesis to Isaac's question in Genesis 22:7: "Where is the lamb?"

The *Akeda* is a principle central to Judaism, as it clearly demonstrates the faith and fervor of both Abraham and Isaac in their service to God's commands.

> Few chapters of the Bible have had a more potent and more far-reaching influence on our people than the story of the binding of Isaac. It has fired the hearts of countless generations of Israel with an indomitable spirit and with unwavering steadfastness to the principles of our faith, however great the sacrifices involved. (42)[8]

The *Akeda's* influence resides in the fact that it offers a brief outline of the entirety of the Jewish experience of *Leidensgeschichte,* while also posing several difficult and perhaps insoluble questions for human beings.

The rewriting and reversals of the *Akeda* in *La Nuit* underscore how radically the original has been transformed, how much more painful is God's silence, and how the miracle that saved Isaac's life cannot transpire in this particular story where death reigns supreme. The reversal is further highlighted by the fact that though father and son walk to the sacrifice together, only the son will survive. The father's death signifies the silencing of the past and its meaning. Faith formerly espoused, the legacy of the tale which the protagonist's father had been telling and that had been silenced, can never be transmitted. The Holocaust *Akeda* becomes representative of total negation, of the utter silencing of Eliezer's world and its Jewish ethos. With its evocation, the *anus mundi* achieves momentary victory. Silence in its vilest guise will reign sui generis.

In the universe of death, where the miracle of life cannot occur, the hope and joy of the outcome of the *Akeda* mock man. Faith destroyed, the legends and stories of the past seemingly forever silenced, the only element in Eliezer's existence that has given him the strength to continue, his last vestige of humanity, has been his relationship with his father. They have endured their "test" together, just as Abraham and Isaac had functioned as one, a notion Wiesel stresses in his midrash on the *Akeda:* "Le mot clé ici encore est *yakh-*

Akeda: The Hebrew term literally means "the binding" and refers to the binding of Isaac on the altar by Abraham. See Genesis 22:1–19.

dav, ensemble" (CB, 82); "Once more the key word is *yakhdav,* together" (MG, 89). From the moment father and son enter the kingdom of night, they have sought to remain together. This has been Eliezer's overriding desire. Together they are marched to a flaming pit; together they lose all aspects of human dignity and identity; together they suffer the ignominious treatment reserved for *Untermenschen;* together they endeavor to combat the void of the night.

Yet even this element of the *Akeda* of the Night contains a cancerous element that will lead to its being silenced. Walking this path together does not imply life, but death. The philosophy of this kingdom quite simply stated is every man for himself. Each person faces the unutterable pain and loneliness of existence alone. Former relationships, be they father and son, mothers and daughters, brothers, sisters or friends, signified death. This idea produces a state of physical impotence first manifesting itself when his father is beaten and brutalized. The ethos of the *univers concentrationnaire* prevents Eliezer from acting. His conscience weighs the frightening reality of the choice between his moral duty to his father, with whom he walks this frightening path, and his responsibility to preserve his own life at all costs. His body cannot and does not react; he stands paralyzed, his muscles "silenced" before the terrors of Auschwitz. Yet despite this episode, Eliezer remains with his father even while other father-son relationships decay. For example, Rabi Eliahou's search for his own son crystallizes into a chilling realization for Eliezer. He recognizes Rabi Eliahou's son's desperate desire to be rid of the burden his father represents, and thus perhaps to ensure survival for himself. This shocking image more sadistically reveals itself during the transfer from Gleiwitz to Buchenwald, when the starving prisoners fight for bread. From the melee, Eliezer witnesses a son strangle his own father in order to extract a molding crust of bread from the old man's mouth.

Such scenes remain engraved on Eliezer's mind as the life of his own father ebbs. The voice that had come to signify life is gradually silenced. Without his voice, Eliezer's father effectively no longer exists in this world. The child assumes the role of father, the father the child. And yet, even as his father weakens, even as their relationship together is gradually silenced—a relationship that represents the last vestige of Eliezer's Jewishness—the protagonist refuses to abandon his father. "Ici, il n'y a pas de père qui tienne, pas de frère, pas d'ami. Chacun vit et meurt pour soi, seul" (NAJ, 115); "Here, every man has to fight for himself and not think of anyone else" (N, 115). This crushing advice is offered by a friendly *kapo* on January 28, 1945. Eliezer's father dies the next morning. Unable to cry, he has but one thought: Free at last! Death has silenced his only link with the past, with the family, with tradition.

Several critics, among them Ted Estess and Ellen Fine, believe that with the death of Eliezer's father the reader has reached the deepest realm of night. I must subjoin a critical subsidiary qualification to their proposal, for this traumatic event only reveals its full power and significance if it is explicitly linked to the *Akeda*. In Genesis, God—albeit through an angel—does intervene, the miracle of salvation does occur. In this instance, however, God is silent and refuses to acknowledge His covenant with the Jews. Hitler alone remained faithful to his covenant: "Il [Hitler] est le seul a avoir tenu ses promesses, au peuple juif." (NAJ, 88); "He's the only one who's kept his promises, all his promises, to the Jewish people" (N, 87). Elsewhere, Wiesel insists:

> Nous avons connu des enfants qui, comme Isaac, ont subi le sacrifice dans leur chair; et certain, devenus fous, ont vu leur père disparaître sur l'autel avec l'autel, dans un braiser qui incendiait le plus haut des cieux. (CB, 87)

> We have known children who, like Isaac, lived the Akédah in their flesh; and some who went mad when they saw their father disappear on the altar, with the altar, in a blazing fire whose flames reached into the highest of heavens. (MG, 95)

The path that Eliezer has trod with his father is now his alone. His father, his God, his world, are dead. This is his inheritance. "In *Night* I wanted to show the end, the finality of the event. Everything came to an end—man, history, literature, religion, God. There was nothing left" (Reischek, 1976, 46). So it is that the protagonist has been swallowed by the silent void of Auschwitz. "Du fond du miroir, un cadavre me contemplait" (NAJ, 119); "From the depths of the mirror, a corpse gazed back at me" (N, 119). Unlike the biblical survivor, Isaac, who pursued a normal life, Eliezer will always exist in a realm of specters. The cadaverous gaze in the mirror at Buchenwald reflects the paralyzed, mute victim par excellence. He signifies Hitler's victory; and, ironically, he likewise represents the seeds of Hitler's defeat. For if *La Nuit* is the vision of the void, that *nihil* similarly serves as the spawning ground for attempts to break or modify the murderous silence imposed in the *univers concentrationnaire*.

L'AUBE

If *La Nuit* is the foundation of Wiesel's work, *L'Aube* (*Dawn*) constitutes the first degree of commentary. The concentric circle formed by *L'Aube* represents a gray, cold, and silent ashen realm that complements the horror of *La Nuit*. The story is, in fact, drawn in shades of night. The opening and closing passages of the novel echo one another and unite to form a zone that is neither day nor night. Wiesel's literary irony likewise mocks the protagonist's struggle to escape the solitary torment of his Parisian exile where days are drawn in "une lumière pâle, déjà fatiguée, couleur d'eau moisie (NAJ, 137); "A pale, prematurely weary light the color of stagnant water" (N, 137). The character and his tale remain closed within this outer realm of hell; and, just as at the end of *La Nuit* where the protagonist is staring into the mirror, so too is the protagonist of *L'Aube* seeking some reflected image at the beginning of that novel, an image that is only realized with the novel's conclusion: "Je regardais ce morceau de nuit. . . . Le morceau noir, fait de lambeaux d'ombres avait un visage. . . . Ce visage, c'était le mien" (NAJ, 198); "The tattered fragment of darkness had a face. Looking at it, I understood the reason for my fear. The face was my own" (N, 204). Appearances would suggest, therefore, that the Wieselian circle remains as static and closed as the *nihil* of *La Nuit*. Maurice Blanchot states in *L'Ecriture du désastre* that "Perhaps writing is a means to bring to the surface something of the absent sense, to welcome that passive pressure that is not yet thought, but is already the disaster of thought" (71) [my translation]. Through the medium of writing, Wiesel places his protagonist betwixt and between. Obscured time refuses to progress, forcing the protagonist to wallow in the silent void that rises to engulf him. Questions obsess him. A burning desire drives him to attempt to comprehend the events that had cast him into the role of victim. These various tests resurrect the hidden, muted beast of the Holocaust, without any mention of the event itself. The *poussée passive* Blanchot mentions in the original French text metamorphoses into a tense cloak of silence, which permeates the textual surface and infuses itself into the very essence of writing. *La pensée,* the thought, does not yet exist; only the silence of the preexistent thought. Furthermore, the specially evoked silence of *L'Aube* will stand as a counterpoint to the word and even to the *désastre de la pensée* (disaster of thought) suggested by Blanchot.

The silent elements of *L'Aube* both represent a continuation of the negative silence imposed by the authority of the *anus mundi* and constitute the initial movement away from the *nihil* toward concealed regenerative forms. François Mauriac advances the proposition that "in the most tormented lives, speech counts little. . . . The drama of a living being almost always transpires and comes undone in silence" (155–56) [my translation]. Mauriac's statement sheds additional light on the general evolutionary course of silence. He perceived everything of importance as passing through a universal atmosphere of silence that molds the destinies of characters, placing them, as M. Parry contends "into a more distant orbit from their fellow men" (790). Parry's observation is equally true with regard to Wiesel's second novel. Though Elisha, the protagonist, has abandoned his Parisian prison for a stiflingly hot, closed room in Palestine, where he is engaged in terrorist activities, he persists in estranging himself from his comrades by his silences. Though he has abandoned his philosophical quest for understanding his situation, and has accepted his role as a maker of historic destiny, silence will continue to open a gulf between him and all he seeks. His silences are negative, destructive. They do not draw him nearer to God or fellow human beings. Thus, the solitary, mute realm in which Elisha exists is not that "sublime world of silence and solitude which is the privileged place of communion with God" (790), which Parry sees in Mauriac's fiction, but rather a silent debate that rages through the night, and will lead, not to God, but cynically back to the ghostly point from which all began. By the novel's conclusion, the negative silences of the Holocaust will again possess him.

Elisha's problem can be defined in Blanchot's words as follows: "It is necessary to cross the abyss, and if one doesn't leap, one will not understand" (*Ecriture*, 23) [my translation]. Blanchot suggests that man must reach out beyond a chasm that separates him from life and others in order to fathom his own existence. Without such an effort to erect a bridge of sorts by which man might attempt to communicate with *l'autrui* (the other), there can be no degree of understanding. Elisha's solitary existence has produced nothing. He must act, for in action he assumes responsibility for his life, his future, and his relations with others. Therefore, he decided to leave Paris for Palestine, exchanging his paralytic impotence for a course of pseudo-Messianic action. But this action achieves nothing. Because of the weight of silence of Auschwitz he bears and which he never honestly faces, any action will result in nothingness, another victory for the negativity of the *anus mundi*, another success for that silence.

From the beginning of the novel, battle lines are plainly delineated for the continued struggle between humanity and God. Placed within the context of silence, the spiritual struggles and physical actions will lead to a further silencing of God's nature in this world, of the past and of the self, thus resulting in a more desperate and pathetic exile for the protagonist—even to the point of rendering his name, Elisha, which means "God will save," useless and redundant.

Before proceeding with an analysis of the role of silence in this novel, a particular element must be mentioned: Gesture. Jean-Jacques Rousseau postulated that gesture represents "an adjunct of speech, but this adjunct is not an artificial supplement, it is a recourse to a more natural, more expressive, more immediate means of communication" (*Langues*, 29) [my translation]. Physical gesture possesses the value of a mute linguistic sign, its origins lying in the phenomenon of speech and the human desire to communicate. Rousseau maintains elsewhere that gestures "by their very nature are more expressive. . . ." (*Oeuvres*

III, 149) [my translation]; they represent humanity's most primordial language, a passionate cry that rises in silence from the depths of the human soul, and as such remain untainted by the ambiguity inherent in the word. It is highly significant, therefore, that Elisha does not gesture to accentuate his state of being during the course of the night's struggle. Vocal articulations are painfully few, gestures freeze in the impotence of the moment. Phenomenologically, it is an absolute, cold, hard silence that results. Again it is Rousseau who in *Les Rêveries du promeneur solitaire* submits that such silences induce sadness serving up an image of death (1047). Despite similarities with those previously expressed views of Brice Parain, Rousseau's evaluation and ideas concerning silence are nevertheless transformed into reality for Elisha. Surrounded by the ghosts of his past, he passes the night in a state of mutism both of word and gesture. Wiesel's ultimate irony lies in the fact that the novel's verbal and gesticular impotence are eventually shattered by a single act: the pulling of a trigger. Rousseau's idea of an image of death indeed metamorphoses into death. Should one accept Emmanuel Lévinas's supposition that "the physical gesture is not a nervous reaction, but a celebration of life" (*Humanisme,* 28) [my translation], that together with the spoken word it amounts to a creative act, then *L'Aube,* with its gesticular sterility and negative, murderous silences, signifies impotence, lack of creativity, and an act of destruction.

Once again, the textual elements of silence build a particular network of thematic levels where the articulated and unarticulated battle for supremacy transpires. The spoken dialogue remains sparse, taut. The conventional use of interior monologue establishes dramatic tension that erodes the moral character of the protagonist. The living and the dead discover no saving balm in the word. Their only shelter is silence.

From the beginning of the novel, silence is evoked. As the protagonist gazes at the descending night, the city appears more silent than ever. In the confines of the terrorists' cell, physical stillness and metaphysical mutism reign. Each episode, every memory or conversation is intensified by silence, especially those generated by inner reflection that highlight the unspoken. Elisha's first encounter with the Zionist activist, Gad, consists of terse statements whose impact is accentuated by the thoughtful silences that in themselves form a sort of interior monologue, or *sous-conversation proustienne.*[9] Though the unarticulated thoughts may occur within a fraction of a second, they do stress the unsaid, setting those elements into direct contrast with the short, articulated dialogue. Such silent elements also permit us to formulate a composite portrait of the protagonist and his torturous psychological composition.

This technique reaches its climax when Elisha faces his victim, John Dawson, whose life will be taken in revenge for the hanging of a Jewish terrorist by the British. Their conversation gradually becomes unbearable for Elisha, as Dawson's questions elicit cryptic responses pregnant with unspoken meanings. By delving into the words left unsaid, into the silent thoughts themselves, we discover roughly undulating movements and secrets that exist below the surface, silent undercurrents filled with echoes from the past, memories of other victims—whose ghosts stand around Elisha—and of other executioners. All of this directly and tragically links the protagonist to the Nazis. Mental images, prophetic flashes, cascade through the protagonist's mind in a masochistic avalanche as the reader is hurled precipitously toward the moment when Elisha will pull the trigger. Each of John Dawson's questions fuels the silent debate burning Elisha's conscience; every question constructs a new tension between past, present, and future. And, once the deed has been accomplished, the protagonist returns to the stifling room where his comrades await his return. Silence still commands the room when he appears, but it is a radically altered silence. Relief, guilt, indifference? This final silence remains oppressively enigmatic.

A far more frightening aspect of silence haunts the novel: That of the dead who arrive to witness the murder. One-third of the novel consists of a silent debate between Elisha and the dead who represent his past and its ethos. Initially, their silence is frighteningly complete. Elisha's father's specter declines to respond to his son's queries; that of his old master remains mute; and that ghost that represents his own youth threatens him with an impenetrable silence. Elisha comes to recognize that the self he is creating, the future murderer, strikes the ghosts mute. Finally, the ghost of the child he had been speaks, almost in a parody of the Four Questions asked by children at the Passover seder, and accuses him: "Cette nuit est différente; et tu es différent cette nuit—ou plutôt, tu vas l'être" (NAJ, 166); "Tonight is different, and you are different also, or at least you're going to be" (N, 171). This remark reflects Wiesel's affinity to Sartre's existentialist views concerning the continuing creation of one's essence. Like Sartre, Wiesel is indicating that whatever one has been can be radically altered by a single action. Thus, in accepting his role as executioner, Elisha becomes a murderer, and I believe Wiesel would argue that, by extension, those people who can be seen as the cornerstones of Elisha's personality would similarly be labeled murderers.

Does the silence of the dead constitute a judgement of Elisha and of the movement he has joined? André Neher views such silences as part of an essential, existential debate: "A life-and-death contestation fought out point by point, scene by scene, between the young unhappy Elisha and these silences embodied in phantoms" (Exil, 231) [my translation]. The silence of the dead Jews weighs heavily on Elisha, instilling terror and despair. Elisha, the silent, brooding protagonist, stands before these shades: "Lorsque tu nous vois, tu crois que nous sommes là pour te juger. Tu as tort de la croire. Ce n'est pas nous qui te jugeons: c'est le silence qui est en toi" (NAJ, 177); "When you see us you imagine that we are sitting in judgement upon you. You are wrong. Your silence is your judge" (N, 183). Elisha's silence in accepting the role of executioner judges him, and by extension the movement that commands him to silence God's law and take a life. Ironically, Elisha's silence in accepting this new role parallels God's silent indifference and active collaboration during the Holocaust.

Elisha has freely chosen to enter the terrorist cell, which now demands the taking of a life. The element of silence that drives these young Zionists to this conclusion is precisely God's absolute silence and the bankruptcy of Judeo-Hellenic civilization. Humanity must now seek to play God, to imitate the Creator in whose image human beings were formed. "En tuant, l'homme devient Dieu" (NAJ, 143); "Why has a man no right to commit murder? Because in so doing he takes upon himself the function of God" (N, 144), a belief that would abolish the ethos of Jewish life. In the face of God's absence, however, humankind feels the compulsion to act in order to affect the course of history. God's laws and commandments, which had framed the pre-Holocaust world, had given it meaning and substance, had constituted and sustained dialogue, now have become superfluous. Thus, when Elisha silences John Dawson's life, he is correct to cry: "J'ai tué! J'ai tué Elisha!" (NAJ, 197); "I've killed! I've killed Elisha!" (N, 203). His action effectively usurpes God's traditional role as the source of all life. The mute God, the impotent Creator of Auschwitz is removed by a human operation. Ironically, the promise of a brighter future merely reduces to another dawn the color of stagnant water. Elisha no longer exists. The dead and all they represent vanish. The understanding so desperately sought remains forever elusive. Only the silence within reaches out to stare back at Elisha from the reflection in the window-pane. Elisha has become one with the night of Auschwitz.

LE JOUR

In *La Nuit*, Eliezer struggled with a silent God, only to lose his faith. In *L'Aube*, Elisha usurped the mute God's primary position in the universe, only to lose his ethical heritage. In *Le Jour (The Accident)*,[10] a nameless protagonist has no God with whom to contend. He merely seeks Death, the ultimate degree of silence. The entire text evolves as a battleground between life and death.

Viktor Frankl remarks that in the concentration camps

> the prisoner who had lost faith in the future—his future—was doomed. With his loss of belief in the future, he had also lost his

spiritual hold; he let himself decline and become subject to mental
and physical decay. (74)

Moreover, having survived the *anus mundi* leaves each survivor tainted. "Notre
séjour là-bas a posé en nous des bombes à retardement" (NAJ, 286); "Our stay
there planted time bombs within us" (N, 303). Thus, the nameless protagonist's pursuit of death, which in Lillian Szklarczyk's words "represents a refusal
to live in a universe that is empty and void" (138) [my translation], underscores another victory for Hitler. Life, even without the weighty burden of guilt
for having survived, presents the anonymous protagonist with no logical reason for existing.[11]

In the first two novels of Wiesel's trilogy, the protagonists have gradually discovered themselves engaged in painful struggles between life and death. In
each, the spiritual self is demolished, a notion thematically linking the novels. Yet, despite the violent metaphysical upheavals that destroy the protagonists' souls, they do emerge alive, though estranged and exiled from God's
creation. In *Le Jour,* Josephine Knopp believes "this estrangement becomes
complete" (46). If, therefore, we accept David Williams's general notion of the
images of exile "as amputated member and as creature without dialogue" (4),
then we must acknowledge the evolving degrees of exile in the Trilogy as steps
toward the ultimate, silent extreme of exile as uncreator: Death.

This evolution poses a fundamental problem: That of the silencing of the
Jewish ethos on a purely personal level. *La Nuit* banishes Eliezer's faith; *L'Aube*
replaced the divine law of life with human will; *Le Jour* appears to shatter the
ideal of Jewish respect for life. This idea is graphically illustrated in the story
of Golda, a woman hidden in a bunker, whose child—a symbol of life and continuance—will not stop crying.

> Alors les autres, auxquels Golda elle-même s'était jointe, se
> tournèrent vers Shmuel et lui dirent: «Fais-le taire. Occupe-toi de lui,
> toi dont le métier est d'égorger les poulets. Tu sauras le faire sans qu'il
> souffre trop.» Et Shmuel s'était rendu à la raison: la vie d'un nour-
> risson contre la vie de tous. . . . Il avait pris l'enfant. Dans le noir, ses
> doigts tâtonnants avaient cherché le cou. Et le silence s'était fait
> dans le ciel et sur la terre. (NAJ, 259)

> That's when the others, including Golda herself, turned to Shmuel
> and told him: "Make him shut up. Take care of him, you whose job
> it is to slaughter chickens. You will be able to do it without making
> him suffer too much." And Shmuel gave in to reason: the baby's life
> in exchange for the lives of all. He had taken the child. In the dark
> his groping fingers felt for the neck. And there had been silence on
> earth and in heaven. (N, 272)

This episode exemplifies the crisis upon which Wiesel strikes in *Le Jour.* The sanctity of life is one of Judaism's most fundamental beliefs, one which supersedes faith in God and all aspects of the law. It is this reverence for life that the narrator places in question. The protagonist's attempted suicide and his protracted desire to die while in the hospital amount to the most supreme challenge yet found in Wiesel's fiction. The protagonist has tired of hollow protestations against God's silent injustice; he has, more effectively, rejected the past. Knopp believes *Le Jour* represents "the ultimate defiance of God, the final rejection of God's role in history" (46). It seemingly depicts the absolute victory of silence's negative role. And yet, by the novel's conclusion, we are impressed by the radical alteration in the protagonist's character. For the first time in the trilogy, a Wieselian protagonist is brought to tears. This reaction marks the beginning of renewal. The nameless protagonist has moved from the sterility of death toward the warmth of human feeling and emotion.

The theme of silence in this novel appears on several levels with varying complexity. In a manner of speaking, this novel is the silence after the horrific scream vocalize by the texts of *La Nuit* and *L'Aube. Le Jour* delineates those sharp, tense seconds after the articulated sound has ended, a moment charged with the silent echoes of the scream, which prolongs and intensifies the physical act. The elements of *La Nuit* and *L'Aube* are here synthesized and crystallized, transformed into new and more threatening forms of silence. Not only is the protagonist reluctant to speak about his past, but when he does vocalize his memories, the listener is threatened by those words and stories. What he recounts does not inspire understanding or hope, but merely engenders hatred that evolves from the listener's having been drawn into the hell expounded by the narrator. Silence would seemingly be safer for both parties. The protagonist comes to view himself as "un messager des morts parmi des vivants" (NAJ, 234); "just a messenger of the dead among the living" (N, 243), and he is on the side of the dead.

If, as earlier stated, the human voice represents life, then *Le Jour* immediately underscores the protagonist's tenuous hold on life. "On parlait avec difficulté" (NAJ, 203); "It was difficult to speak" (N, 207). Gestures prove difficult to accomplish. "Faire le moindre geste, c'était tenter de soulever la planète. J'avais du plomb dans les bras, dans les jambes" (NAJ, 203); "The slightest gesture was like trying to lift a planet. There was lead in my arms, in my legs" (N, 208).

The accident, which we later learn was a deliberate act of self-destruction, reduces the protagonist to a mute, his voice having temporarily been silenced. Moreover, he now finds himself excluded from all human contact and any bodily movement by the plaster cast and bandages that literally shroud him. In this specially designed cocoon proceeds the struggle between life and death. And yet, the protagonist's situation of extreme physical/metaphysical alienation that manifests itself in vocal and physical paralysis still permits a near-animal instinct to seize him. "Je fis des efforts surhumains pour crier" (NAJ, 213); "I made a super-human effort" (N, 218). This raging against death, represented by his desire to break the silence, is indicative of a shift in attitude. It is the initial phase of a radical metamorphosis. And, when finally he does speak:

> Ma voix n'était qu'un murmure. Mais je pouvais parler. J'en ressentis une joie qui me fit monter les larmes aux yeux. . . . La preuve que le pouvoir de la parole ne m'était pas ôté m'inonda d'une émotion que je n'arrivais pas à dissimuler. (NAJ, 213)

> My voice was only a whisper. But I was able to speak. This filled me with such joy that tears came to my eyes. . . . But the knowledge that I could still speak filled me with an emotion that I couldn't hide. (N, 219)

There is a fundamental paradox in this novel. For the first time in Wiesel's fiction we encounter two diametrically opposed forms of silence. The first represents the negation of life as exercised in *La Nuit* and *L'Aube*. In effect, this silence signifies separation of an individual from the group and a denial of a social or moral contract. The very existence of this negative silence, however, proves to be the germinating factor for a new and regenerative silence absent in the preceding novels. It is this more positive silence that produces the revolt against death, providing support for the protagonist's burning desire to speak. Thus in this novel, the text alternates between the negative silences of the Holocaust and those that produce joy at being able to speak.

The novel does witness, however, the birth of another degree of negative silence: The lie. Lying becomes a part of the protagonist's nature, as it allows him to exist in the realm of the living. Sartre defines lying as "a renunciation of expressing an impossible truth and using words not to get to know others but to be accepted, to be loved"[12] (*Situations I*, 200) [my translation]. A liar knows something but chooses to conceal it in a willful silence. By lying, the protagonist believes he will be marginally accepted by society, while his authentic self will pass undisturbed beneath the falsehoods. The question here is what truth does this protagonist choose to hide? An initial response would be that the horrors of the Holocaust lurk submerged beneath the placid surface of his language and actions. There is also the reality that his mind focuses on one abiding truth—death. But, more to the point, his frightening secret is his attempt to take his own life. For these reasons, the truth must be concealed.

Thus, when asked to recount his past, he flatly refuses. This imposed silence must be seen as a lie, as it obliterates and betrays the echoing voices of the countless dead. And, when some partial truth is spoken, either hatred or silence are the residual effects. Truth only appears to injure and to deform. Truth forces the protagonist to become a torturer who inflicts misery on those individuals as yet unscathed directly by the horrors of the *anus mundi*. As a result, the protagonist resorts to prevarication. The lie denotes an abandonment of one's responsibility to express the truth. In order to conceal the unspeakable, lying becomes an active adoption of euphemisms, or words possessing multiple meanings, or silence itself. Veracity emerges as another victim of the *shoah*.

Even if the protagonist were to discover those words that might best express his plight, they possess a degree of impotence and ambiguity that would require further elaboration. Thus, lying or silence would be best. As he tenuously exists in the realm of the living, he opts for speech, carefully, shrewdly choosing his words and phrases. His articulated lies easily silence truth. But, as with most liars, the protagonist lives in fear of discovery. In the novel, he himself is unsure whether under sedation this facade of lies had been shattered by a subconscious desire to purge himself of the many sublimated secrets he conceals. One example should suffice to illustrate this point. When he is no longer critically ill, his doctor, Paul Russel, initiates his own investigation into the protagonist's desire to die. "—De quoi donc avez-vous peur? A nouveau, j'eus l'impression qu'il me cachait quelque chose. Se pourrait-il qu'il sût? Avais-je parlé dans mon sommeil, pendant l'opération?" (NAJ, 243); "What are you afraid of, them? Again I had the impression that he was keeping something from me. Could he actually know? Had I talked in my sleep, during the operation?" (N, 254). The text plunges into a dense silence that conceals the protagonist's thoughts. His anxiety mounts with every query and each statement. This painful tension—transpiring as it does in silent Proustian undercurrents—produces its own piercing, threatening silence that tortures the protagonist. The hospital room becomes, by extension, another of the many symbolic prisons in which the early Wieselian protagonists find themselves. Moreover, the room signifies the continued existence of the *univers concentrationnaire* and of its menacingly negative silences that impose an impotent muteness on the protagonist. Unable to express his emotions, his tongue has become paralyzed. His silence signifies nothing more than a lie and, as such, represents a victory for the powers of death and evil. The world beyond his hospital room ironically echoes within, enticing him to join the living—an invitation he rejects. Russel strives to dislocate his patient's morose facade, only to encounter further silence. Even when queried if he loves his mistress,

Kathleen, the protagonist mutely considers before asserting the fidelity of his love. An obvious crisis arises between the conflict between the animal desire to live and the survivor's need to reject life. His affirmation of love for Kathleen, therefore, persists as nothing more than a lie; and, once he has stated this, a potent authorial silence imposes itself upon the text. "Rien ne bougeait plus. Le silence était complet" (NAJ, 244); "Nothing stirred. There was complete silence" (N, 255).

The various elements of silence do indeed stifle the aspects of life represented by Dr. Russel, the unseen world beyond the hospital room, and Kathleen. Kathleen especially represents life. Her verbal imperatives have continually pressed the protagonist through the motions of existence. When she visits him in the hospital, her incessant talking is juxtaposed to the protagonist's deathly silences. Thus, it is Kathleen who suffers most from the lies that mask the profound hidden secrets. One particular episode best exemplifies this situation. She happens to ask about the enigmatic Sarah. After some initial disquietude, the protagonist replies that Sarah was his mother's name, an answer embracing an element of truth while still subsisting as a lie. Sarah also happened to be a young girl whom the protagonist had encountered in Paris long before knowing Kathleen. More to the point, Sarah is the antithesis of Kathleen. She symbolizes death and the terror of the *univers concentrationnaire*. Forced at the age of twelve to become a prostitute in the camps, the innocence of her childhood torn from her, she is an extension of the protagonist's own tormented psyche. Her story haunts him and drives him to hatred. Sarah's regulated monotone voice and her prolonged, intense silences torment him from the depths of the monstrous silence of oblivion to which he believed the memory exiled. But Kathleen remains ignorant. Sarah, the silence of Auschwitz, will be Kathleen's eternal rival.

The lies and their accompanying silences imply other elements of the same night in which all early Wieselian characters exist. Arguments for life are negated by silence. Dr. Russel argues that life wants to live, to continue, to struggle against death. His logic merely draws an awkward silence. The protagonist unquestionably realizes the danger he represents for Russel. And yet, even this drama of interrogation ensues in nothingness, its conclusion a cold, disastrous silence. Thus, Michael Berenbaum would apparently seem correct in postulating that

> Death ultimately triumphs. Though the correspondent does rage against death and though he does outwit death a second time, the external forces of death and his own desire for death remain. The ashes of the past will inevitably return to haunt him as they have haunted him before. All being is being unto death. In *Le Jour* Wiesel

exposes a world in which God is at best absent in the struggle
between life and death. At worst, God may even be an ally of the
forces of death. (29)

Yet despite such firm support for death's supremacy, evidence exists within the
narrative that underlies the evolution of silence's role from a purely negative
pole to one in which it becomes a positive presence.

The protagonist's silences change to more transparent forms as Kathleen
attempts to understand him through the medium of silence. While he has been
ill, she has attempted to interpret his silences, daring to invade the reserved
region. With his defenses down, she has been able to penetrate the shadowy
void; or, has she been allowed to enter owing to an alteration in the type of
silence that predominates? For whatever the reasons, the protagonist's ten-
week physical isolation and recuperation have imposed changes, and have prepared the way for spiritual regeneration. The catalyst appears to be personified
in the character of Gyula, who alone appears capable of comprehending the
meanings and directions of the protagonist's silence.

Gyula represents life, but unlike Kathleen, whose timidity often borders on
the passive, he is a celebration of life. His name in Hebrew means redemption
or redeemer.[13] Gyula transforms the protagonist's words and silences into a
portrait, a metaphorical mirror, in which the latter is finally able to recognize
himself and his absolute estrangement from life. In the concluding pages of
the book, Gyula stands at the center as he emphasizes life, offering the protagonist redemption from death. Gyula's initial protestations appear merely
analogous continuations of those so strongly voiced by Dr. Russel and
Kathleen. What element in the friendship between Gyula and the nameless
protagonist passes in silence, unnoticed, a factor that will favor the former with
a degree of success? Gyula is also a survivor, a factor based on two textual
clues. First, the statement that only Gyula has been able to divine the protagonist's secrets suggests that he alone possesses some special quality allowing
him to comprehend the hidden significance of the protagonist's words and
silences. Second, Gyula comes to see the protagonist daily, in the afternoon.
The key-word here is afternoon. It offers sufficient insights to explain Gyula's
ability to fathom the text's morphological silences, and similarly establishes his
connection to being a survivor.

This time of day corresponds to one of the daily services of the Jewish
liturgy: *minha.* Tradition attributes the institution of this religious service to
Isaac, a survivor.[14] In *Célébration biblique,* Wiesel relates:

> Isaac a survécu. . . . Devenu poète—il est l'auteur de l'office de *minha*
> —il ne rompt pas avec la société, il ne s'oppose pas à la vie. . . . Il

s'établit dans son pays . . . il se marie, il a des enfants, il fonde un foyer; le destin n'a pas fait de lui un homme amer et aigri. (CB, 87)

What did happen to Isaac after he left Mount Moriah? He became a poet—author of the *Minha* service—and did not break with society. Nor did he rebel against life. . . . He married, had children, refusing to let fate turn him into a bitter man. (MG, 96)

Isaac like Gyula is a survivor who has come to accept life. The names *Isaac* (he who laughs) and *Gyula* (redemption) speak of joy, redemption, and a sense of life. Gyula, himself a survivor, is imbued with a sixth sense that assists him in understanding the protagonist's dilemma. It similarly explains his relative success in the wake of Kathleen's and Dr. Russel's failures.

Through his words, his own particular silences, and eventually his portrait of the protagonist, Gyula forces a transformation. He endeavors to convince the protagonist that suffering is given to the living; only the living can derive significance from suffering. Before the dreadful pictorial representation of the protagonist, Gyula's words resound like an incantation of exorcism: "Kathleen est vivante. Moi, je suis vivant. Il faut penser à nous" (NAJ, 297); "Kathleen is alive. I am alive. You must think of us" (N, 316). The protagonist has come to the brink. Gazing at himself in the portrait much as Eliezer had viewed his spectral reflection in the mirror at Buchenwald—and as Elisha had seen himself in the pane of glass—the nameless protagonist must choose. "Tout était dit. Le pour et le contre. Je choisirais les morts ou les vivants" (NAJ, 297); "Everything had been said. The pros and the cons. I would choose the living or the dead" (N, 317). As a coup de grace, Gyula burns the portrait, leaving only its ashes. But the novel's conclusion is far from inconclusive. The tears the protagonist now sheds reflect a limited return to life, a regeneration of the emotions of a living man.

Berenbaum's aforementioned statement that "death ultimately triumphs" in this novel now has limited validity. Man must die; life's expected culmination is death: "For dust thou art, and unto dust shalt thou return" (Genesis 3:19); "Man born of woman is short-lived and sated with trouble" (Job 14:1). Yet, despite the bitterness and negativity of the text, *Le Jour* reflects a subtle resurgence of and toward life. The essence of silence, its metamorphosing significance, create a tension that leads to speech, and this action eventually erupts in fire and water, both archetypal symbols of purification. Though crushed, the nameless protagonist is not defeated. He can now prepare to be born into an imperfect world where he must continue the struggle.

CONCLUSION

Wiesel's trilogy guides us on an exploration of hell and its aftermath. The three protagonists exist within the void of Auschwitz, amidst the destructive silence unleashed there. The *nihil* that destroyed their lives and beliefs reaches beyond 1945 and corrupts them, annihilating bodies and souls. Though they have survived, though they live in a lifeless exile, they too become victims. Their voices cry out as a single one. Moreover, the various levels of silence do evolve in the course of the trilogy and effect alterations in the protagonists.

As exiles, the three might appear shattered and lost. Yet Emile Cioran emphasizes that "it is a mistake to think of the exile as someone who abdicates, who withdraws and humbles himself, resigned to his miseries, his outcast state" (63) [my translation]. Eliezer remains alone, isolated, exiled from God and humanity. His world has been shattered by the greater silence of Auschwitz. Elisha, the survivor, opts for action in order to free himself from the painful solitude of his Parisian room. Ironically, the negative silence that predominates transforms his choice into an act of deicide. Both protagonists are victims of the Holocaust and its aftermath.

Initially, the same appears true for the nameless protagonist of *Le Jour*. Yet the silences at play in this novel crystalize into actions that reflect both negation and regeneration. The attempted suicide is symbolic of the most destructive silence: Death. But the protagonist demonstrates a faint though inexplicable desire to live. Despite his lies and silences, he does speak and, as Parain recognizes "speaking implies that one is not alone" (*Métaphysique*, 25) [my translation]. His is no longer a vegetative life where negative silences stifle words, thoughts, and deeds. The protagonist has recognized that life can be lived, though of necessity its essence will be monumentally altered by the events of the past. The words and silences of this third novel return to their origin in the Holocaust, and then emerge with a new sense of vigor and direction. *Le Jour*, bleak though it appears, promises a renewal of life and its unique dialogic relationships. The ambiguous conclusion does indeed present a possibility of "return;" the protagonist has shed the chains imposed by the negative silences of Auschwitz in order to accept the yoke of different silences. No longer tied down, he can progress. He emerges, in a peculiar way, a victor. Max Picard suggests: "In silence . . . man stands confronted by the original beginning of all things: everything can begin again, everything can be re-created" (22). If we accept the *nihil* of Auschwitz as the beginning of Wiesel's literary universe, which is a creation wrenched from that absolute nothingness by the Logos, then Picard's statement does indeed offer hope. The victor's hope will be realized in unique acts of *teshuva*, return, in Wiesel's fourth novel, *La Ville de la chance (The Town Beyond the Wall)*.

CHAPTER **3**

Images of *Teshuva:*
The Beginning of the Return

La Ville de la chance (1962)

Writing is a form of prayer.   *In my end is my beginning.*
   F. KAFKA   T. S. ELIOT

I n the trilogy, Wiesel had produced a sense of silent, frustrated impotence—
the silence of voices suffocated, the painful silence of others. While many
of these uses of silence are easily uncovered in *La Ville de la chance (The Town
Beyond the Wall),* one also senses a radical shift. Wiesel's fourth novel is remarkable in form and content, as it serves as a *point de tournant,* or turning point,
and a *point de départ,* or point of departure, for this reconciliation.

 La Ville de la chance marks that moment when the protagonist, though constantly beset by the problems of his lost youth, and pursued by ghosts from
the earthly paradise so cruelly stolen from him, attempts a return to the mainstream of human and Jewish existence. Wiesel, through his hero Michael,
moves toward the first authentic reconciliation with the past, as well as toward
the realities of a post-Auschwitz future. An act of purgation of ravaging guilt
is played out before the reader's eyes, the struggle moving to its powerful and
complex climax in a pattern reminiscent of the spirit of the *yomim ne'orim,**
the Days of Awe, and of Yom Kippur, the Jewish Day of Atonement.

---

*yomin ne'orim: literally, Days of Awe. These are the ten days of penitence that begin with Rosh
Hashanah, the Jewish New Year, and terminate with Yom Kippur, the Day of Atonement.
They are, in fact the culmination of a full month's introspection and repentance.

A critical feature that must be considered at this initial stage of analysis is the notion of *teshuva,* or return, which is an exceptional and integral element in the Jewish process of atonement, as it indicates a return not only to God and His commandments, but also to a fuller life, one in which a person devotes himself to establishing a human existence that is richer, more humane, and more godly.[1] *Teshuva* conveys spiritual and physical movement, a commitment to oneself, and to humanity. The "return," or the repentance, is based on reflection, prayer, and charitable deeds. Wiesel himself defines *teshuva* as "an act of consciousness, of awareness of willingness to take sides and responsibility for the future. One cannot modify the past, but one is given the power to shape the future" (FBP, 151). Through this process, the soul averts physical and spiritual degradation, and is illuminated and regenerated. The process unites the many facets of being, and molds them into a new wholeness.

On Yom Kippur, Jews do not merely seek forgiveness for their sins, but pray to be allowed to prove they have truly returned and are prepared to enrich their lives. Yom Kippur becomes a festival of the soul when "material things of life that tend to make us neglect our spiritual condition until our souls become numb and our hearts unresponsive to the higher values of life" (Rubinstein, 1972, 73) are set aside, while the penitent seeks to fan the minute spark of life and Jewishness still within the soul into a flame. Remorse for past action or inaction, penitence, and understanding form the essence of *teshuva* and Yom Kippur. The penitent longs for spiritual rejuvenation and for the granting of renewed life.

La Ville de la chance is far from being an account of a traditional, religious Yom Kippur where the contrite sinner begs forgiveness from the divine judge. The protagonist's acts of *teshuva* will seek to expunge that which is evil—that is, the ungodly elements implanted in him by the Holocaust and which continue to distort his life. Yet before confronting God, Michael must first fully comprehend himself, fathom his feelings of culpability, his fears, and his passionate desire to return to the dead town of his youth. Shrouded in silence, these elements constitute the foundations of his return, for his need of a Yom Kippur. The walls of silence and isolation that time and events have erected around him must now be destroyed, and he must recognize his own uniqueness as a survivor. Michael must recognize the importance and sanctity of life, and of the primary requisite to live life for others, and consequently for God. He is driven to return to himself in order to rediscover what it is to be human, for only then can he begin the lengthy process of rediscovering God and forcing Him to beg forgiveness of humanity.

The structure of *La Ville de la chance* is patterned after the Jewish day. By rabbinic tradition, each day commences with the setting of the sun at which time prayers are recited, the *ma'ariv*. Prayer is resumed in the morning, the *shaharit*, at times coupled to a reading from the Torah (Law) and occasionally joined to a full additional service, the *musaf*. Late afternoon sees the concluding prayers for the day, the *minha*. In his novel, Wiesel has divided the text into portions entitled *prières,* or prayers. In the novel's context, the word prayers ironically refers to the torture used by the secret police in Communist Hungary: "nommé ainsi par un tortionnaire érudit . . . parce que les Juifs prient debout . . ." (VC, 16); "named [thus] by an erudite torturer . . . because the Jews pray standing" (TBW, 7). This ironic touch is all the more sharp as Michael has rejected the God of his childhood and has very nearly refused his own Jewishness. He is a man who has refused to pray, and is now subjected to this cruel and inhuman travesty of prayer. But, it is precisely this "prayer" that will facilitate Michael's descent into the depths of his soul where he will reflect upon his life. In this sense of introspection and confession, "the prayer" evolves into a traditional prayer, one which responds to a need and signifies a "movement inward and outward, a movement toward life" (PE, 172) [my translation].

William James notes that in real prayer "something is transacting" and that "through prayer . . . things which cannot be realized in any other manner come about: energy which but for prayer would be bound is by prayer set free and operates in some part, be it objective or subjective, of the world of facts" (455, 456). In purely Judaic terms, Abraham Joshua Heschel believes that

> prayer is the essence of spiritual living; [it] takes the mind out of the narrowness of self-interest, and enables us to see the world in the mirror of the holy. . . . Prayer is a way to master what is inferior in us. . . . Prayer is an event that comes to pass between the soul of man and the word. (199; 198; 203)

It should be noted that the Hasidic world of which Wiesel was, and continues to be a part, has placed strong emphasis on prayer. Whereas traditional rabbinic Judaism stresses study, the Hasidic tradition introduces prayer to the center of life. It is in prayer that man found himself on the *dereh emet,* the way of truth, as it is through prayer that an awareness of God and the spiritual self can be achieved.

As noted earlier, Wiesel has defined prayer as that which responds to a need. Prayer in this novel stands as a metaphor for the creative act in which the protagonist purges his own guilt. The "prayers" are, therefore, responding to some deep need in the psyche of the protagonist. The "prayers" that Michael will undergo in the course of the novel's action will indeed become real prayers responding to actual needs profoundly rooted in the protagonist's spiritual self. More attention must be given to these prayers, to their structure and number, and to the manner in which they literally move Michael from solitary silence to active dialogue with others.

On closer examination of the number of prayers endured by the protagonist, we find the standard three, this recalling the cycle of the typical Jewish day; but at the end of the novel, Wiesel has added a *Dernière Prière*, a last prayer. On only one day in the Jewish year is a further set of prayers appended to the routine number: Yom Kippur The *ne'ila* (closing or concluding) prayers set forth again the themes of the day. Wiesel thus establishes a conscious metonymic allusion not simply to the structure of the Jewish day, but more precisely to the Day of Atonement. I must stress here that I am not referring to services on Yom Kippur of which there are five: *kol nidrei/ ma'ariv, shaharit, musaf, minha* and *ne'ila* but to combinations of prayers that form meaningful liturgical groupings: *kol nidrei/ ma'ariv; shaharit/ musaf; minha; ne'ila*. These prayers will serve as specific means to a necessary end, a method to effect Michael's return from the night into which he had been exiled.

The prayers of Yom Kippur bear a marked similarity to the "prayers" that Michael undergoes. The essence of the Yom Kippur liturgy accentuates the nothingness of man's solitary existence, his need of God, and his fellow human beings in order to survive as human. The prayers are laced with confession, history, and acceptance. Confession is an essential component of the prayers of Yom Kippur. In general, confession "corresponds to a more inward and moral stage of sentiment," which according to William James "is part of the general system of purgation and cleansing which one feels one's self in need of, in order to be in right relations to one's deity . . . shams are over, realities have begun; the man has exteriorized his rottenness" (452). The confessional prayers do not imply that the rottenness has been utterly purged, but rather indicate an attempt has been made to begin anew "upon a basis of veracity" (James, 1952, 452). In the case of Michael, I shall endeavor to prove this is so.

While standing at his private "wailing wall," Michael confesses his guilt for having survived, and recalls memories of those people who had touched his life, only to be cruelly removed. He calls upon everything he has ever known or loved to come to his aid, to help him regain the lost paradise. With his knowledge of Jewish tradition, Wiesel realizes that Michael's confession alone cannot ensure his "return," as "confession of sin alone, however, is not sufficient: words alone, however beautifully framed, cannot annul sin and gain forgiveness. *The whole course of life must be improved*" (Rubinstein, 1972, 88) [my emphasis]. Michael must move from bitterness and preoccupation with his solitary lot to a position of taking action to improve his life and the lives of others. He is required to learn compassion for a "return" to be assured. This is the general direction his "prayer" assumes, as he moves through his ordeal, retracing each step that has led him to this peculiar and personal Yom Kippur.

From the very outset of the tale, there is an awareness of the special nature of the descending evening. The twilight falls heavily, imbued with power and fearful solemnity that overcomes humankind and animals. Wiesel further underscores the extraordinary nature of this evening, and draws parallels with notions that rabbinic tradition establish in relation to Yom Kippur. These ideals evoke qualities of power, majesty, and ultimate truth. Humanity quakes in fear and awe before the judge of the universe. The liturgical poems *Ya'ale* and *Om'num ke'n* recall this fragile finitude of human existence. God is besought to recall our good deeds, and is requested to find some favor in our lives and actions to warrant renewed life. These prayers are chanted standing before the open Holy Ark: The unveiled book of our deeds paves the way to the moving penitential prayers.

Michael's personal ordeal begins in much the same way. As the sun sets, as nature and humanity prepare themselves for a unique day, Michael stands before the cold stone prison wall, and before the wall of silence within himself. He is poised to open a Pandora's box of memory, which represents his first step toward offering his own confession. Ironically, he is warned of the weighty consequences of this "prayer" when his tormentors tell him "on en sort vaincu, humilié" (VC, 17); "You finish them defeated and humiliated" (TBW, 8). Yet Michael is encased in his own silence, a silence he has borne from the man-made hell he had witnessed and continues to endure. Beyond the walls of his physical prison a storm breaks, pathetic fallacy mirroring the soul in torment. And through his fascination with the storm, Michael is drawn into the depths of his soul, into the inner self where the silence of his cell and of his self is broken by the thundering sound of the inner voices. The spiritual storm within the protagonist hovers ready to shatter the silence of the Hitlerian inferno. Thus begins Michael's *descente aux enfers.*[2]

This *descente,* this abandonment of the self to the self, is indeed necessary to break the hold of the negative silence that has stifled the protagonist. It prepares the way for his spiritual rebirth and for the reestablishment of dialogue. Michael is the imperfect iron ready for the smith's hammer. His mind remains lucid, and actually commands a degree of intensity necessary for elevation to higher levels of spiritual awareness, where he will confront himself. "I stress the word *return,* so basic in our tradition," states Wiesel. "Whoever returns to the source does not remove himself from the present. On the contrary, he lends it new dimension. For he then realizes that in Jewish thought, everything is connected" (*Rebirth,* 3).

The Hebrew term for the intense spiritual state necessary to achieve honesty in prayer and to effect true return is *kavana.* It implies a power of self-possession, a depth of concentration, and faith in prayer. Often the pious Jew will pray with his eyes closed, thus allowing the surges of *kavana* to pull him or her above the ordinary, and fix the individual on a purely spiritual plane where the inner self might commune with the voices of eternity. For Hasidic Jews, *kavana* is the means by which the soul rises toward the *shehina,* the divine presence in this world, joining with it for an instant of totality, rapture, ecstasy, and joy. In addition, *kavana* aids in the mystical transformation of words of prayer into holy names that serve as landmarks on the upward climb to the *shehina.* Michael, in much the same way, enters into his "prayer" of penitence.

The attainment of this loftier spiritual plane is likewise facilitated by an imposed ascetic rigor, namely fasting, itself another symbolic hallmark of Yom Kippur. The association of fasting and prayer has long been viewed as an essential combination in the process of "return" for the Jew. The way to human and divine reconciliation is frequently paved by fasting. This personal affliction serves as a sign of remorse for past misdeeds and indicates a spiritual determination on the part of the penitent to conquer baser instincts. Fasting clarifies and heightens *kavana,* allowing one to project the mind and soul within the self, rather than dwelling on aspects of physical existence. Williams James notes that "ascetic mortifications and torments may be due to pessimistic feelings about the self, combined with theological beliefs concerning expiation" (291). Such an ascetic expression as fasting can be deemed a form of sacrifice when freely accepted. Michael, however, has no choice, as the secret police ironically impose this upon him as one of the aspects of *la prière.* Nevertheless, the result of this forced fasting produces much the same effect as voluntarily accepted abstinence. In fact, there are several references to Michael's being fully cognizant of his physical state. Yet with each physical lapse comes the realization of the necessity to return to the spiritual plane where the struggle for *teshuva* must continue. Moreover, Michael will later remember the numerous times he had spent with the *clochards* of Paris, times often passed in fasting when his inner perspective was keener: "A jeun, il voyait les choses et les êtres dans une clarté parfois saisissante" (VC, 84); "Fasting, he saw things and beings with often striking clarity" (TBW, 69). Thus, the trope of fasting is established here both to parallel an aspect of penitence associated with Yom Kippur, and simultaneously to act as a metonymic device stressing Michael's forced return to "prayer," action that will result in his confronting truths about himself.

Another element that this novel shares with Yom Kippur and *teshuva* is the remembrance of the dead. During the traditional period of *teshuva,*[3] it is customary for Jews to visit the graves of family members and those of the sages of Israel, where prayers are offered for the eternal peace and salvation of the departed soul. Jewish legend recounts that on the eve of Yom Kippur the dead gather with the living to pray. Some traditions actually believe the dead assist the prayers of the truly penitent to reach the throne of the eternal judge.[4] On Yom Kippur itself, special memorial prayers, the *yizkor,* are recited, when Jews publicly recall the departed. The pious Jew believes that if this is done, the Almighty will allow the meritorious deeds of the departed to help gain atonement for the living. In other words, the living gain insight and benefit from the dead. This technique is constantly employed by Wiesel throughout this novel, as Michael seeks answers to his simplest questions from the dead who inhabit his murdered past. There exists something in that former life and with those ghosts that should provide Michael inspiration and atonement, perhaps even peace.

Early in the novel, as Michael enters the realms of the dead, he expresses his profoundest desire to his former teacher, Kalman, when he says: "Maître, je veux enfin connaître Dieu, je veux le tirer de sa cachette" (VC, 19); "Master, I want finally to know God. I want to drag him from his hiding place" (TBW, 10). The use of the adverb *enfin* (finally) interestingly implies that Michael has previously sought God halfheartedly, but now has a firm desire and need to find Him. One ought not forget that this represents the first time since the opening passage of *La Nuit* that any Wieselian character has expressed a longing to know God. Kalman's response, however, is not that which Michael desired. His former teacher has recognized that the former pupil does not comprehend himself. How can one then aspire to discover and understand the divinity? One cannot hope to discover God by running away from oneself, or from the responsibilities life bestows. The first lesson of Michael's "return" is then quite simple: The journey to God will not lead directly to Him, but rather first to the self, then to fellow human beings.

The task of self-evaluation, soul-searching, and telling oneself the truth creates an arduous route. For Michael, it signifies a journey into a past ripped from him, a return to a childhood replete with the secrets of happiness and remorse. In order to locate God and to return, Michael must seek those truths concealed in the silence of the past that he carries within himself.

This particular "Yom Kippur" service unrolls as Michael encounters the first ghosts: Moishe-le-fou (Moses the Madman) and Varady—the mystic and the apostate. Their lesson lies in the constant imperative to pursue truth and to acquire understanding, elements that had characterized Michael's youth and had then been silenced in the *anus mundi*. Until this "Yom Kippur," these features had been wanting. The biting torment for Michael is to know where this quality of honesty currently hides itself. Is Michael honest and true to himself? Furthermore, why does he appear to fear to retrace those steps that have led him to this particular moment? The reply to these questions temporarily eludes him, remaining hidden in silence.

Michael's "first confession," his initial intimate glimpse of the past, establishes the fact that he has lost his love of questioning and the desire to pursue truth. In their place, silence has descended, silence mingled with a sense of guilt. This guilt arises not simply from his being a survivor, but also from Michael's inability to give direction to his life, to seek truth within himself. In many ways, Michael is akin to Albert Camus's Meursault. Both exist in psychological and physical prisons where spiritual liberation weighs more importantly than actual liberation. Both search for that portentous and liberating light. In *La Ville de la chance,* Michael's early encounters with the dead and with himself form a meager means of asking for that guiding beam that might provide direction. A liturgical parallel can be found in the special *yotzer* prayers for the morning of the Day of Atonement: *Oz b'yom kippur.*[5] The lengthy series forms a pressing supplication for the divine light of forgiveness as well as expressing the desire of each man to know the light of God in his life, which in turn will enable him to know himself and his unique personal direction.

The first prayer reaches its emotional climax as Michael fights against memories concerning his desire to know God and to hasten the arrival of the Messiah. In parallel fashion to his present condition, Michael had earlier renounced all ties with reality and had plunged into the study of Cabala. Not eating, not speaking, he attempted self-purification. He had constructed a wall of silence, a barrier between himself and the impurities of the human race. No one had mattered. In this separate universe he had sought God, a project doomed to failure from its inception. His father's pleas had been ignored, though, ironically, their message is now understood: "Dieu est dieu parce qu'il est trait d'union: entre les choses et les êtres, entre le coeur et l'âme, entre le bien et le mal, entre le passé et l'avenir" (VC, 55); "God is God because He is bond between things and beings, between heart and soul, between good and evil, between the past and the future" (TBW, 43). Later, in those memories constituting the second prayer, we again find Michael divorced from the world and imposing a silence in which he has sought God. But this silence is the negative silence of the camps, a silence that indicates lack of dialogue. His failure to discover God, his inability to follow his masters or his fellow students haunts him. Only his father's message remains, and it grows in clarity and intensity reminiscent of the prayers of a Jewish congregation on Yom Kippur, prayers that are chanted more courageously and determinedly as the Day of Atonement progresses.

The essence of Michael's father's message is repeated by Kalman in one of the last passages of the first prayer. Michael had once overheard a prayer uttered by a travelling stranger: "O, Dieu! Reste près de moi quand j'ai besoin de toi, mais surtout ne me quitte pas lorsque je te renie" (VC, 56); "O God, be with me when I have need of you, but above all do not leave me when I deny you" (TBW, 44). This, Kalman explains, is Michael's unique prayer. He informs Michael that each person must find his or her prayer, then set out to discover his soul and God. The inference here is that one day Michael will need this particular prayer to assist him in his quest for God, despite his "rejection" of Him. The keys to all questions, the path to God Himself lie within the soul. Thus, from this point to the novel's conclusion, Michael's raison d'etre becomes a pilgrimage to reclaim his soul and his lost self. As the first prayer concludes, Michael, though humbled and tired as promised by his guards, appears prepared to proceed. He has become obsessed with discovering a beginning by working backwards from the bloody ending accorded him by the Holocaust. And, though moved to new spiritual heights in this initial stage, he has yet to purge any of his sins, or the guilt and intense anger still held captive within.

The second prayer continues the process of liberating the truth from the ashes of the past as well as the word trapped within. Structurally this "prayer" serves as a narrative device to relate the story of Michael's life since the end of the war. The second prayer stands as both "prayer" and Torah reading. On Yom Kippur, the portion of the law that is read thematically concentrates upon the ancient promises of pardon from sin and then focuses on the *avoda,* the Yom Kippur service in the Tabernacle, and the various means God had directed the priests to pursue in order to achieve such at-one-ment. This particular theme of expiation predominates throughout the remaining prayers. Similarly, in reading Michael's story, we encounter the tale of Yankel, a haunting series of memories that will overshadow all subsequent action in the second prayer and that will be significantly and repeatedly echoed in the remaining "prayers." For Michael, the tale of Yankel pinpoints several instances of guilt and misunderstanding, a notion to which the protagonist alludes numerous times in the course of this "prayer" and that commences to provide Michael some means of exorcising his debilitating sense of culpability.

The tone at the beginning of the second prayer is fully reminiscent of that established in the trilogy, situations bathed in negative silence in which the protagonists were incapable of action. In this text, one learns that Michael has lived alone in Paris, severed from society and all meaningful dialogue, inhabiting the periphery of human existence where he vainly has sought to wrestle with a God he no longer knows.

Yankel's arrival disrupts the negative, silent abyss into which Michael has fallen. "On avait frappé à la porte. D'abord timidement, puis plus fort, avec insistence" (VC, 65); "Someone had knocked at the door. At first idly, then more firmly, insistently" (TBW, 51). Michael is roused, frightened, and agitated by this knocking that acts like the blasts of the *shofar,* the ram's horn sounded during the period of *teshuva,*[6] or like the insistent, repetitive, mantra-like prayers of Yom Kippur. But Michael's initial response is one of explosive fright: "Va t'en! Va t'en, Yankel! Et ne reviens plus! Je n'ai rien à te dire, rien à te donner!" (VC, 65); "Get out! Get out, Yankel, and don't come back! I've nothing to tell you and nothing to give you!" (TBW, 51). This irrational reaction together with its subtext of phobia require exploration. Why does Michael fear Yankel and refuse to see him? What silently lies beneath this outburst? The significance lies in the fact that Michael believes he has nothing to offer the boy. His isolated, silent state has rendered him psychologically impotent. Yankel's very presence would persist in reminding Michael that they were together in the *anus mundi* and, notably, Yankel had witnessed Michael's behavior. Yankel's arrival wrenches silenced memory into the light of reality and demands to be confronted. Michael has not merely desired to retreat into his silent exile, he has also wished to drown certain voices within himself. The silence he longs to achieve is absolute: Death. Yankel must then be viewed as a symbolic representation of the manifold degrees of silent guilt, fear, and anger sublimated within Michael. Yankel is the accusing witness who in the past had indeed seen Michael become another being. Yankel likewise represents the millions of others who, on this particular "Yom Kippur," have come to pray with Michael, alluding also to that silent, impotent band of sad phantoms who had filled the stifling room in Palestine as Elisha, the protagonist of *L'Aube,* sought answers and direction. Yet the thousands with Yankel are no longer impotent nor silent. They threaten Michael's existence and would pull him apart; no one would ever know why. The key to this puzzle, and to the myriad of other silent obsessions harbored within Michael, lies with Yankel.

Yankel's appearance transports the reader into perhaps the most heavily guilt-ridden sections of the novel, perhaps even in all of Wiesel's novels: The death of Michael's father. Two narrative voices appear to link at this juncture, since like his protagonist, Wiesel himself had witnessed the deterioration and eventual death of his own father. Both remained silent, impotent. Neither could halt the steady process of death. Both were incapable of tears before the absurdity of such a meaningless end. In this specific context, Yankel had been witness to Michael's behavior. A vision of that silent, impotent Michael exists within Yankel, an image of a person who had devolved into utter inhuman indifference. That unspoken truth, more than Yankel's physical presence, haunts Michael. The "other" Michael lives on in Yankel and instills in the protagonist a sense of rage and self-hatred for that which he had become. It is precisely this concept of "the other" that stands at the center of Michael's guilt. At this instant, Michael, the shattered man, standing like the penitent Jew seeking forgiveness and understanding, has reached the bottom of the pit and must now discover the path to at-one-ment. The key resides in the questions: who and why. Who is "the other?" Why must Michael seek "the other?" These seminal riddles are to be sounded and resounded by the enigmatic character of Pedro in the third prayer.

Michael is confronted with two additional important bits of information in this second prayer: One, a confession; the other, an unwelcome invitation. While living in postwar Paris, he had encountered Meir, a former student friend. Meir has become a smuggler and invites Michael to join him. Michael callously rejects this proposal, as he believes Meir's "profession" to be despicable. Meir reciprocates by blasting Michael's naiveté and blasts Michael's reasoning for being alone: "Tu divagues! Tu vis encore dans le passé" (VC, 77); "You're a dreamer! You're still living in the past" (TBW, 62). These words, analogous to the knocking sounds on Michael's door at the beginning of the "prayer," stun Michael. He has relinquished his hold on reality while constructing his walls of silent solitude. Meir challenges Michael to act, to become a man, to face life and its challenges. But Michael appears unable to imitate his friend. He remains incapable of seeing that Meir, despite his illegal occupation, is alive and establishing himself in the world of the living, while Michael stagnates in the past.

An analogous revelation is advanced in Michael's vision of Martha, the drunken prostitute of his boyhood town. She vividly invites Michael to copulate with her, an invitation, repugnant though it may be, that represents another opportunity for Michael to destroy the walls of silence that keep him from life. Like Meir, Martha represents another vision of life. Though she is repulsive: "une odeur de terre et d'excrément se dégage de son corps. . . . Son ventre est blanc, sa peau craquelée, ses cuisses flasques" (VC, 102); "an odor of dirt and excrement hovers about her body. . . . Her belly is white, her skin crisscrossed with wrinkles, her thighs flabby" (TBW, 85), Martha represents one facet of human existence. Michael must strive to remember that life is not always beautiful, especially for the survivor. The survivor must do what he or she can, living and hoping to effect change in an imperfect world. Michael is hunting for absolute truth and beauty where none exist. He has ignored the notion that beauty and truth are ushered into the world by the actions of people doing God's work in their relations with their fellow beings. "This affirmation is related to an important dimension in Wiesel's understanding of the Jewish concept of man. In creating the world, the God of Israel did not entirely destroy formlessness and darkness, but He made man in His image to continue the fight against them" (Estess, 1980, 63). Yet Michael remains apathetic, incapable of action. He stands on the threshold of life, but declines to participate. The world as represented by Meir and Martha does not entice him; they repulse him, and, consequently, the world with its realities sickens him. The progress effected to this point is not enough to dispel the past and the specters of silence.

Despite this rejection and the momentary repulsion of the world, Michael is offered a curiously unique message, one that remains with him and that is sharpened during the remaining prayers, especially through the influence of Pedro, that singular figure who appears at each critical juncture in the story. While Michael has relived his past seeking answers and formulating additional questions, Pedro has repeatedly demanded why. On Yom Kippur, penitent Jews pray *s'lah lanu, m'hal lanu, kaper lanu* (forgive us our sins) and *zohraynu l'hayim* (remember us to life) in the quest for a route of return. The penitents examine themselves, probing ever deeper into their soul for some truth, attempting to reestablish life on a proper course. Likewise, Pedro insists upon Michael's seeking out truth by asking appropriate questions. By the end of the second prayer, Michael confesses to Pedro: "Je me voyais tel que j'étais et tel que j'aurais voulu être. Simultanément j'étais moi-même et un autre. J'étais enfin arrivé à me libérer de moi-même" (VC, 110); "I saw myself as I was and as I wanted to be. I was at once myself and another. I'd finally been freed from myself" (TBW, 93). The key word is again *un autre* (other). Pedro pressed Michael: Who is the *Autre,* this Other? Why does he seem to hold fast at the center of Michael's guilt? Moreover, Pedro wishes to know how Michael's returning to his native town could assist him in unravelling that fundamental mystery? The confessions, the questions, the visions in profound and rapid succession have created a garbled message that Michael must now attempt to decipher. To break free of the guilt and the ghosts, to smash the silent barriers about him, Michael must first acknowledge life, then act as a living soul. He must attempt to respond to those pertinent questions posed by Pedro. So it is that in the closing pages of the second prayer, Michael inches nearer the turning point in his quest. The secrets of liberation are producing a light, the *yotzer,* so necessary for him to effect a full "return." The catalyst rises in the third prayer.

The names of Wieselian characters impart great significance, frequently hiding meanings that could resolve certain puzzles posed by the text. It would be efficacious to examine the name of the protagonist and that of his alter ego, Pedro. Michael's name is closely associated with the Hebrew phrase: *mi el kamoha,* which in a paraphrastic translation is rendered as "who is like unto the Lord." First used in Exodus 15:11, the Hebrew verse celebrates the power and glory of God. Yet the protagonist who bears the name based on this meaning has found neither power nor glory in a God who during the years of the Holocaust demonstrated His impotence and silence. Like the protagonists who preceded him, Michael has forgotten or abandoned that God. One can, however, uncover yet another root for Michael's name: מה, *mah,* indicating being feeble, poor, or demonstrating weakness. Thus, Michael's name can be rendered *God is weak,* a point confirmed in a talmudic exegesis by Emmanuel Lévinas in *Quatre lectures talmudiques* (123). The Michael of the first two "prayers" has found his God wanting, a weak God worthy only of being relegated to oblivion. And yet, Michael's name metamorphoses, losing this negative connotation. That which Michael had endured in the opening "prayer" of the novel has not merely served as *descente aux enfers* or even as an act of *teshuva;* these spiritual ventures have served as a subtle, silent initiation which, as Mircea Eliade believes "in the most general sense denotes a body of rites and oral teaching whose purpose is to produce a radical modification of the religious. . .status of the person to be initiated. . . . The novice emerges from his ordeal a totally different being: he has become *another"* (112) [my emphasis]. Michael will rise from this ordeal a different man, and this will be reflected in a significant alteration of the spirit of his name.

The other key name is Pedro, meaning *rock.* Though to this point in the story Pedro has merely been a vision, a voice whose existence might be called into question, he represents the power that has scrupulously conducted Michael through the hell of his past. Michael has undertaken the spiritual journey that has laid the foundation for his understanding, not merely of his own past, but also of the silence that has shrouded and choked him. In his friendship with Pedro, silence has phenomenologically altered, extending its positive elements. "Parfois ils marchaient en silence côte à côte. Michael découvrait alors la densité du silence, sa profondeur, sa musique" (VC, 135); "Sometimes they walked in silence side by side. Michael discovered the texture of silence, its depths, its music" (TBW, 115). This silence shared with Pedro transmits meaning. Wiesel, it would seem, has imbued Pedro with unique powers. A clue can be discovered in a question Michael poses to his friend: "Est-ce toi, Dieu?" (VC, 134); "Pedro, are you God?" (TBW, 115).

From the beginning of the novel, Wiesel has established a purely metaphysical state through a lack of description and physical detail. The characters and the decor of the novel remain purposefully vague, as these elements possess minimal importance. The novel primarily treats the psychological evolution and spiritual regeneration of the protagonist. A text replete with excessive, realistic description would unnecessarily encumber such metaphysical developments. This spiritual state accounts for more than the ephemeral nature of

physical reality, for in this novel and throughout his work, Wiesel's preoccupation focuses on the spiritual essence of humanity as he attempts to redefine
us in the light of the Holocaust. In such a context, we can therefore accept
Michael's perception that perhaps Pedro is God, or at least an emanation of
the Divine.

In Jewish tradition, God has numerous appellations. One of these names is
Shaddai, שדי. Both Rashi, the medieval Jewish commentator, and the twentieth-
century scholar André Neher link this divine name, *Shaddai,* with silence:

> This God who is sufficient unto himself is likewise self-sufficient in
> His Word: He is the *God beyond dialogue.* He requires no partner, nei-
> ther to whom to address the Word, nor from whom to receive a reply.
> He is the God without echo, without yesterday and without tomor-
> row,the God of Absolute Silence. (*Shaddai,* 155)

It is my supposition that just such a divine being, God known as *Shaddai,*
haunts the novels of the trilogy. This God of silence, whose presence is felt in
the Book of Job (chapters 3 to 37, where God is silent) likewise hovers over
the pages of the Wieselian universe in those first three novels. Only with the
fourth text is a difference discernible as a new dialogue painfully emerges
between God and humanity. Pedro is representative of that transmutation in
the divine manifestation.

In Judaism, another of God's names is *Tzur* (צור), or *rock,* which is Pedro's
name. Another image that points to a change in the divine presence's attributes is seen in Pedro and Michael walking together, an action that echoes various references in Genesis to man and God walking together, chapters 5:24
and 6:9 serving as two examples. Time and again the protagonist and his
guide set out on long walks, which conclude with Michael better understanding himself. The silence that surrounds them serves to encourage this
positive evolution. One of these sublime insights refers to one's not being
alone, for as Pedro explains, God is the silence that frames human existence,
especially when we share our life with another living soul. Solitude and
silence elicit a presence. Not only has the very nature of silence shifted from
stifling negativity into something positive and pregnant with meaning, but this
revelation is effected by Pedro, the rock, the positive, communicative manifestation of God.

Another interesting aspect of this omnipresent/absent Pedro, a third party
to everything, lies in his ability to persuade Michael to act while still in prison
so as to re-create the life of the Silent One, a fellow prisoner. Michael's efforts
are silently observed by Pedro's unseen eye, an action reflecting the talmudic
teaching that God is an unseen partner in all human dealings. In this analysis

of Pedro's name, I do not wish to suggest that Wiesel has cast Pedro as God. Such an interpretation would run counter to all of the author's fundamental religious beliefs. However, Pedro's metaphysical role in the novel, especially in the penultimate third prayer, must be viewed in cabalistic terms, with Pedro as representative of one of the various manifestations of God. Such cabalistic interpretations have already been suggested with reference to portions of Wiesel's work, especially to another mysterious, mystical character, Katriel, in the novel *Le Mendiant de Jérusalem,* a point I shall develop more fully in Chapter Five. For the moment, however, these characters must be returned to their context in the third prayer so as to examine their exceptional interaction and the means by which their "dialogue" assists in Michael's "return."

The *minha* service of the Day of Atonement, like the third prayer, is relatively short. *Minha* on Yom Kippur finds the penitent physically and emotionally fatigued, though still endeavoring to demonstrate remorse for sins, persisting in the hope that through intense introspection and good deeds during the *yomim ne'orim,* and by prayers on Yom Kippur, will merit renewed life. The essence of the Ten Days of Awe and the true meaning of *teshuva* are reiterated in this service by the haftorah* reading from the prophetical Book of Jonah, a structural device that provides a direct, positive link to Michael and the metamorphosis of his name. Indeed, the ancient rabbis added a brief passage from the Book of Micah at the conclusion of the reading from Jonah, a passage that begins with the Hebrew phrase: *mi el kamoha,* who is like unto the Lord—the positive sense of Michael's name. The thematic parallels between the text of the Book of Jonah and the events portrayed in the third prayer imbue Michael's name with this alternative and evolutionary significance. One could infer, therefore, that the rites of initiation, the *descente aux enfers,* the period of personal *teshuva* have achieved a transformation in the protagonist's character.

In a series of lectures given at Boston University and at the 92nd Street YMHA (Young Men's Hebrew Association) in New York City, Elie Wiesel spoke of Jonah and the lessons to be derived from this seemingly minor prophet. "On reading his [Jonah's] story, we realize that he moves us to think more deeply" (FBP, 130). In "reading" his own story, Michael is forced to ponder seriously all aspects of his life and their meanings in order to grasp some degree of understanding. Jonah is taught through difficult experiences just as Michael must learn from his own life, from those people who had touched it, as well as from *all* the events that have assisted in shaping his experiences and existence. Two important lessons in the Book of Jonah are simple: One cannot run from God or from one's responsibilities; nor can one begrudge

---

*haftorah: special portions read from the books of the prophets on sabbaths and festivals.

any human being the care, love, and forgiveness due to a fellow creature. These become, in time, Michael's lessons.

Michael has been running from God; but in attempting an escape from the divine presence, he ironically finds himself on the route that will lead to God. Michael has constructed walls about himself; and within that lonely fortress he has tracked a god of his own making. In this silent solitude, he has rejected living and dead: Yankel, Meir, and all the others. Like Jonah, the more one runs, the more quickly one meets oneself and one's God. One cannot avoid one's attachment to humanity or one's responsibilities to others. This was what Moishe had warned him of, what Varady had similarly instructed, and what Michael's father had preached. That which Wiesel said of Jonah easily applies to Michael: Jonah was a "displaced person living in an internal exile" (FBP, 135).

Another parallel between the two stories is encountered in the prevalence of the number three. Jonah is cast overboard to quell the storm and is swallowed by the "great fish," where he languishes for three days in its belly, during which time he comes to prayer, and through this prayer to an understanding and acceptance of his prophetic mission to do what he can to save the people of Nineveh. The notion of three days recurs constantly through Michael's thoughts as he is in prison, forced to "pray," and knowing that in so doing he will certainly save Pedro's life. And, too, it is during the first three "prayers" that Michael comes to a better understanding of his own past, and to a degree of acceptance of life and of his unique human charge to assist others.

Michael, like Jonah, is a frustrated character. In his midrash* of the Jonah story, Wiesel indicates how the readers and listeners wait along with Jonah for a host of events to transpire: For escape, for death, for liberty from the divine will, for the city of Nineveh to be destroyed. None occurs. Michael, like Jonah, has a singular destiny; his will is perpetually frustrated. He wanted to go mad as had his fellow students Hersh-Leib and Menashe, but he did not; he seeks answers to his obsessive queries from others while it is he who possesses the answers; he yearns to be freed from the burden of his past, liberated from his cancerous guilt, yet he continues to be pursued by them.

The message of humanity and reconciliation with God becomes paramount to an understanding of Jonah and to a more complete comprehension of Michael's anguish in this third prayer. Jonah, says Wiesel, is taught by God that "justice must be human, truth must be human, compassion must be human. The way to God leads through man, however alien, however sinful he may be"

---

*midrash: the rather copious body of literature compiled during the Tanaic and Amoraic periods. The midrash expounds scriptural ideas by legend and parable.

(FBP, 148). The quintessence of the "return" is therefore bound up in the nature of human relationships, of humanity itself. As the memories of his friendship with Pedro deepen and acquire new meaning, Michael reaches a shocking realization:

> Michael réalise soudain qu'il avait atteint un *tournant:* il vivait un de ces moments où le destin regardait. Il sentait son coeur bondir. Voilà le carrefour. Aller à gauche ou à droite? Quel que soit le choix il engage l'avenir. (VC, 133) [my emphasis]

> Michael realized suddenly that he had reached a *turning point:* he was living through one of those moments when destiny sat up and took notice. He felt his heart leap. He was at a crossroads. Left or right? Whatever his choice, it would determine the future. (TBW, 113–14) [my emphasis]

Michael stands at a crossroads, as had Jonah. Life beckons him in the guise of the silent future. "La nuit s'éloigne" Pedro remarks. "Le noir s'en allait, traînant derrière lui des nuages gros foncé aux franges rouges. Encore une fois le jour eut le dessus, il chassait l'ennemi à coup de bottes" (VC, 133–34); "The night's disappearing. Night was disappearing, dragging behind it dark gray clouds fringed with red" (TBW, 114).

It is indeed unfortunate that at this crucial point, Stephen Becker's translation omits a crucial sentence in the original text: "Encore une fois le jour eut le dessus, il chassait l'ennemi à coup de bottes" (VC, 134); "Once again, day had the upper hand and was forcibly chasing away its enemy" [my translation]. In the Wieselian vocabulary, *night* has become synonymous with the *shoah* and its negative aftermath. It is, therefore, eminently significant that Michael, with Pedro at his side, notes the retreat of the night before an authentic advancing dawn, symbol of new life and resurrection. And, if creation can renew itself, Michael, as an integral part of that creation, is similarly capable of change. Pedro subjoins the idea that "qui pense à Dieu en oubliant l'homme risque de se tromper de but: Dieu peut-être le voisin d'à côté" (VC, 134); "He who thinks about God, forgetting man, runs the risk of mistaking his goal: God may be your next-door neighbor" (TBW, 115). Pedro's insight profoundly affects Michael in this observation, as the story of Jonah unites with Michael's.

During the third prayer, Michael's evolution accelerates, and the "return" commences its full, visible manifestation. The lonely, self-exiled rebel who had sat in silent solitude seeking the God of his past is now a changing man, who has rediscovered the joy of sharing life with another living being. In silent and spoken conversation with Pedro, he has uncovered and explored the dead moments of the past, and has come to comprehend those events. In Pedro's company, Michael has likewise gained insight into the future. Pedro's presence is akin to that of God in the Book of Jonah. Both represent links between past and present; both give impetus and meaning to the silence of an unknown future, and lighten the burden of the silent past.

Step by painful step, Michael progressed through retrogression. In his personal *descente aux enfers* he has been afforded precious intuitive views of himself, of who and what he is and what his own duties in life must and should be. The sinner aches to "return"; he approaches God slowly, hoping his remorse will result in a rebirth free of sin, pain, and guilt. Other prayers of Yom Kippur likewise remind the penitent that to indulge in sin again would render atonement useless. Like the people of Nineveh who were spared (*Cf.*, Jonah 3:10), so Michael must go beyond mere recognition of the fact that one must choose life. One must act to secure it. Pedro warns him: "Camus a écrit quelque part qu'il faut créer du bonheur pour protester contre l'univers du malheur. C'est une flèche qui indique le chemin à suivre: il mène à autrui et non par l'absurde" (VC, 138); "Camus wrote somewhere that to protest against a universe of unhappiness you had to create happiness. That's an arrow pointing the way: it leads to another human being. And not via absurdity" (TBW, 118). The key is others. In order to prove we choose life, we must act for and with others. This choice, to be complete, must effect absolute harmony between chooser and that which is chosen. Turning again to Wiesel's definition of *teshuva*, it is "willingness to take sides and responsibility for the future" (FBP, 151). Michael cannot resurrect the past; he is incapable of altering it even one iota. But he can possess the future by opting for life, just as did Jonah, "however filled with anguish in order to prevent others from dying" (FBP, 153).

The role that Pedro plays in this Third Prayer is as important as Michael's. As noted above, Pedro is the bridge between past and future; he is the catalyst that precipitates Michael's "return." The keys ignored by Michael are collected by Pedro and presented to him so as to allow the protagonist to unlock the chains of guilt and pain that shackle him. Through Pedro, Michael is able to recall and recognize the lessons of his past, to discover meaning in his own actions, and to dispel the negative silences of the *anus mundi*. Pedro's wisdom, his clarity of vision, fall on fertile soil as Michael is edged toward the brink of absolute awareness. Michael has vaguely hinted at direct action: A physical return to his native town. This desire to return to the site of his youth marks the dawn of Michael's spiritual rebirth. Through Pedro, a physical return will be effected. The two friends are poised at the beginning of the day as "ils marchaient côte à côte, silencieux, unis dans le jour qui allait se lever" (VC, 143); "They walked side by side, silent, together in the day about to dawn" (TBW, 123). Like Elijah and Elisha, they march together into the coming light. Pedro, the guide, in a manner one can only describe as prophetic, places his hands on Michael's shoulders as if to anoint him and repeats his message: Seek to help others, no matter how many or how few. Action increases godliness in the world. This becomes Pedro's testament to Michael. With these words, Michael has been blessed, and he has inherited the mantle of life and of the future. As a result of Pedro's blessing, the negative silence that had choked and stifled the protagonists of the trilogy has been dispelled. In its place, a new, more meaningful silence has evolved, one which initiates action. And as Michael returns to his prison cell, into the metaphysical world of vision, the silence about him is no longer barren and sterile, but has become a silence in which the calming voice of Pedro is perceived. In this environment of tranquil silence, Michael begins to live again, something demonstrably evidenced by his passionate desire to save Pedro's life by enduring the "prayers" of the Hungarian secret police.

From this point to the novel's conclusion, Pedro's role diminishes. He has provided Michael with reasons to live. At the conclusion of the third prayer, Pedro warns Michael of the possibility of torture should they be caught in Szerencsevàros, but Michael does not falter. No longer repulsed by life, he indicates he will merely do his best. One who repents can only promise to attempt to affirm life. As the pain and ghosts of the past lift from his soul, Michael's mind and his very essence are geared to life, and are coupled in the text to a physical need of love, as well as a return to authentic prayer to the God of his childhood. The reconciliations, though still incomplete, have indeed commenced as the text highlights Michael's love and need of Pedro, his mentor and companion.

The final and concluding prayer presents several structural problems with the more obvious parallels to Yom Kippur. The imposed torture has ended, the twenty-four hour period of "atonement" having run its course. Michael is alive, though physically exhausted. He is spiritually regenerated. The philosophy of action has, to a limited extent, been implemented. Yet for the reconciliation to be whole, Michael must both achieve the expiation of his lingering guilt, and similarly realize some means to help another being.

The prison cell into which he is cast is inhabited by three radically different men: The Impatient One, the Silent One, and Menachem, a pious Jew. Menachem, whose name means the comforter, assumes a portion of the role previously exercised by Pedro, as he confronts and comforts Michael, while pressing him into his duties as a man by making him aware of his responsibilities toward God and others. Menachem is described as a saintly beggar, a *navenadnik,** an eternally wandering Jew who anonymously seeks to assist

---

navenadnik: the Jewish notion of the "wandering Jew." He is most frequently depicted as a beggar seeking to gather together the various sparks of the divine in creation.

those in distress. In Jewish folklore, the role of the wandering beggar is to search out sparks of the divine presence, the *Shehina,* comfort them, set them right and gather them together.

One issue from an earlier "prayer" persists in clinging about Michael's neck. Though he has recognized the importance of life and friendship, one element of guilt silently oppressed him—his inability to act or react when his father was dying, an inaction subconsciously related to another act of indifference. This truth has remained insoluble, until this concluding prayer when Michael achieves that level of spiritual elevation and truth required to comprehend utterly his profound and visceral need to return to his native town. To understand the human capacity for being less than human, to understand himself at the moment when his father died, these become the ultimate veiled mysteries Michael must penetrate. Over the years since the loss of his home, his family, and his childhood, one face has remained etched in his memory: That anonymous face of the contemporary everyman symbolizing all that is not human. Michael has seen good and evil and recognized them to be human; but, this "Other's" complete indifference is incalculably inhuman. For Michael, this "Other" by extension represents Michael's own inhuman impotence when his father died: "De comprendre les autres—l'Autre—ceux qui nous regardaient aller vers l'inconnu; ceux qui, impassibles, nous obversaient alors que nous devenions objets—du bois vivant—et victimes numérotées?" (VC, 172); "To understand the others— the Other—those who watched us depart for the unknown; those who observed us, without emotion, while we became objects—living sticks of wood—and carefully numbered victims?" (TBW, 148). This becomes Michael's final task. Jonah had eventually fathomed the compelling relevance of his obligation to act so as to save the inhabitants of Nineveh. Michael is now fully cognizant of his own need to force this indifferent "witness" to act, to explain his refusal to take sides. Such a confrontation will also furnish Michael with the opportunity to understand and purge his own frustrated anger, and ultimately, to comprehend that element within himself and all human beings that possesses the potential to deform moral and ethical character—that interior sense of the divine nature—and transform humanity into beasts.

The final expiation of guilt occurs during this encounter with the silent "Other." Michael approaches him and demands to be given some reason for the "Other's" absolute lack of action, for his cowardly inability to speak out. He attempts to smash the plastic image of the contemporary "Average Man, the Bureaucratic Cipher, the man who is afraid only of the police" (Friedman, 1967, 25). At the thematic level, this encounter with the "Other" symbolically represents the conflict between indifferent silence and the emerging positively oriented silence that leads to human action. By unmasking the contemporary "everyman" and accusing him of complicity in introducing additional evil into the world, Michael's violent accusations act as double-edged swords. His words not only condemn the "Other" of evil, inhuman indifference, but the cutting edge also strikes Michael, giving rise to the remorse, shame, and anger that have been seething in him. Furthermore, Michael realizes that the Jews have behaved in much the same fashion: They had neither spoken out nor reacted to prevent their deportation into the unknown, though they had been warned. They had permitted themselves to play their role in passive silence, in seemingly perfect obedience. Everything appears as some gruesome inhuman drama. Michael, his teachers, his comrades, his family, had refused to act; at the death of his father, Michael remained incapable of action. His guilt and resentment are consequently directed not entirely at the pathetic surrogate whom he faces, as at himself and at the Jewish people who proved to be such exemplary victims. The "Other," the Jews, Michael—all had stood passively by enacting their collective roles as silent automatons. All had been guilty, as had humanity. This represents the silent curse that has been consuming Michael since his liberation from the camps.

The confrontation ended, the text suggests that the guilt and its accompanying hatred are being purged:

> Le passé sera exorcisé. Je vivrai, je travaillerai, j'aimerai. Je prendrai femme, j'aurai un fils, je lutterai pour défendre son avenir, son bonheur futur. Fini. La tâche est accomplie. Plus de colères dissimulées. Plus de travestis. Plus d'existence double menée sur deux plans. Me voilà entier. (VC, 187)

> The past will have been exorcised. I'll live, I'll work, I'll love. I'll take a wife, I'll father a son, I'll fight to protect his future, his future happiness. The task is accomplished. No more concealed wrath, no more disguises. No more double life, lived on two levels. Now I am whole. (TBW, 162)

Michael will continue to act. And yet, the juxtaposition of the final sentence of the passage with the first seems to construct an oxymoron. Though Michael claims to be whole, though he resolves to live, though he pledges to create a life in the future, a small vestige of his past will always remain with him. In beginning anew, Michael will not forever be without his ghosts, without some guilt and self-hatred, without the stifling silence of Auschwitz; for like sin they are omnipresent, lurking in the shadows of existence, waiting for the opportunity to lay hold again. In like fashion, at the conclusion of the Yom Kippur service, Jewish tradition requires that the *ma'ariv* prayers of the newly-born day be recited with the same fervor and devotion as those of the Day of Atonement. Moreover, as one cannot be completely free of sin, one recites *s'lah lanu avinu* (Forgive us, Father) during the *amida* (silent devotion). One day sin will be conquered, but for the moment we are fragile beings: "le passé sera exorcisé," one day the past *will be* exorcised. In choosing the dawn, in returning to the light of life, Michael will gain the force of spirit to fight and repulse the dark powers of the night of his own past.

This same statement can, however, be read in a radically different light: as that of a biblical command. The evil decree can still be averted by being fully human and dedicating one's life to the creation of a new life through meritorious deeds. One chooses to be human, to work with others and to create *anew*. And, making that choice, one becomes responsible for establishing universal harmony. As Menachem expresses it, each being must be human before God since "la dernière porte qui se referme au ciel, la toute dernière, est celle des larmes" (VC, 158); "The last door that closes in heaven, the very last, is that of tears" (TBW, 136). It is interesting that Wiesel has chosen the expression the *last door,* or gate, that closes, as his metaphor, as this is again reflective of the meaning of the last liturgical service of Yom Kippur, the *ne'ila,* literally the closing of the gates. Tradition states that this is the solemn hour when God is begged to seal the penitent to life, to view each soul as being worthy of life, of being human. Tears make us human, reflecting our remorse and our joy, as well as the strengths and weaknesses of the human condition. As Menachem states: "Dieu nous attend au-delà de toute chose. Laisse-toi aller, ami. Pleure et tu trouveras l'écorce de l'existence moins épaisse, moins dure" (VC, 192); "God awaits us beyond all things. Let yourself go, friend. Weep and you will find the crust of existence less thick, less hard" (TBW, 167).

The bonds of the past are severed when Michael saves Menachem's life from an attack by the Impatient One. This act of positive choice to help preserve life finally releases that which is uniquely human in Michael: he cries. Josephine Knopp remarks that "for the first time the protagonist can cry and, in so doing, releases a bit of pent-up horror. The physical recovery from near death now holds out the promise of a spiritual recovery as well" (*Trial,* 81). This is not a singular reaction to that particular moment, as several days later he cries a second time. Michael becomes fully human, complete with all elements that form part of the human experience. Not only has he physically returned from the Night, but we recognize that Michael has become a man who is prepared and willing to respond, to act, to create, and to choose. At this juncture, Menachem, the comforter, is removed from the cell he has shared with Michael: "soudain, appauvri, il appuya sa tête contre le mur et se mit à sangloter, à bout de nerfs"

(VC, 193); "So suddenly impoverished, he leaned his head against the wall and broke into sobs, at the end of his tether" (TBW, 168). The key word here is *appauvri,* impoverished. Without human contact, Michael is poorer, almost worthless. In such conditions, he may well go insane.

Mi el kamoha, who is like unto the Lord? Events in the story appear to be manipulated by a deus ex machina, for once again Michael is called upon to save a life. When the Impatient One attacks the Silent One, Michael again springs to the defense of the mute boy. As a result of this attack, the Impatient One is removed, leaving Michael alone with the pathetic, silent being lost in the incommunicative void of his own night. From the weighty silence of his cell, Michael perceives Pedro's voice. Like the God of old, Pedro visits a chosen one and charges him with a task: Save the boy; bring him forth from his state of catatonia. To renew human life, to continue to perfect the otherwise imperfect world, to retrieve another from the void and bring him into the light of life, all evidence the magnitude of Michael's shift of character. Michael proves himself worthy of his return to life. Now he must demonstrate his full humanity and accept all incumbent responsibilities.

> Michael accueillit l'aube *en homme nouveau.* La vigueur lui revenait. Du coup, il se sentait responsable d'une vie qui se confondait avec celle du genre humain. Il lutterait. Il recommencerait la création du monde à partir du zéro. (VC, 198) [my emphasis]

> Michael welcomed the dawn *as a new man.* His strength flowed back. He was suddenly responsible for a life that was an inseparable part of the life of mankind. He would fight. He would resume the creation of the world from the void. (TBW, 172) [my emphasis]

At the conclusion of this paragraph, an abrupt change of narrative voice breaks into prayer: "Dieu d'Abraham et d'Adam, cette fois-ci, je t'en supplie, ne sois pas «contre»!" (VC, 198); "God of Adam and Abraham, this time, I beg you, don't be against us!" (TBW, 172)

This modification of narrative voice jolts the reader, while subtly underscoring a vital factor. It is imperative to note how in this short prayer, Michael finds expression in Jewish tradition and in a degree of revolt. He implores: "Dieu d'Abraham" and "d'Adam," a highly unorthodox manner for a Jew to begin a prayer. Jewish prayer traditionally implores *elohenu velohe avosenu* (Our God and God of our Fathers), *elohe Avraham, elohe Yitzhak, v'elohe Ya'akov* (God of Abraham, God of Isaac, and God of Jacob), but never the God of Adam, and rarely is the God of Abraham addressed alone. This manner of addressing God in prayer propounds a two fold significance. First, in speaking to the God of

Abraham, Michael is firmly establishing himself within Jewish tradition. Abraham is the father of the Jewish people, and in the Jewish tradition is the first man to recognize God's unity and to express the notion of a single, universal God of ineffable, unrepresentable proportions. Michael's experience of "return," of his being born again, is similarly reflective of the name Abraham, who when introduced in the Bible is called "Abram the Hebrew." The Hebrew word for Hebrew is *evri* (עברי), whose Hebrew characters can be arranged in another fashion to form the word *ubar* (עובר), or embryo. The inference is that Abraham was ceaselessly becoming, existentially evolving throughout his life. I would propose that Michael has engaged upon a similar course. Moreover, Jewish tradition similarly teaches that each individual in every generation must find God in a personal way; hence the sequence of "God of Abraham, God of Isaac, and God of Jacob." Michael is placing himself into that context. Like Abraham, he is affirming God's existence; like Abraham, Michael is within a tradition, a covenant. However, rather than listing the other patriarchs, as in traditional Jewish prayer, Michael speaks of the "Dieu . . . d'Adam," Adam the first human. Herein lies the second significance of Michael's prayer.

In *Célébration biblique* (*Messengers of God*), Wiesel says of Adam: "Au commencement, l'homme ne s'orientait que par rapport à Dieu—et toute la Création se définissait par rapport à l'homme" (CB, 15); "In the beginning, man oriented himself solely in relation to God—and all of creation defined itself in relation to man" (MG, 3). God, humanity and creation are linked. Adam was given the unique task of completing and perfecting creation. Michael recognizes his task to be as great as Adam's. Out of the silence and chaos of the Holocaust, the universe has need of *a* human being, an Adam (אדם) who is willing to reestablish the essential rapport between humanity and God, a soul capable at least of beginning again the act of creation. As Wiesel notes: "Il appartient à l'homme de recommencer. Il recommence chaque fois qu'il décide de se ranger du côté des vivants, justifiant ainsi l'ancien projet du plus ancien des hommes, Adam" (CB, 35); "It is given to man to begin again— and he does so every time he chooses to defy death and side with the living. Thus he justifies the ancient plan of the most ancient of men, Adam" (MG, 32). Therefore, in this short prayer, Michael prays for the spiritual faith of an Abraham, and for the strength of an Adam, as he undertakes his task.

The tedious struggle to free the Silent One from his psychological prison begins. Michael, who had been encased in silence, must now attempt to liberate a fellow being likewise trapped behind a wall of negative silence. During this journey into the mind of another, Michael expounds the lessons he has finally learned. He realizes that no one can know or even pretend to know the answers of life's mysteries. One can merely affirm ones own humanity by dealing rightly, fairly, and justly with other human beings. As the questions life poses will remain eternally unanswered, each person must seek to accomplish something else that will render life meaningful. All must seek to be human, to establish links with others, and to learn to appreciate all human actions. As human beings, all must strive to be human. "L'homme n'est homme que parmi les hommes" (VC, 203); "A man is a man only when he is among men" (TBW, 177), Michael says, speaking with the strength and conviction of Jonah, the compassion and compassionate understanding of Pedro, the humanity of Varady, the burning mystical intensity of a Kalman, and the madness of a Moishe. Michael has become one with the voice of humankind. In this rediscovery of his voice, he has become cognizant of the relevance of ordinary words, as well as the silences that precede and link them. Like saints and simple men, holy persons and horrific demons, one must act—and act within the parameters life delineates. Only then can he hope to find himself and God. "Michael arrivait à la limite de ses forces. Devant lui, la nuit, telle une montagne avant l'aurore, reculait" (VC, 204); "Michael had come to the end of his strength. Before him the night was receding, as on a mountain before dawn" (TBW, 178). Michael has won; humanity has won. He has accepted the yoke of life. The walls of silence he had so skillfully constructed have fallen. The act of "returning" has been initiated, and once fully and authentically undertaken, no force can impede it. Most important of all, for the first time in Wiesel's literary universe, a true dawn is breaking.

Michael has faced the past and himself in a daring manner, so that by the end of the novel, the protagonist is purged of guilt and pledged to a future. Michael has learned to pray again despite the reality that his present prayers are far removed from those of his childhood. Nevertheless, he has learned the need to pray, to speak, and to be a part of humanity, thus reflecting some of Wiesel's fundamental thoughts concerning prayer: "Man cannot pray if he is alone. Only if man is put in society, part of the universe and part of God does prayer have a meaning. Then prayer becomes a song" (Cargas, 1976, 98). And one can realize that at least one prayer has been answered. The Silent One has progressed out of his catatonic state into the peripheral shades of human existence. "L'autre portait le nom biblique d'Eliezer, ce qui signifie Dieu a exaucé ma prière" (VC, 204); "The other bore the Biblical name of Eliezer, which means God has granted my prayer" (TBW, 178). Interestingly enough, Eliezer is Wiesel's proper name, Elie being a diminutive form. From this we can infer that Wiesel himself has been wrenched from the silence of the abyss of the *anus mundi*. And, in the context of the novel, Michael's prayer for the faith of an Abraham and the strength of an Adam has been answered: Eliezer has been resurrected from the savagery of his night.

The Midrashic epilogue of the novel notes that God and mankind reestablish dialogue, though from radically altered positions. Questions persist; additional questions remain to be posed; specters lie hidden and wait to be encountered; silence hovers, always prepared to threaten the refound voice. But as sure as the true dawn that is breaking, hope has been reborn. Michael's period of *teshuva* has allowed him to accomplish this. The "prayers" before the wall in the prison cell permitted him to wrestle like Jacob with his deep-seated guilt. It is the purity of the newfound voice and the joy of the promised dialogue, despite its altered form, that touch us in the closing paragraphs of the novel. Allen Kronfeld argues that "Wiesel's traditional orientation finds a way of saying that the universe, though terribly out of joint, is still redeemable by man, on a cosmic level" (309). Thus, within the context of renewed dialogue, God and humanity must work together toward redemption. The critical struggle between silence and dialogue will, of necessity, therefore continue, and will be refined in Wiesel's fifth novel, *Les Portes de la forêt (The Gates of the Forest)*.

CHAPTER 4

The Dialogue of Peniel

Les Portes de la foret (1964)

> L'authenticité . . . c'est de vivre
> jusqu'au bout sa condition de Juif,
> l'inauthenticité de la nier ou de
> tenter de l'esquiver.
>
> J.-P. SARTRE

> Ma condition de Juif, je n'ai jamais pu
> la nier tout simplement..
>
> A. MEMMI

The role played by silence in Wiesel's first four novels has indicated a particular path that culminated in the "return" to a more complete, responsive, and responsible human spirit. In *La Ville de la chance* (*The Town Beyond the Wall*), silence exhibited a more metaphysical nature, eventually being personified in the Silent One. This transformation permitted Michael to sacrifice himself within a physically and temporally delineated environment for the sake of a fellow human being.

In "Creative Power of Silence," G. A. Maloney quotes Carl Jung, who states: "To make sacrifice is an act of self-recollection, a gathering together of what is scattered—the things in us that have never been properly related, and a coming to terms with oneself with a view to achieving full consciousness" (59). It is precisely this process of sacrifice and profound examination that began in *La Ville de la chance*. The negative powers of silence that had murdered the voices and identities of earlier protagonists can never fully be abolished. The silence that emerges at the conclusion of Wiesel's fourth novel expresses positive, creative directions. To permit the continued silence of Auschwitz, a posteriori, would grant a victory to all powers of negation. In *La Ville de la chance* Wiesel has deliberately harnessed these forces and propounds a priori a modification of the ontology of silence. Therefore, *Les Portes de la forêt* represents a refinement of this evolution.

A single obstacle would appear to impede the easy evolution of the affirmative ideas upon which *La Ville de la chance* concluded. In Jung's view, "an act of self-recollection" and "a coming to terms with oneself with a view to achieving full consciousness" are necessary for responsible, positive sacrifice. Jung continues: "To sacrifice proves that you possess yourself, for it does not mean just letting yourself be passively taken. It is a conscious and deliberate self-surrender, which proves you have control of yourself, of your ego" (60). From the very outset of *Les Portes de la forêt* these elements are missing. The protagonist, Grégor, has willingly silenced his Hebrew name, Gavriel, and then freely offered it to a nameless stranger who stumbled into his hiding place. Lillian Szklarczyk sees in this action "an abdication of faith, a condemnation of a silent and merciless God. In abandoning the name Gavriel, Grégor is killing the believing child he had been" (133) [my translation]. This conscious silencing of the name, a human being's unique possession, represents a distinct lack of Jungian self-recollection and full consciousness. Sacrifice cannot proceed because of this obstacle in the protagonist's own psyche.

In his seminal text, *I and Thou,* Martin Buber asserts: "Spirit in its human manifestation is man's response to his You" (89). Once, however, humankind has rejected her or his essence, once she or he has negated the very name through which she or he has established her or his link to creation, then the spirit spoken of by Buber cannot evolve. "Spirit is word," Buber continues (89). With full acceptance of the self, with, as Jung states, full consciousness and self-recollection, a sort of metaphysical language develops in which humanity exists and from which each individual speaks. This spirit exists within and beyond humankind; it is humanity, and it links all human beings to the constituent bits of creation. Yet, once a person rejects herself or himself, there is no spirit, no word; only negative silence.

In *Célébration biblique,* Wiesel notes that humanity is the keystone of creation. Man and Woman were fashioned to combat chaos within creation. The first act in which Adam exercises this specific role occurs in naming the elements of the world. Adam establishes the centrality of humankind in the universal scheme by means of this enumeration. Humanity becomes a partner with the God, the Creator. Adam accepted this role in tandem with God. The elements of chaos and darkness were diminished by the light of their special dialogue.

In *Les Portes de la forêt,* the act of silencing the name signifies far more than Szklarczyk suggests. This action grants tacit approval to the forces of Auschwitz, and controverts the most basic idea advanced throughout *La Ville de la chance:* The way to God leads through humanity. *Teshuva* had been realized only once Michael accepted his human responsibility to himself, to Pedro and to the Silent One. Wiesel has further complicated matters in *Les Portes de la forêt:* Grégor would appear to have cut himself off from mankind and from God. His refusal to view himself as he is, or the world for what it is, assures the triumph of ignorance, impotence, and deceit.

For the protagonist to rediscover God, he must search through humanity. Returning to Buber's notion, the self must first achieve total reconciliation with itself, thereby ensuring the establishment of a unique creative spirit that will manifest itself in the word, the primary tool for the construction of dialogue. Dialogue will, in turn, extend beyond the framework of human relationships toward union with God, or as Buber suggests, "Every single You is a glimpse of that eternal You. Through every single You the basic word addresses the eternal You" (123). Here, then, the role of silence evolves into a metaphysical struggle whose end should be the abolition of negative silence, and a full recognition of the self and one's inherent responsibilities.

Grégor's silencing of his Hebrew name attacks the fundamental Jewish tradition dealing with names, the onomastic element conveying profound relevance and concealing distinctive powers. In an interview in *La Tribune juive,* Wiesel postulates:

> Israel, the name of the Jewish people, contains the word "God". . .
> is exceedingly important in our history and in our conscience. It is
> a matter of God and of man's combat against God from within the
> tradition, from within the name itself. (171) [my translation]

"Il y a quelque chose d'éternel, d'immortel dans chaque nom" (PF, 24); "Every name has something immortal and eternal about it" (GF, 16), Grégor is told. In one naive act of abnegation, however, Grégor has exiled the divine element concealed within his name, his action ironically achieving that which the Nazis desired: The *absolute* eradication of the Jewish people, including their names.[1]

The rejected name does not, however, remain totally silenced. Grégor has been disturbed in his sheltered cave by another Jew who happens to be nameless. In what appears as a touching act, Grégor confers his Hebrew name upon this mysterious man. Is this deed merely one of human communion, as proposed by Thomas Indinopulas (122), or can one find in it the seeds of a silent struggle that extends throughout all episodes of the novel?

In his study, *La Libération du juif,* Albert Memmi analyzes the reasons why Jews often alter or entirely change their Jewish names. Memmi seeks to define the attitude of some Jews who modify their names, yet oddly retain some vestige of the original. In such practices he perceives that "essentially it seems to be a double contradiction: self-rejection immediately counteracted by a profound resistance to that rejection"[2] (33) [my translation]. A similar existential struggle marks the bestowing of the name in this novel. Grégor abandons his name but cannot altogether reject it. To assuage his guilt, the name is bestowed upon the stranger, to whom we shall refer in this discussion by the Hebrew appellation Gavriel. Thus, the name is preserved, and the novel becomes a tale of Grégor's struggle to regain his silenced name and to accept its significance, as well as gaining the full reconciliation and recollection of the self to which Jung alludes.

Before extending the present analysis, a curious issue must be addressed: The literal existence of Gavriel. He plays a highly substantive role in the novel's silent struggle. Yet, when Grégor attempts to convince some Jewish partisans to rescue this mysterious man, they demand to know if Gavriel exists. Gavriel is the character whose presence permeates all aspects of the narrative, its structures, even its language. Who then is this mysterious being whose presence so radically alters Grégor's life? Does he exist? Or, is he merely a projected shadow, an angel?[3] At the purely mechanical level of plot, Gavriel does exist. Whether he is a living, breathing character who exists in space and time is not a major issue. He is a part of the textual universe, operating within it, and as a result does exist, be it on a physical or metaphysical level.

The struggle to free Gavriel, Grégor's struggle to "rediscover" his name, lies at the core of the novel's action. Grégor is forced to work toward the ultimate battle in which he must face himself and wrestle for his identity. In *Célébration biblique,* Wiesel relates that Jacob's struggle at Peniel speaks "ni d'homme, ni d'ange, ni de mirage" (CB, 110); "he himself never spoke of man or angel, or self-reflection" (MG, 125). Jacob's life had one course: "Comme son père et son grand-père, c'est avec Dieu qu'il cherche à engager le dialogue—et advienne que pourra. C'est Dieu qu'il désire affronter" (CB, 112); "Like his father and grandfather, he wanted to engage God in dialogue, no matter how great the risk. It was God he wished to confront" (MG, 128). What happens at Peniel becomes an "acte conscient et délibéré, provocation de la part de Jacob. Le combat? Jacob l'a souhaité et arrangé. L'initiative est de lui, la mise en scène est de lui, la mise en condition aussi" (CB, 112); "A conscious, deliberate act, a challenge by Jacob. The battle? Conceived and arranged by Jacob. The initiative was his, so was the stage setting" (MG, 128). Grégor's struggle for Gavriel, the man and the name, is the same. Like Jacob, Grégor is an individual desirous of dialogue with a silent God. This dialogue must begin with the individual and lead through humankind. To achieve this, Grégor must free Gavriel; he must struggle for his name and assume his full human essence. He must learn that "qui choisit la solitude et la richesse qu'elle abrite, se déclare complice de ce qui en nous agit contre l'homme" (PF, 232); "The man that chooses solitude and its riches is on the side of those who are against man" (GF, 221). Dialogue with God can only result from human interaction. In this light, Grégor becomes Wiesel's paradigm of humanity after the Holocaust.

The underlying leitmotiv of the novel is that of struggle, a conflict that is expressed through the implementation of numerous techniques. The protagonist must search and battle first to liberate, then to win back his silenced name. Much like the biblical antecedent at Peniel, this leitmotiv reaches its climax during a nocturnal struggle with a mysterious stranger. Grégor encounters his stranger in a Hasidic synagogue in Brooklyn, an unknown man who bears a remarkable resemblance to Gavriel. Through their verbal wrestling match, Grégor effects self-recollection and moves into a position from which he can strive for renewed dialogue. Only after this struggle in the dawn's breaking light can Grégor affirm his true name.

To arrive at that sublime moment of reconciliation, various silences operate upon Grégor, serving as stimuli to guide him. In addition to the more commonly used textual aspects of silence, Wiesel introduces new forms that reflect the evolving role of silence, while also confirming the existence of silent struggle. The novel conveys a sense of confrontation both on the level of the individual and on that of the world beyond. The negative silences that had previously reigned unchallenged, exiling the word and destroying the protagonists' belief in the word, are here threatened by words, by new degrees of silence, and by iron wills not prepared to accept passive annihilation. The characters recognize the importance of positive silence. Grégor's struggle will reflect the mounting revolt against the silences of Auschwitz.

The most visible uses of silence in the text are *la page blanche* and *le grand silence typographique-respiratoire*. In the earlier novels, this technique indicated the stifling of the voice, the painful inability of the protagonists to relate their experiences and the nightmarish reality in which they exist. This silencing technique approximated to a metonymy for the supremacy of the *anus mundi*. By contrast, in this novel one finds the use of this convention signifying augmenting strength. It serves to introduce positive memories that regenerate the individual character and fuel the escalating revolt against a world that imposes death and negativity upon him.

The initial application of *le grand silence typographique-respiratoire* acts as a transition to Grégor's memory of Leib the Lion, his childhood friend. The anamnesis within this silent pause conveys imprimis a tense, anxious silence that plagues the young Grégor, a silence reflective of the dangers that await him on his route to the *heder*. He knows that *la Bande,* a group of young anti-Semites, hides along the way, ready to assault Jewish children. When he is joined by Leib, the two boys cautiously follow their course, until eventually the anxious silence is shattered by an attack. This instant of revolt explodes as Leib protects himself and strikes back, an action elevating Leib to the pantheon of heroes of Jewish history. No longer is the Jew impotent or cowardly. And, Grégor imitates his comrade, as together they effect a small, though highly meaningful, victory. This particular memory, introduced by silence, fortifies Grégor's spirits and encourages him to survive.

Near the novel's conclusion, *le grand silence typographique-respiratoire* marks a similar direction. The Holocaust has ended; the nightmares of Europe have been left behind. Grégor and his wife, Clara, live in New York City, where memories and ghosts of the past persist in haunting them. At a Hasidic celebration, Grégor argues with the rebbe about the meaning of the Holocaust. At its conclusion, Grégor appears to accept the necessity of returning to his former, true self. His admission catapults him into a near-mystical state introduced by *le grand silence typographique-respiratoire.* This white fissure eases the transition into the metaphysical realm, where the final struggle of the narrative transpires. The sphere of action for this wrestling match lies in a nebulous region between that of common reality and the netherworld. A zone of silence seems to shroud Gavriel as Grégor attempts to construct a dialogue with this strange man. The bit of introductory white page has created a cleavage, a silent matrix in which the creative battle will occur. In this instance, the circle of silence, drawn by an initial use of *le grand silence typographique-respiratoire,* evolves into smaller concentric circles, realms of memories each possessing a key to the locked doors of the future. Each circle is introduced, first by *le grand silence typographique-respiratoire* and later by *la page blanche.* Each bit of white page emphasizes that which preceded and silently announces that which will follow. These spaces interrupt the normal respiration of the text, punctuating it with staccato beats that intensify our awareness of being drawn into the essence of the matter. Each new recourse to this technique signifies another hold in the wrestling match, until Grégor emerges as Gavriel.

Not only has Wiesel altered his application of these two techniques to underline the modification of silence, as well as Grégor's struggle, but we discover a conscious evolution of the ontology of silence itself. In the earlier novels, silence had demonstrated and exercised its most negative elements. With the previous novel, silence became Michael's means of accomplishing his *descente aux enfers* and the ensuing acts of *teshuva.* Silence reflected a positive, generative prepotency. In the text under consideration, the contest for the discarded name will be shown to act positively upon silence, effecting a modulation in its very essence, so that by the novel's conclusion, as André Neher believes "what has changed is men, the ontological vibration of their silence that has ceased to be solitary and egotistical" (Exil, 240) [my translation]. This altered silence, in turn, presses for evolutionary modification in the mode of the protagonist's behavior.

Silence's earliest appearance in this text recalls those of La Nuit. Evoked by Gavriel's words, this silence links this story directly to the anus mundi. Silence would appear to manifest the selfsame essence as in earlier works. How, then, near the conclusion can Grégor say to Gavriel that he has learned the value of silence? What has, in fact, been learned? The key resides in the act of listening, for if one truly listens, one can hear everything—even the silences and their significations. Listening signifies a silent, positive function, for as Shmuel Trigano postulates: "The ability to listen . . . is like the ability to give birth, of bearing dialogue into the world, of giving birth to that which is unknown—the future—and what might be other and different from that which currently exists" (16) [my translation]. Listening permits one to penetrate the hidden words and meanings behind the articulation in silence. "Vous vous arrêtez aux mots. . . . Apprenez à les traverser. Apprenez à écouter ce qui ne se dit pas" (PF, 186); "You stop at words. . . . You must learn to see through them, to hear that which is unspoken" (GF, 174).

The best example of this afforded by the text occurs in the second section of the novel. Grégor has abandoned the cave where he had hidden, and openly seeks a new refuge with a former family servant, Maria. Well aware that the villagers would gladly deliver Grégor to the police—and certain death—if his Jewish origins were discovered, Maria concocts an ingenious plan. To conceal his identity, something that would be patently evident if Grégor were to attempt to speak, Maria determines that he shall be mute. The young man who had discarded his Jewish identity must accept yet another role in silence: that of the mute. This idea is speedily transformed into a major act of deception, a mise-en-abyme that initiates a Holocaust ludus replete with elaborate schemes. But the charade does permit the protagonist one positive action: Listening.

Maria counsels him to listen without speaking. This silent state of listening to which Grégor has been elected presents a multitude of positive features. He can effortlessly observe the depths of the interior struggles that occupy the lives of ordinary people. These confessed hidden truths subtly act upon Grégor, altering his being. The metamorphosis results in Grégor's being bound more completely to Gavriel, to Gavriel's ideas of humanity's need of itself, of the human spiritual thirst for truth. To speak would jeopardize these lessons, threatening them with silence and death. Thus, Grégor discovers himself capable of remaining mute.

In the previous novels, silence had frequently been equated to impotence, or even to human imperfection. In contrast, Grégor's silence now represents a firm resolve and a strength previously unknown. At another level, however, the old significations persist. The peasants' reactions to the mute boy range from expressions of sympathy, to more sinister and vengeful ones that interpret his "affliction" as heaven's curse on "his wicked mother" and her sordid past. The village teacher synthesizes these two views when he resolves that Grégor should play the role of Judas in the annual Passion play. The teacher believes one can easily adopt a role, another name, and identity. But the entire essence of the silent struggle in this novel is diametrically opposed to this notion, as one cannot assume another name, another existence, another identity, with impunity.

In the novel's structure, this play within the charade not only serves as an opportunity for Wiesel to demonstrate the culturally transmitted anti-Semitism of these people,[4] but also allows Grégor to listen silently to the powerfully violent reaction, to the psychological deformation that the power of a single name elicits. As the public cries for the blood of Judas, Grégor senses that something has been grossly transformed. A vicious rite has begun, one which Grégor cannot fathom. The villagers he had known have devolved into a barbaric horde screaming for his blood. The goodness and charity that had previously characterized these people have disappeared. He now stands before vicious strangers silently bearing their primitive hatred, suffering their blows, all because of a name.

This scene serves as a crucible in which Wiesel ignites the thoughtless, bigoted hatred that Judas evokes. Judas is the paradigm of the Jew.[5] As Grégor is attacked during the play by the howling mob, he himself is metamorphosed into the name, the role, and the essence of Judas. Under various layers of deceit and subterfuge, beneath the silent mask he has worn, Grégor passively endures the pain of persecution and threat of death. Grégor has become one with Judas, with the suffering Jew whom Judas represents. He has for this moment joined with that primary aspect of his own character previously silenced.[6]

A curious event occurs during this violent scene. Among the spectators sits Petruskanu, the local lord and titular mayor of the village. He has silently observed Grégor as the rabble have raged. Like Grégor, he remains alone in this sea of hysteria. Silent communion instantaneously unites them when their eyes meet, bridging the gulf of hatred and inhumanity erupting in the room. This silent union, this ability to communicate fully by a glance or a gesture, occurs only after Grégor has reassumed a purely Jewish identity. The lucidity gained in that action stresses the Jungian idea of self-recollection, and from it is born that unique communicative spirit to which Buber alludes. In that moment, a sudden indefinable sensation of happiness engulfs the boy as he senses the spiritual union with Petruskanu.

This feeling of friendship guides Grégor to another fundamental realization: He cannot lie to this man. Petruskanu stands in this appointed place at this particular time as an ally and guide. The test of listening, the endurance of the deaf-mutism have led to this particular instant. Lying would mean betraying the advances he has made. Petruskanu becomes another indicator in Grégor's silent struggle for the reclamation of his name, to the reunion with the self.

The scene climaxes when Grégor breaks his silence and casts aside the mask fabricated while living with Maria. Shock silences the villagers in their ravings, but it is a weighty silence, pregnant with fear and expectation, replete with the negative elements that Grégor's voice has temporarily muted. The villagers' initial reaction is to declare Grégor's "refound" voice a miracle, and they prostrate themselves before him, acclaiming Grégor/Judas a saint.

Grégor endeavors to demonstrate to the people their own ignorance, to force them to understand the injustices they have wrought over the centuries, but Grégor's lesson is futile. Their hatred cannot be exorcised by hastily chosen words, nor can the antagonism the villagers have silently harbored against Grégor's "mother" be mitigated by their realizing that Grégor, in reality, is not her son. Grégor's final revelation, his coup de grace, is to admit his Jewish origins: "Je ne m'appelle pas Grégor. Je suis juif, j'ai un nom juif: Gavriel" (PF, 122); "My name is not Gregor. I am a Jew and my name is a Jewish name, Gavriel" (GF, 111). This confession releases those destructive forces previously held in abeyance by the shocked silence. The villagers' hatred elicits a more terrifying silence, an horrific sense of the approach of death in which Grégor is again identified with the Jews.

> En ce moment même, dans les champs rouges de Galicie, des officiers élégants et à l'allure distinguée lancent des ordres: feu, feu, feu! Et cent Juifs, dix mille Juifs basculent dans la fosse: on ne meurt donc pas seul. (PF, 123)

> At this same moment, in the crimson fields of Galicia, smartly turned-out officers were shouting the order: "Fire! Fire!" A hundred Jews, ten thousand Jews were tumbling into the ditches. He would not die alone. (GF, 113)

His death, like theirs, becomes part of a nightmarish operetta.

At this critical moment, Grégor is miraculously saved. Just as Gavriel had surrendered himself to the Hungarian police in order to protect Grégor,

Petruskanu now dashes on to the stage and races off with the boy. Grégor has again experienced that ultimate moment in a human relationship when one individual is prepared to sacrifice his or her own life to save another. Once spirited away, and before metaphorically confronting the next locked gate in the forest, Grégor requests that Petruskanu protect Maria from any retribution. His concern demonstrates a genuine desire to protect and ensure the safety of the woman who had aided him. This conscious sentiment reflects his expanded sense of responsibility and humanity, and is demonstrative of his acceptance that the path toward God must lead through humankind. This action represents Grégor's "final examination" during this phase of his struggle to regain his silenced name.

Despite what has transpired, further steps remain to be taken. If we examine Grégor's extreme moment of truth before the villagers, we see that he openly asserted his Jewish origins and indicated the existence of his Jewish name. But he has failed to resurrect and possess Gavriel. Thus, the struggle will continue.

In the two concluding sections of the novel, "L'Automne," and "L'Hiver," the leitmotiv of struggle assumes new dimensions, passing from the realm of textual elements and passive activities to those of aggressive moves taken to combat the silence of the *anus mundi*. This new action can be divided into two distinct categories: physical combat and metaphysical revolt.

The former occurs in "L'Automne" when Grégor again enters the forest and joins forces with a group of Jewish partisans. At the beginning of this section, the ontology of the forest is altered. In the opening pages of the book, the forest had frightened Grégor, just as had silence. For the youth, the "negative" forest existed everywhere, a constant menace to his very survival. And, one could postulate that the most savage elements of that forest were manifested in the villagers' attitudes, in their profoundest thoughts and actions. Now, however, as Grégor returns to this primeval venue, he becomes aware of the creative sounds that explode from the once frightening silence. Though the forest still exists everywhere, its essence has altered, and silence's ontology reflects this modification of the forest. Silence exists in various forms, with numerous shadings and nuances. Grégor's experiences have obliged him to realize the multiple possibilities hidden within silence.

The forest alone does not demonstrate this modification in Grégor as the various levels of silence act upon him. Grégor senses the need to bridge the chasm between his solitary self and humanity. Thus, Grégor's act in joining forces with the partisans signifies another step toward the realization of his complete self, and toward the ultimate struggle for his silenced name. This can be more clearly seen in his initial role with the partisans: as a messenger.

When Gavriel stumbled into Grégor's cave at the novel's beginning, he had carried with him the weighty silence of the night of Auschwitz. The silenced voices of the murdered Jewish communities sounded again in his voice as he retold their tale. This simple act of serving as messenger implies a great deal for Grégor as a human being, for not only has Grégor opted for positive action by becoming one with others, but he has also recognized his responsibility to act as messenger, to transmit, despite the reality that often words are considered inadequate to bear the charge of meaning required. But despite this inability of language to communicate absolutely the message, he speaks. He watches as the silence of the *anus mundi* invades the souls of his comrades. As Leib completes the report that Grégor has brought, an insupportable silence crushes the unsuspecting partisans. Grégor has transmitted a message which, though it stuns and wounds, contains the essence of mutual salvation.

Earlier protagonists often floundered in such silences as those unleashed by Grégor. Those characters discovered in such silences the unbearable absurdity of their abandoned status in an evil universe. Nevertheless, the basic manner for dealing with such an untenable situation has been a recourse to prayer in a God in whom they may no longer believe. Bruno Bettelheim suggests that "when religion stopped being the essence of man's awareness of himself as a human being, he henceforth had to rely on himself alone to set up the barriers against encroachment by society" (65). This attitude has been adopted by the partisans, and now by Grégor himself. They can no longer rely on God; they can no longer afford to await the arrival of a mystically heaven-sent messiah. They must act, not merely to ensure their own survival, but also that of the Jewish people.

Wiesel presents another important element that underlines the novel's leitmotiv of metaphysical revolt. A prime expression of this revolt occurs during the novel's concluding section when, at a Hasidic celebration, Grégor engages the sect's rebbe in an acrimonious war of words over the nature of the Holocaust and the role and culpability of the divinity. Their conversation opens in hostility as each man's views are clearly defined. The rebbe seeks to probe beneath the bitter mask Grégor displays. Grégor, for his part, wishes the rebbe to admit the fallacy of belief in a pre-Holocaust creator.

To accentuate his case, Grégor recounts to the rebbe the story of four talmudists who convened a *beth din** in the *univers concentrationnaire*. The indicted: God. These four scholars wished to try God for murder, viewing Him as being responsible for the eradication of His chosen people as well as for the abrogation of His own law. The trial ends in a unanimous verdict: Guilty. But,

---

beth din: a rabbinic law court.

the ultimate irony of the tale lay in the fact that the following day the four judges themselves were found guilty by merely existing, and were summarily marched off to the gas chambers.

The rebbe has silently and patiently listened to Grégor's story. Now, in turn, he asks the tormented Grégor if one should cease praying, abandon all hope, and howl madly. Grégor's affirmative response is countered by a calculated, emotional reply from the rebbe, who in his own way is rebelling against God. Each activity of his community constitutes a form of revolt:

> Tu [Dieu] ne veux pas que je danse, tant pis, je danserai; tu m'ôtes toute raison de chanter, eh bien! prête l'oreille, je chanterai. . . . tu ne t'attends pas à ma joie, elle te surprend, eh bien! elle est là, elle monte et ne cessera de monter. (PF, 210)

> You [God] don't want me to dance; too bad, I'll dance anyhow. You've taken away every reason for singing, but I shall sing. . . . You didn't expect my joy, but here it is; my joy will rise up; it will submerge you. (GF, 198)

Not wanting to halt at this, the rebbe continues:

> Il [Dieu] est coupable, crois-tu donc que je ne le sache pas? Que je garde les paupières close et les oreilles bouchées? . . . Oui, il est coupable, oui il s'est fait l'allié du mal, de la mort, du meurtre. (PF, 210)

> He [God] is guilty; do you think I don't know it? That I have no eyes to see, no ears to hear? . . . Yes, he is guilty. He has become the ally of evil, of death, of murder. (GF, 199)

But the rebbe's anger appears to offer Grégor no solution: We must even query whether he has succeeded in surmounting the negative silence within Grégor, the silence of those individuals whose lives have crossed his and are now dead. According to André Neher, the rabbi's challenge was "the 'challenge to silence'. . . a challenge that exonerates none of the murderous qualities of silence, for, rising up out of the depths of silence, prayer, dance, and song become cries and daggers" (Exil, 240) [my translation]. The ontology of silence has altered; nothing more.

This sharp encounter has deeply touched Grégor. Ted Estess feels that "the rebbe reawakens the voice of eternity within him [Grégor]" (86–87). It should be remembered that a part of Grégor's Hebrew name is El (אל), a name of God, that trace of the eternal within Grégor. Moreover, the rebbe has demonstrated the depth and proliferation of revolt, and he has likewise given Grégor a degree of courage and direction. Each question, each statement has acted to draw Grégor back to the essence he had earlier rejected. The rabbi's direction has prepared Grégor for the final battle. "Le Rabbi avait raison. Il fallait revenir" (PF, 215); "The Rebbe was right; he had to come back" (GF, 204). The time has indeed come to return.

The leitmotiv has prepared us for the final struggle, for that moment when Grégor, like Jacob, must ford his own Jabbok. It has been suggested here that silence in *Les Portes de la forêt* denotes a struggle for the muted name which, within a Jewish/Wieselian context, is equated to the primary essence of the individual, and that there exist certain parallels with Jacob and his encounter at Peniel. Jacob's life had drawn him to that night by the Jabbok, where he encountered the mysterious being with whom he struggled. In a similar manner, Grégor's existence has pursued a course guiding him to his own nocturnal struggle. Grégor's final experience, and its significance in relation to silence, can be elicited by a detailed intertextual structural analysis of these two stories.

In *La Nuit,* Wiesel presented his own version of the biblical *Akeda* in which several key elements of the original were altered or reversed. The *Akeda* of the night necessarily deformed all positive features of the original. The word, life, and hope appear as superfluous elements in a universe where death and evil reign; as a result, they are silenced. In the retelling of Genesis 32:23–33, the story of Jacob at Peniel, the original is likewise altered, though the negative veil of *La Nuit* conspicuously absents itself here.

That a struggle takes place in both stories is beyond doubt, though the biblical text recounts a physical struggle, while Wiesel's reconstruction describes one of metaphysical dimensions. In both stories, the protagonists' opponents remain unnamed beings. And yet, are they unknown? Both stories offer insights into who the nocturnal strangers might be. In the biblical text (Genesis 32:31), no name is evoked, yet "Jacob called the name of the place Peniel: *for I have seen God face to face,* and my life is preserved" [my emphasis]. The phrase in apposition hints at the identity of the nocturnal opponent. As Barthes suggests in his analysis of this biblical tale: "It is necessary to extract the said from—the unsaid" (*Analyse,* 29) [my translation]. Thus, I agree with Wiesel in *Célébration Biblique* when he stresses that Jacob speaks of God. Though from a traditional Jewish viewpoint, this would seem heretical, the textual evidence would suggest that the "other" in the biblical text is God.[7]

In Wiesel's reconstruction, the nameless stranger who comes to be known as Gavriel says of his name: "Mon nom se prononçait et s'écrivait de différentes façons" (PF, 17); "My name was written and pronounced in different ways" (GF, 10). This lone, cryptic phrase presents a vital clue, for it recalls the problem of the tetragrammaton, the ineffable name of God. In the Talmud, Kiddushin 71a, one discovers the following statement with regard to the name: "Not as I am written am I pronounced," and it points to the identity of the unknown being. Jewish law and tradition have not permitted the four-letter word, transcribed in English as YHVH, to be pronounced as the word is written. The common articulation has become *adonai,* and among Orthodox Jews even this appellation of the divine name is uttered only in prayer, while the term *Hashem*—the name—is pronounced in common reference to God. It would seem, therefore, that the nameless stranger whom Grégor encounters possesses an ineffable name whose orthographic and phonetic forms have nothing in common. Thus, the biblical and Wieselian opponents who, though unnamed, may very well be God.

Looking at Genesis 32:25, the biblical story painfully attempts to dispel the possibility of Jacob's adversary being God, for in the text, the Hebrew word *ish* (איש), *man,* is stressed, though as the story reveals, he is no ordinary mortal. Wiesel's text reflects a similar notion, especially in those pages that represent the ultimate nocturnal struggle.[8] In the initial moments when Grégor engages the "other," the reference is constantly to *l'homme,* the man. In both texts, the stranger is confirmed as being human.

Biblical and rabbinic sources remain vague as to which character first engaged the struggle on the banks on the Jabbok. In Wiesel's text, the instigator of the struggle clearly is Grégor, who wishes to engage the mysterious man in dialogue, a thought not shared by the opponent. Grégor does not achieve any degree of success until he pleads: "Rends-moi ce que je t'ai confié. Je suis seul, j'ai mené une vie fausse, je veux changer, redevenir moi-même, reprendre ma liberté" (PF, 217); "Give me back what I gave you. I'm alone and leading a false life. I want to change, to become again what I was" (GF, 205). We can safely assume that the constant struggles Grégor has faced have reached the moment when the ultimate choice must be made so as to secure his liberty; he must act in order to be that which he is, and accept in toto his responsibility to himself and to others, "Rends-moi mon nom" (PF, 217); "Give me back my name" (GF, 205). Only at this juncture does the "other" finally acknowledge Grégor's presence, and the two enter into combat.

Wiesel's tale describes the struggle in purely metaphysical terms, again a point differentiating it from the story in Genesis. Nevertheless, certain rabbinical sources stress the singularly metaphorical and metaphysical nature of the conflict in Genesis, which indicates Jacob's need to evaluate his past in order to accept his future role as Israel. The wrestling becomes one of conscience as the patriarch inventories his life. Much the same is true of Grégor's situation as this confrontation allows him to review his life's course since the abandonment of his true name and the adoption of the facade, Grégor.

Grégor's attempts to regain Gavriel evolve into a dual struggle: To become one again with his most basic self, to reassert and revive his muted name; and, to construct that unique link between what is and what was, to establish basic and meaningful human relationships, dialogues that will lead to God. Grégor recognizes the fact that God has not changed; His silence remains unaltered. Mankind, however, has altered, and must continue to evolve. The silence of the *anus mundi* that had threatened Wiesel's protagonists is in its turn threatened. The first step toward its exile resides in human beings helping one another, linking forces regardless of the burden. One cannot attempt to save all humanity; rather, one must begin with a single life. In assuming this philosophy, Grégor's attitude announces an evolution of the ontology of silence, and his own preparedness to assume his rightful name, a name that contains, as stated earlier, something eternal, something immortal.

In Genesis 32:26, the nocturnal stranger "touched the hollow of his [Jacob's] thigh" in a desperate attempt to overcome the patriarch. This event is echoed in Wiesel's tale. Grégor, having related numerous episodes of his life, the friendships in which he has engaged since the silence of the cave, finally speaks of his marriage to Clara. Love, the union of two souls, ultimately represents the greatest element in creation, symbolizing the creative act that can lift the world out of chaos, an act that diminishes solitude and helps unite the diverse elements of creation. And yet, the stranger notes that Grégor's language silently conceals some truth. "Tu vas la quitter?" (PF, 228); "You're leaving her?" (GF, 217), the opponent asks. He has understood the words left unsaid in the meta-silence framing Grégor's statements; he has recognized the failure of the union and now uses that knowledge to stun and cripple Grégor.

At this point in Wiesel's reconstruction, we uncover a reversal. In Genesis 32:27, the opponent pleads: "Let me go, for the day breaketh." Now, however, it is the wounded Grégor who wishes to break off the encounter. The opponent refuses and demands Grégor list all his failures, a remark that deals another wound, but a catalytic one that results in a *grand silence typographique-respiratoire,* a silence of truth and a sort of silent decor for the final phase of the novel's struggle for the muted name.

In this silence, Grégor recognizes that his failure to achieve unity within himself has resulted in the impossibility of creating a full, harmonious union in his marriage. Grégor understands that he is what he has chosen. Free to be himself, free to accept his Hebrew name, its significance and its fate, Grégor has, as Sartre would term the act, demonstrated *lâcheté* and *mauvaise foi* in his denial of his own freedom. Grégor has been *l'en-soi,* a labyrinth of chaotic meaninglessness that offers a sort of challenge that Grégor has thus refused to accept. Yet since his encounter with Gavriel, Grégor has gradually accepted the necessity of becoming actively engaged in order to free himself. Each action has created a *pour-soi* situation in which Grégor has fought to express his responsibility by means of his actions and assistance to others.

In this moment of silent lucidity within the struggle, Grégor approaches himself, actively directing himself to continued action. Despite his development and the progress already realized, Grégor is no more than a *salaud,* having robbed himself of his name and of his conscious freedom to readopt it. He remains Grégor, seemingly locked in the choice made years before.

Grégor realizes he can be whole and authentic, but only by accepting the freedom at hand, by choosing again, and by rejecting the solitude of a false name.

> Je suis tel que je me choisis, je suis dans mon choix, dans ma volonté de choisir. Point de divorce entre le moi et son image, entre l'acte et l'être. Je suis cette image, je suis cet acte. (PF, 231)

> I am what I choose to be; I am in my choice, in my will to choose. There is no divorce between self and its image, between being and acting. I am the act, the image, one and indivisible. (GF, 221)

In order to achieve the Jungian notion of full consciousness and to establish viable dialogue, Grégor must first choose himself, and then link that authentic self to others. He must accept the Jew within and become authentic in his choice, or as Sartre proposes:

> Authenticity consists in possessing a true and lucid consciousness of the situation, in assuming the responsibilities and risks that are involved, in accepting it in pride or humiliation, sometimes in horror and hate. (*Réflexions,* 109) [my translation]

The text abruptly dissolves into *la page blanche.* We must assume that in this textual lacuna something transpires, for when the printed text resumes, it is morning, and though Grégor is still in the Hasidic *shteible,** the mysterious opponent has vanished. In his place sits a young yeshiva student. This boy symbolizes the believing Jewish student of *La Nuit.* Past and present have met, and create a hope for the future. The boy, assuming the role of messenger, announces the need for a tenth man for the morning minyan, the traditional quorum of ten

---

**shteible:* a Yiddish word referring to a small synagogue. The word is frequently associated with the Hasidic world.

men necessary for public prayer, and which represents a community. Grégor's affirmative response signifies his willingness to rejoin the community, to opt for life and some degree of a future. The text now echoes the question posed by the nameless stranger at the beginning of the novel: What is his name? And, as before, the protagonist replies: "Grégor;" but, the text continues: "Il rougit et se corrige: —Gavriel. Je m'appelle Gavriel. Grégor n'est pas un nom juif, tu sais" (PF, 235); "He blushed and corrected himself: "Gavriel. Gavriel's my name. Grégor isn't a Jewish name, you know that" (GF; 224). .

Grégor/Gavriel become one. The struggle for the muted name has ended. The night that appeared to have concluded far less dramatically than had Jacob's has not ended in the silence of *la page blanche*. That blank page now signifies more than a purely technical transition; it is a lengthy silent pause in which a mysterious and powerful transformation has occurred. Though outwardly emerging as Grégor, just as his biblical counterpart appears to remain as Jacob,[9] his character has undergone a final metamorphosis. To persist in being Grégor would be to negate the silent, mysterious victory that has been achieved.

The final element in this act of revoicing the Hebrew name comes in the kaddish, the unique doxology recited as both prayer for the dead and sanctification of God's majesty. The prayer is characterized by an abundance of praise and glorification of God. Far from being a lamentation for the dead, the kaddish stands as a sublime expression of hope for the speedy establishment of God's kingdom on earth. More importantly, the kaddish is a congregational prayer only recited in the presence of a minyan where the congregation intones its responses, an action that has the power of influencing heavenly decrees in humanity's favor.[10] The kaddish also signifies humanity's means of praising the creator even for the evil that has befallen him. Thus Grégor/Gavriel prepares to recite the kaddish, which had previously been exiled from Wiesel's literary universe.

The kaddish also signifies and serves as a powerful and holy initiatory act. In this context, the kaddish symbolizes both an acceptance of, and a challenge to, renew the struggle. Though Grégor's name and Jewishness have been restored, elements of creation remain in chaos, encased in negative silence. "Reprenons la lutte" (PF, 235); "Let's resume the struggle," he states (GF, 225). His next task must establish unity in his relationship with Clara. She must be freed from the past. "Ce sera une bataille âpre, austère, obstinée. La lutte pour survivre commencera ici-même".(PF, 236); "It will be a bitter, austere, obstinate battle. The struggle to survive will begin here, in this room" (GF, 225). Men and women must work to create life, to free the caged messiah. By accepting life as it is and taking risks in order to change it, Grégor/Gavriel enters into dialogue with other men and perhaps, eventually, with God.

Grégor/Gavriel has finally achieved that full consciousness that Jung prescribed as necessary to sacrifice of oneself. Grégor/Gavriel has likewise attained a loftier degree of autonomy, that which Bruno Bettelheim defines as "one's sense of identity, the conviction of being a unique individual, with lasting and deeply meaningful relations to a few others" (73). Fully conscious of himself, prepared to act autonomously, Grégor/Gavriel is prepared to challenge God and humankind, to establish viable dialogue, and once more to build together. The kaddish may be the means "par laquelle l'homme remet à Dieu sa couronne et son sceptre" (PF, 236); "by which man returns God his crown and scepter" (GF, 225), but it also symbolizes the promise for continued, revitalized encounters with Him, as Wiesel persists in his quest to understand the silent creator.

CHAPTER **5**

The Mystical Union
Le Mendiant de Jérusalem (1968)

*Il ne s'agit pas de supprimer la parole
articulée, mais de donner aux mots à peu
près l'importance qu'ils ont dans les rêves.*
A. ARTAUD

Leur code est indéchiffrable aux non-initiés.
E. WIESEL

A s Wiesel's novels have evolved from the epicenter of *La Nuit*, his techniques have become more ethereal, more mystical. In that first novel, the invasion of the *univers concentrationnaire* into the world of innocence and faith disrupted the passage of time. The telos of the other stories continued to remain vague, with past and present uniting to open a way to the future. Characters appear to exist in Chagall-like kingdoms where reality and dreams fuse. Wiesel weaves complex tapestries of phantasmagorical testimony and Hasidic fantasy in which the memories of his personal past and the collective history of the Jewish people mingle amid cabalistic signs and symbols. Wiesel has attempted to articulate these elements in much the same manner as Antonin Artaud proposes in *Le Théâtre et son double*—that an author should attempt to impart to language the importance it happens to have in dreams (112). Wiesel has sought to integrate the silence of the nightmarish reality of the *univers concentrationnaire* and the living, colorful legends of his youth into this quest. The result has not produced a curse of Babel, but rather the creation of a mystical universe richly layered with sacred and profane silences in which the Wieselian protagonists have persisted in their struggles.

Le Mendiant de Jérusalem (A Beggar in Jerusalem) represents, one of the author's most complex and dense creations. Though critics and scholars refer to it as a novel, the author clearly stresses it is a *récit,* a multilevel, complicated text founded upon shrift, stories, and parables. Wiesel's conscious choice to employ the *récit* as the means to narrate this tale propounds a particular relevance. As the *récit* is viewed as confession, this narrative approach permits a narrator to relate past events in his or her life that have led to a present moment of moral crisis. The *récit* correspondingly demonstrates a degree of inevitable inconsistency between the narrator's accepted truths, perceptions, and intentions, and the enigmatic reality of the actual moral predicament. As a reader, one can never know with certainty precisely what transpired to the narrator who occupies a privileged place from which to survey past endeavors. At the moment of narration, the narrator of the *récit* enjoys a specific cognizance that could never have been possessed when the events had happened. These somewhat ironic discrepancies engender a variety of silences and consequent questions concerning the verisimilitude of the narrator's account, inviting the reader to engage the text in active dialogic fashion.

Moreover, Wiesel, the self-styled storyteller, believes the tale possesses enormous powers to effect changes in humanity and in the universe. In *Le Mendiant de Jérusalem,* he has abandoned the novel's traditional form in favor of a technique in which the protagonist, David, sits among the beggars, madmen, and mystics of Jerusalem during their nocturnal vigil, where he shares their stories. These tales reflect the mystical aspects of the Jewish experience, and include contemplations on the recently fought Six Day War. Every story and parable offer the reader a revelation of a truth concealed in David's life, as well as of a distant light, some semblance of a transcendent reality in a world of nightmares.

The tales that comprise the greater part of the *récit* appear to be founded on silences that project themselves across Jewish history. They recall the Midrashic tales of the Talmud and the esoteric stories of the Hasidic rebbes. The preponderance of these stories becomes all the more crucial when we consider they reflect something more. Like the Hasidic masters who occupied so formative a position in Wiesel's youth, his tales possess similar properties, silences, and hopes. His stories alter themselves and echo through our minds as they engage us in mental acrobatics. Such stories, because of their particular power to move the minds and hearts of human beings, as well as to enjoin heaven's support, remain central elements in Wiesel's work. Hasidic masters entertained the belief that their tales, their faith, their mystical invocations would, to a degree, have some influence on human events.

This work is unique for another reason: It alone is set in Jerusalem. Jerusalem is the capital of the contemporary State of Israel, but as André Neher suggests in his study, *Jérusalem, vécu juif et message,* it is also the capital of Judaism, one which "is not linked to a particular place and time but rather a portable capital that each authentic Jewish community would carry with itself in its Diaspora" (23) [my translation]. Jerusalem resonates "like a deep, mystical chord in us all" (Wiesel, *Jerusalem,* 15), and it is this mystical element that is continually reflected in the *récit*. Jerusalem represents certain mystical links between God and humankind.

According to Neher, Jerusalem exists in constant tension. Though temporal and spatial, if effectively transcends such limitations, representing the eternal as well as the finite. For Neher, Jerusalem exists in a state of tension between the real and the ideal, between that which is accessible and that which is not. This view tends to reinforce Wiesel's choice of setting, as in Jewish thought the eternal, otherworldly Jerusalem can be reached only by means of the physical reality. This idea can be extended, as in the Talmud where we discover the proposal that God Himself must seek out the true path to the Eternal Jerusalem through the earthly one. Jerusalem represents the vestibule of eternity. Beyond all other venues, humanity and God may more easily encounter one another there. Thus, Wiesel's reasons for setting the *récit* in Jerusalem reflect this simultaneous, silent quest of Creator and creation for one another. Moreover, two additional factors place Wiesel's choice of setting clearly within the context of silence.

First, Wiesel stresses the omnipresence of silence in Jerusalem: "ces silences de peine, ces silences de joie" (UJA, 32); "those silences of pain, those silences of joy" (JT, 20), silences that speak to individuals and unite them to the distant past and an uncertain future. Of all aspects of the city, none demonstrates this quite as exceptionally as the Wall. The symbol of walls had previously been used in each of Wiesel's preceding novels. After the warmth and protection of the *shtetl,* the earlier protagonists have found themselves increasingly trapped by physical and metaphysical walls erected to ensnare and deprive them of their liberty and humanity. The ghettos of Sighet and its walls, the barbed wire within the *anus mundi,* the enclosed execution chamber in *L'Aube,* the hospital room and plaster body cast in *Le Jour,* Michael's prison wall before which he offers his "prayer," and the metaphorical walls of the forest with its locked gates that Grégor/Gavriel had to open; all were obstructive walls that hindered the evolution of the characters. But these walls gradually became catalysts, the means by which the protagonists entered into themselves and into the silences imposed from both beyond and within. Walls assumed mystical properties that facilitated the development of the protagonists, eventually setting them on a route that would lead beyond the quagmire.

The modification of this symbol is completed in this sixth book, where the metaphorical wall becomes tangible in the Wall. The Wall, symbol of the past, present, and future, becomes that unique venue where all aspects of creation are gathered together, and where at midnight the *shehina,* the female aspect of the Godhead representing God's presence, comes to mourn, along with the beggars, mystics, and madmen who sit before it, the destruction of the Temple. The Wall becomes man's *point de départ* into the mysteries of the universe, and toward union with God.

Standing before the Wall after the 1967 war, Wiesel relates: "Je me souviens de la qualité, de la densité du silence qui s'appesantit sur nous: nul n'osa le briser, pas même par l'incantation des prières" (UJA, 39); "I recall the quality, the density of the silence that fell upon us: nobody dared breach it, not even by the incantation of prayers" (JT, 26). The Wall becomes a silent witness to Jewish and human history—no longer a wall of separation, but a wall of union, a mystical wall. It is thus fitting that the action of the *récit* unfolds before it.

The Wall lends its mystical power to the second manner in which the choice of Jerusalem reflects silence. In the text, once the Old City of Jerusalem has been liberated from Jordanian forces, thousands of Jews flood the narrow alleys as they race toward the Wall. This crowd is suddenly altered as the Wall elicits ghosts of the past.

> Ainsi, à force d'appeler l'hallucination et de lui résister, tour à tour, j'y plonge [dans la foule] et retrouve amis, parents et voisins, tous les morts de la ville, toutes les villes mortes du cimetière que fut l'Europe. Tous se firent pèlerins, et les voilà, à l'heure crépusculaire, intemporelle, envahissant le Temple dont ils sont à la fois les fondements de feu et les gardiens. (MJ, 179)

> Thus, by inviting hallucination and then rejecting it, I plunge into it [the crowd] and find friends, parents and neighbors, all the dead of the town, all the dead towns of the cemetery that was Europe. Here they are, at the timeless twilight hour, pilgrims all, invading the Temple of which they are both fiery foundation and guardians. (BJ, 201)

The Wall has silently, mystically resurrected the six million murdered Jews. In an arcane manner, the Wall not only symbolizes Good, but it also signifies the intrusion of the *anus mundi,* of evil into the victory of the 1967 war.

Jerusalem with its complex and unique elements ideally suits Wiesel's silent, mystical search for God. God and humanity, past and present, legend and history, fuse into a single story that must be transmitted. These various elements of the *récit* recall André Neher's belief that such opposites, such contradictions, do not exist and that "in the manner of a fugue, two themes intertwine, each seeking the other. They are unable to encounter, and yet they are condemned to an inseparable companionship" (*Jerusalem,* 97) [my translation]. Jerusalem most significantly presents that point where the divergent themes of the fugue join in harmony. Moreover, as Michael Berenbaum postulates, this is where "all the characters from the earlier novels are present . . . to witness another aspect of the human mystery, the mystery of good" (69).

As proposed earlier, Wiesel's use of silence in *Le Mendiant de Jérusalem* evolves into the realm of mysticism. It is imperative therefore to seek to define mysticism and to substantiate its links to silence. The generally accepted definition of mysticism is that which renders possible union with the divine nature, most frequently by means of ecstatic contemplation. Mystics seek to efface their empiric selves and to exile conceptual thought as they attempt to perceive God. Often, such experiences result in images of a negative nature, or as Dom Cuthbert Butler proposes: "The mystics heap up terms of negation—darkness, void, nothingness—in endeavoring to describe that Absolute which they have apprehended" (123). According to E. Herman, this negative approach to God is "really the way of analogy reversed. It proceeds upon the assumption that, since the finite is the complete antithesis of the infinite, everything that can be affirmed of man must logically be denied of God who can only be described by negative" (299). Thus, mystics who have desired to represent the *mysterium tremendum* have been obliged to refer to the nothingness, the darkness, and the silence beyond normally perceived reality.

According to Herman, the truly renowned mystics "invariably found that the Eternal can only be experienced in a profound and brooding silence" (28). Silence is the means by which God manifests His presence in the world. In Max Picard's view, "the mark of the Divine in things is preserved by their connection with the world of silence." He goes on to propose that "just as language constitutes the nature of Man, so silence is the nature of God; but in that nature everything is clear, everything word and silence at the same time" (20; 229). Within our temporal framework, silence would appear to be an important sign of the divine. For the mystic, silence becomes a means of tracking God, perceiving God as a negative silence that metamorphoses into a silence filled with meaning, a paradoxical silence where nothing is articulated and yet all is said.

Mystics have gone from the word to the negative silence of God in order to discover its positive nature. Wiesel has proposed that "c'est en cherchant le silence, en le creusant, que je me suis mis à découvrir les périls et les pouvoirs de la parole" (PE, 7); "it was by seeking, by probing silence that I began to discover the perils and power of the word" (K, 14). The residual silence of Auschwitz, the chaotic, negative elements of silence that persist to affect humanity, have led Wiesel to a contemplation of our mortal condition. These silences have placed him in contact and combat with the divine silence. Each encounter with the silence of the *anus mundi* has heightened Wiesel's awareness of the eternal silence that is God. Like other mystics, Wiesel has attempted to gain some appreciable knowledge of God by means of that silence, and *Le Mendiant de Jérusalem* represents his effort to effect a degree of harmony and peace in the post-Auschwitz world.

The mystical path that Wiesel follows is that of Cabala.[1] I do not wish to propose in these arguments that Cabala is to be considered a unitary, monolithic term. Jewish mysticism is a variegated, richly heterogeneous tradition. What I would suggest, however, is that Wiesel has used certain aspects of Cabala *in its broadest sense* as ludic, metaphoric devices in the text under consideration. Thus, it is imperative that the reader possess a modicum of information about those elements that the author employs, thereby ensuring an appreciation of the literary subtleties that emerge.

Cabala is Jewish mysticism that represents not merely esoteric teachings but combines esotericism and theosophy with mysticism as it seeks an apprehension of God and His creation, whose intrinsic elements lie beyond the grasp of human intelligence. Cabala attempts to draw the mystics' conscious awareness of the transcendence of God and of His immanence into a context of true religious life. All facets of life are a revelation of God, although He may not be clearly perceived through human contemplation and introspection. Cabala seeks to unveil the mysteries of the hidden life of God in all things, and to establish direct relationships between the divine life and that of creation, especially that of humankind. "No religious knowledge of God, even of the most exalted kind, can be gained except through contemplation of the relationship of God to creation" (Scholem, *Kabbalah,* 88). Within Cabala, mystical and esoteric elements coexist in a highly confused manner. The mystical knowledge, by its very essence, cannot easily be transmitted, whereas the esoteric knowledge can. These two elements contemplate one another as together they guide the mystic toward the desired encounter with God.

Cabala would appear to offer Wiesel three basic elements to weave into his *récit*: the presence of the *sefirot,* or the ten emanations of God; the *shehina,* along with its notion of exile; and *tikkun,* the gathering together of the pure elements of creation with hopes of effecting universal redemption. Though these principles would not necessarily belong naturally or logically together in an analysis of orthodox cabalistic movements and certain significant departures (*e.g.,* the Lurianic tradition), Wiesel has employed them within this literary context to develop and to extend his silences, as he attempts to reconcile the Creator with His creation in the light of the reality of the *anus mundi.*

The *sefirot* represent the ten emanations of the divine presence in the universe, elements of God that can be perceived by those mystics who seek to unveil them. The *sefirot* emanate successively from above to below, each one revealing an additional element of the divine process and representing a particular attribute of God, each containing all that preceded. Each *sefira* signifies itself and other emanations to which it is intrinsically linked.

In this text, Wiesel has structured his own "tree of life" in the characters of the beggars at the Wall. "Leur code est indéchiffrable aux non-initiés" (MJ, 15); "Only the initiated can decipher the code they use to transmit information" (BJ, 6), that is, something transpires in their lives and stories that transcends our commonplace sense of reality. Michael Berenbaum has suggested elsewhere that each beggar's name represents a specific quality of the Jewish people: compassion, wisdom, the spirit of waiting, etc. (72–75). I wholly concur with Berenbaum's observation, though I would significantly extend it. Based upon their Hebrew names and some circumscribed information tendered in the stories, certain of these beggars personify various *sefirot* in the cabalistic "tree of life." For example, the second *sefira* is *hohma,* or wisdom. In Cabala, this sense of wisdom refers to genius, inspiration, or revelation—that flash of active intellect from which other degrees of intelligence and understanding stem. There is one beggar whose name would suit this: *Moshe.* In the Jewish tradition, Moshe (Hebrew for Moses) had the law revealed directly to him by God, and this revealed wisdom formed the basis for Jewish life, thought, and tradition. Moreover, it is, as Bernebaum demonstrates, this character who symbolizes the wisdom of fighting in June 1967, just as the biblical Moses had been forced into action by urging the liberated Israelites into the waters of the Red Sea to flee Pharaoh's chariots. Another example relates to the fifth *sefira: gevura,* translated either as *power* or *judgment.* This *sefira* is also known as *din* (judgement). Among the beggars sits Dan, whose Hebrew name stems from the word *din.* Hence, he would seem to correspond to the fifth *sefira.*

Such parallels, though intriguing, are not always clear. I believe Wiesel has purposefully done this so as to limit our focus to three specific *sefirot* and their relationships: *keter, yesod,* and *malhut,* which are respectively represented by Katriel, David, and Malka. These particular elements of the divine being as personified by these three characters, epitomize Wiesel's silent quest for God. Wiesel is probing for a proper mode of action, for "whenever we act with the right intention and devotion . . . we convene the divine presence around us" (Hoffman, 1981, 55). I would here add the corollary that the interplay and relationships between these three characters and the representative *sefirot* constitute Wiesel's attempt to effect *tikkun,* or redemptive reunion of the elements of creation presently in chaos.

Keter, yesod and *malhut* demonstrate more interaction than other elements of the cabalistic "tree of life". *Keter,* the highest *sefira,* has "traditionally been viewed as the primary generative force" (Hoffman, 1981, 55), and is represented in masculine terminology and symbols. The *kav* (beam of light) descends from it into our temporal universe. Its goal is the creation and establishment of the rule of God's kingdom in our dimension. The notions of kingdom and kingship are represented by the lowest *sefira, malhut,* the complement of *keter* and that attribute of God given feminine qualities by the cabalists. But *keter* requires an agent to direct the generative forces of God so it may establish itself. *Yesod,* symbolized by the phallus in cabalistic writings and iconography, becomes the means by which this impregnation is achieved. Thus, these three *sefirot* are fundamentally linked: *keter,* signifying force and harmonious union; *yesod,* the foundation of all creation that "guarantees and consummates the *hieros gamos,* the holy union of male and female powers" (Scholem, *On the Kabbalah,* 104); and *malhut,* the root of the universe and life, as well as the representation of God's kingdom in this world.

These *sefirot* share yet another element: Jerusalem. As earlier demonstrated, Wiesel's choice of Jerusalem as the setting for the *récit* emphasizes the silent struggle between opposing characteristics in the Jew and within the world, as well as the capacity of Jerusalem to resolve such conflicts. An additional reason for his choice can be found in the Zohar II: 157a and b. This esoteric exegesis expounds the richness of the land of Israel derived from the plenitude of God's omnipresent spirit. The rabbinic argument found in Zohar II, 157a first discusses the poverty of unleavened bread (*matza/*מצה) that for them is "symbolic of the female principle, which without the male principle is, so to speak, in poverty." For the rabbis, this poverty was altered by the addition of the Hebrew letter *vav* (ו), symbolic of the missing male element. The word *matza* is thus transformed into *mitzva* (מצוה), or good deeds or commandments, and represents a positive guiding force and the union of male and female principles. The poor bread of affliction is thus enriched and can nourish humanity, the subsequent passage noting how it awakens within the human soul "intelligence and power of discernment" (Zohar II, 157b). The key feature of this rabbinic exegesis is the setting where the male element, *vav,* is inserted: The Land of Israel (Erez Yisrael). The Zohar II, 157b offers the following explanation: "When Israel left Egypt they were devoid of all knowledge until God made them taste bread of that earth called *erez* (viz., Erez Yisrael). . . . Then Israel began to know and to recognize God."

Erez Yisrael possesses the nourishment that elevates all human beings to a higher spiritual plane. Later rabbinic and cabalistic commentaries, especially the first chapter of Joseph Gikatila's thirteenth-century work *Sha'arei Orah,* and

Nachmanides's commentaries on Genesis, extend the Zohar's text and state that as the *even shetiyya,* the "foundation stone of the entire world[2]" is in Jerusalem, then Jerusalem represents that point to which heaven's goodness flows down directly, and from which all else is nourished. Only in Jerusalem does *reshit hohma* exist, which is to say that no curtain separates the holy city from God, which thus permits harmony to flourish. Thus in Wiesel's *récit,* it is in Jerusalem that the three *sefirot* represented by Malka, David, and Katriel seek out each other. The story tells of their quest for nourishment, unity and harmony.

The *sefira keter* contains all that was, is, and will be. Its position in the metaphoric "tree of life" is located beyond the limits of our universe in the *ayin sof or,* the endless light that surrounds the magnitude of the *ayin sof,* the endlessness of the divine being. *Keter* represents the beginning and the end, the point from which creation emanates, and to which all will eventually return. Traditionally, the divine name, *Ehyeh asher ehyeh,* or "I am that I am," is associated with *keter,* establishing a mystical bond with God. Moreover, within the mystical patterns of *gematria,* where each Hebrew letter possesses a corresponding numerical value, the tetragrammaton has a numerical value of forty-five, the same value found in the word for human being, *adam* (אדם). Thus, the principal rabbis of the cabalist movement suggested there was a strong perfectible element of God in every human being. David's search for Katriel represents that human quest for the divine spark hidden within all, as well as a search for those elements apparently exiled or silenced by the smoke of Auschwitz.

"Vivant ou mort, Katriel reprendra sa place dans le récit" (MJ, 13); "Dead or alive, Katriel will claim his place in this tale" (BJ, 3). Real or imaginary, Katriel must have a place in the story. Though the tale told by the protagonist implies Katriel may have died, no clear textual evidence of his death exists. His absence approximates to a metonymy of exile. Katriel, like God, belongs to the story. His qualities of innocence, simplicity, and love resound throughout, and suggest he represents the positive, good qualities of the Almighty to be discovered in life and humankind. Katriel's essence becomes David's obsession and his hope for escaping his own schizophrenic plight. But David only remembers and recognizes the horrors of the Holocaust that recall the eternal contradiction of evil as a constituent element of a loving God, a problem presented in biblical texts, and a notion that has frequently posed a cumbersome obstacle for all theologians and commentators. The Zohar, II, 163a, however, perceives evil as providing a background for good; it facilitates the channelling of good into the universe. Though David remains a prisoner of the evil of the *anus mundi,* that very power has driven him toward a force of good: Katriel. The latter's voice silently reaches out to David, a recurrent whispering that imparts three vital concepts: The importance of both language and silence in the transmission of a story, the individual's role as a bridge between past and future, and the ultimate power of love in effecting *tikkun*. David's quest can effectively usher Katriel's message into an otherwise imperfect world.

The first principle deals with language and silence and their complementary role in the transmission of any tale. David, the witness of the night, dislikes words. His visceral reaction has been to reject them, opting instead for silence. But Katriel reminds him that human beings must learn to impart silence more carefully than words. "Tous les silences ne sont pas purs. Ni féconds. Certains sont stériles, maléfiques" (MJ, 98–99); "But beware: not all silences are pure. Or creative. Some are sterile, malignant" (BJ, 108). Katriel presses David to the following realization: "J'aime que le silence ait une histoire et qu'il soit transmis par elle" (MJ, 99); "I like silence to have a history and be transmitted by it" (BJ, 108). Not only are the audible and visible silences important, but one must, like Katriel, become aware of the silences within words. It is at this juncture that Katriel offers advice learned from his father: "C'est lui [son père] qui m'a appris à me mesurer aux mots et à me concilier le silence, sinon la vérité, qu'ils recèlent" (MJ, 98); "He [his father] taught me to measure myself against my words and to attune myself to their silence if not always to the truth they conceal" (BJ, 107). That Katriel has learned this principle, that he practices it and urges David to follow suit, are important elements in the cabalistic puzzle. As previously stated, *keter* presents no contradictions. Existing above the contracted void in which our universe was brought into being, *keter* represents the nearest emanation to the *ayin sof*, so that within it all contradictions are resolved. Language and silence, light and darkness, good and evil, are gathered together in cosmic harmony as part of this divine attribute. Katriel appears to know these truths; David's duty is now to learn and to implement them in this world.

The first truth, much like Katriel's existence within the *récit*, rests on a rather solitary plane, whereas the second and third appear more concrete and linked. The first message deals with a mystical, esoteric union of opposing poles; the second and third are complementary and require one another for full recognition and realization. As such, I see these two emanations from Katriel as being directly linked to the male and female elements: David and Malka.

Katriel must have his place in the *récit*; *keter* must be introduced into our chaotic world. But this can only be achieved through the union of *yesod* and *malhut*, David and Malka. This vital relationship, however, remains enigmatic. When Malka had first appeared at the Western Wall, she had initially been mistaken for a divine apparition, a physical manifestation of the *shehina*. It was David, however, who perceived her quite differently: Katriel's widow. He hastily recalls those bits of "information" he had learned from Katriel about this woman whom David would have us believe he has never met. And yet, as they speak, the reader is struck by the fact that the truth concerning their relationship is buried in a silent subtext. Malka's responses to David's questions and bizarre statements categorically stress they have met before. Moreover, it becomes patently obvious she does not know her alleged husband, Katriel.

The textual contradictions mount throughout the story as David vainly attempts to tell Malka about her lost "husband." But David's story is no more than a farcical charade. Finally, at the end of the night, Malka breaks the tense, frightened silence—unable to tolerate these absurdities any longer. The central question remains: What relationship actually exists between Malka and Katriel, or between David and Malka? The protagonist does, in fact, offer several significant clues.

The first step to resolving this conundrum lies in the protagonist's silent narrative: "Pauvre Malka. Sait-elle qu'il n'est pas facile de revenir en arrière. Elle le sait. Cela ne la décourage pas. Que lui répondre" (MJ, 182); "Poor Malka. Does she know how difficult it is to retrace one's steps? She does. And it doesn't discourage her. What could I answer?" (BJ, 204). The subtext indicates that the two, David and Malka, do indeed know one another and that she has been striving to understand him. David proffers additional silent evidence that conclusively establishes the exact relationship between himself and Malka. "Je regarde *ma femme,* je la touche et j'aime l'aimer, et cependant quelque chose en moi se crispe, se convulse" (MJ, 182); "I look at *my wife,* I watch her and I love touching her, yet something in me shrivels and rebels" (BJ, 205) [my emphasis]. Several pages later, as Malka is leaving David by the Wall, he reminisces: "Et je revois *le jour de notre mariage*" (MJ, 186-87); "And I see myself again *on the day of our marriage*" (BJ, 209) [my emphasis]. Though to date all critics and Wiesel scholars have supported the notion that Malka is Katriel's wife as proposed by the protagonist, David, I believe the textual evidence permits me to state with assurance that David and Malka are husband and wife, though their marriage is fraught with problems, ghosts, and contradictions. It is a relationship haunted by madness.

For Malka, this relationship is particularly frustrating. David's erratic behavior represents more than a deranged game of hide-and-seek in which the wife is obliged to find her husband. Yet despite such frustration, Malka has learned to wait patiently for the end of her exile from her husband, for she anticipates her future union with David.

It is here that one perceives another of the cabalistic elements operating within the text: The notion of the *shehina,* that female counterpart to the divine presence in the world. The *shehina* has traditionally been considered in exile since the destruction of the Second Temple in 70 C.E. Cabala teaches that the *shehina,* like Malka, is desirous of reunion with the male aspect, but this eventuality depends primarily upon the actions of humanity. The lack of direct action by God to effect this union would seem to indicate a degree of unwillingness or impotence on the part of the creator. God's plan, however, has entrusted the success of this reunion to humanity in the act of *tikkun.* Within Cabala, two primary and contradictory elements or influences underline every aspect of creation. The primary dichotomy lies in the male-female principle. Without the union of these two forces, chaos persists in the world. Redemption is distanced from humanity, and the *shehina* remains in exile. The Zohar II, 176a and b declares: "Whoever obstructs such a performance [of the sexual act] causes the *shehina* to depart from the world." In Cabala, sexual union represents an act of sacred meditation if both partners focus their full attention on the experience, and thus encourage the fusion of two contradictory but creative elements that will ensure the introduction of harmony into the world. David's game, or perhaps his madness, precludes Katriel's messages from having their rightful place in the story. Katriel's return will not be possible; David will remain a king without a crown, without God, a man waiting for his own Godot.

David's inability to recognize Malka as his wife, to possess her and to love her illustrates a significant obstacle that the Holocaust has implanted in David's psyche. David, the survivor, has witnessed the barbarity of the *univers concentrationnaire* as well as the victory of "redemption" in the Six Day War. Yet he cannot aspire to unite the divine mysteries of good and evil while he himself remains incapable of loving another living being.

Malka's role in this struggle demonstrates her profound, maternal-like desire to assist David in his desperate efforts to effect reunion of the scattered facets of his own life. Their estrangement is extreme, as evidenced by his use of the formal *vous* when speaking to her; yet even this does not impede or deter her ability to play the game David has initiated. She presses him into recalling his own memories of her as "transmitted by Katriel"; she encourages his mad wanderings, and offers clues to the importance of their unified role. It is Malka who stresses the element of love that has the capacity to raise humanity above the agonies of life. Love comes to represent the ultimate means of reuniting the exiled elements of creation and of directing Katriel's message into reality.

To emphasize the urgency of this message, Wiesel goes beyond mere words. Gestures become evocative means of expression between the two estranged partners.

> Tout en parlant, nos mains tâtonnantes, nerveuses, comme celles d'enfants craintifs, se cherchent, se nouent, s'épousent. . . . Il y a en moi une telle soif d'amour, de pardon, elle pèse sur ma poitrine et m'écrase. (MJ, 130)

> We talk, and our nervous, groping hands, like frightened children's, seek one another, knotting and intertwining. . . . There is in me such hunger for love, for forgiveness, that I think it will stay with me forever. (BJ, 143–44)

David senses the power that his union with Malka could generate, a force metaphorically represented by the mystically floating lovers in Chagall's paintings:

> Une force irrésistible s'est emparée de nos corps et les emporte dans un tourbillon, et tout tourne autour de nous, avec nous. Le ciel au-dessus de la ville, la ville elle-même, et les hommes qui rêvent en elle: tous se joignent à la ronde. (MJ, 131)

> An irresistible force has seized our bodies and sweeps us away in a whirlwind along with the stones and the steps, the stars and the trees. The sky above the city, the city itself, and the people dreaming within its gates, all are spinning around us, with us. (BJ, 145)

But this ecstatic moment has been tainted. The silent shades of the Holocaust erect a barrier between David (*yesod*) and Malka (*malhut*). Love cannot evolve; and, as a result, Katriel will linger in exile.

David's obsessive task of bearing witness to the dead, of questioning and of seeking out his true self appear as his primary goals and the focal point of the *récit*. If one accepts this message and concedes to his being chained to his past, the muted optimism for the future, that glint of hope hidden in the book's ludic devices borrowed from cabala are roundly repudiated. The silent mysteries of good and evil constitute the perplexing essence of David's struggle within the story. In order for him to formulate those questions that will facilitate his effecting *tikkun,* the protagonist's quest has led him into confrontations with various emanations of God. Though David has not yet succeeded in his task of uniting them, I believe Wiesel's choice of setting again has the added significance of signaling a silent hint of reunion: "the reunification of Jerusalem is a sign, perhaps marking the twilight of our world and the dawn of another," (A.M.G., *Terre,* n.p.) [my translation] or as David indicates: "Voilà pourquoi je reste encore sur cette place hantée, dans cette cité ou rien ne se perd et rien ne s'éparpille. Transition nécessaire, indispensable" (MJ, 187); "That is why I am still here on this haunted square, in this city where nothing is lost and nothing dispersed. An indispensable, necessary transition" (BJ, 210). There is prodigious intention in this necessary transition and the events surrounding it. Malka, symbolic of the *shehina,* would seem to possess no rightful place in the *récit;* she decides to depart, thus exiling herself again. But, before leaving, she inquires if David wishes her to return. He responds: Yes. Though temporarily exiled, though the elements of *malhut* continue to remain impoverished in their separation from *yesod*, Wiesel offers hope that reunion may yet occur, though it will require time and patience.

Silence in the content of *Le Mendiant de Jérusalem* has become a meditation which, though it includes painful memories, has evolved into a meaningful and generative force. The cabalistic elements woven into the fabric of the *récit* prophetically herald the gradual regeneration of the protagonist and the renewal and revitalization of life. Contemporary humankind must learn to live in the fiery shadow of the *anus mundi* and to reconcile absolute good with absolute evil. The mystical silences in the *récit* have gradually led David to this final realization. God is the source of all. More importantly, He must be brought into this world, not merely to assist in universal redemption, but also to offer sufficient responses to the painful questions asked of Him. The key to the entire scheme resides with humankind.

CHAPTER **6**

Apocalypse and Life
La Sermet de Kolvillàg (1973)

*L'Occident ne subsistera pas
indéfiniment—il se prépare à sa fin.*
E. M. CIORAN

A time to be silent and a time to speak.
ECCLESIASTES

"**J**e ne parlerai pas. . . . Ce que j'ai à dire, je ne tiens pas à le dire. . . . Il n'y a plus de demain" (SK, 9); "I will not speak. What I have to say, I don't care to say. . . . There is no more tomorrow" (O, 3). Thus, mysteriously shrouded in silence, begins Wiesel's seventh novel, *Le Serment de Kolvillàg (The Oath),* a story that evokes "scènes d'apocalypse, cauchemars issus du sommeil des cadavres" (SK, 13); "Scenes of apocalypse, nightmares begotten by sleeping corpses" (O, 7). As with *Le Mendiant de Jérusalem,* this text's setting underscores its relevance. Despite objections from Vincent Engel as to the linguistic origins and semantic intentions of the town's name,[1] I concur with the proposition that Kolvillàg stems from a curious etymological marriage of Hebrew and Hungarian roots. Others have submitted that the town's name is based upon the Hebrew word *kol* (כל) meaning all or every, and the Hungarian *villàg,* the world, and read together is symbolic of the entire human family currently living under the threat of global annihilation. Other scholars and critics, perhaps unfamiliar with the Hungarian language, have read the seemingly cognate word *villàg* as *town* or *village,* thus positing that Kolvillàg

is a representative "everytown," an allegorical European town whose Jews will
be exterminated, therefore viewing the novel as being emblematic of the
shoah. I accept as authorial intention this Hebraic-Hungarian etymological
union, though I believe one is likewise obliged to view *kol* as another, homony-
mous Hebrew word, (קוֹל) meaning voice. Such a reading imparts a vitally penetrating message of hope to an otherwise apocalyptic text, for it is in re-voicing
the town's story that a human life is saved, and through that humanity may
finally discover salvation.

The novel is haunted by six forces, six characters in search of meaning, and
desirous of terminating their collective nightmare. Azriel, a survivor, a home-
less wanderer, a *navenadnik;* the Pinkas, a closed book that has not been read
for over half a century and is now jealously protected by Azriel; Kolvillàg, the
town where "la mort fut victorieuse" (SK, 19); "death was victorious" (O, 15).
Moshe, the madman who enjoins a vow of silence upon Kolvillàg's doomed
Jewish community; a nameless young man who wishes to take his own life;
and finally, the omnipresent specter of silence that surrounds the past and
clouds the present. Each of these "characters" maneuvers in such ways as to
weave a curious tale that draws us from death to life while never permitting
us to lose sight of the gruesome realities of the past, which it silently enshrines,
and its future implications.

Though the novel's vision of destruction might seem contrived to symbolize the *hurban** of European Jewry—a point that certainly should not dismissed—I believe the metaphorical decor, Kolvillàg, sets the book apart from
Wiesel's other works that are more directly linked to that event. Kolvillàg allegorically does represent the archetypal, timeless European town that has suffered all cultures and influences in its long, painful history. But, Kolvillàg is
almost forgotten in its obscurity, like some mystical kingdom in a fairytale. The
town that the novel is constructed around gradually evolves beyond allegory
and projects Wiesel's vision of Apocalypse.

A late and decadent development in scriptural writings, apocalyptic literature expresses the central themes of eschatology and the "end of days."
"Apocalypticism and the literature embodying it seems to represent to some
measure a linear development out of prophecy . . . a literature of perceived
adversity" (Hauer, 1980, 208). It is a literature that evolved from its authors'
belief that they were the "last generation" prior to the final, apocalyptic con-
flagration between the powers of Good and Evil. For these writers, the past and
present were evoked so that all human history became intrinsically linked.

**hurban:* a Yiddish term used with reference to the Holocaust. Originally employed to indicate
the destruction of the First and Second Temples, the word connotes a rupture in the
spiritual life of the community.

Above all, a mood of intransigent fatalism manifests itself as the envisioned Armageddon approaches. Apocalyptic literature does not permit any deviation of history from its determined course. Even repentance, so fundamental an element in mainstream Judaism and Christianity, does not slow the momentum toward the final event of human history.[2]

Many of these elements find expression and modification in *Le Serment de Kolvillàg*. Just as Wiesel has restructured various biblical tales and Jewish legends to suit the historical and psychological framework into which he casts his literary works, so too does he fashion his own particular vision of Apocalypse. The single most prominent element that he shares with traditional apocalyptic literature is the ultimate conflict between Good and Evil. The notion of the struggle between these opposing forces in apocalyptic literature has its foundation in the human fall from Paradise. Such an approach does not represents Wiesel's basis. In traditional Judaic thought, human beings have been given the power to discriminate between good and evil, and eventually possess the ability to choose. Everyone must decide the direction of his or her life and thereby direct the course of history. Traditional apocalyptic literature does not permit each person the freedom to choose, but views people as pawns in the cosmic struggle in which Good will eventually defeat Evil, while Wiesel's Judaic background encouraged "human participation in the great movement of redemption" (Alter, 1966, 65). Robert Alter says of Wiesel's vision that "even after directly experiencing this terrible turn of history [the Holocaust], he refuses to look at the world in an apocalyptic light" (65). Thus, his vision of Apocalypse projects a modified conception, one in which the characters of the literary universe are free to choose, and thus affect the course of history.

The choice found in this novel reflects the essence of Deuteronomy 30:15 and the opening words of verse 19: "Behold, I set before you this day life and prosperity, death and destruction. . . . This day I call upon heaven and earth as witness against you that I have set before you life and death, blessings and curses." In the novel, it is the non-Jewish community of Kolvillàg that chooses to believe and promulgate the libelous myth of ritual murder,[3] a choice that allows hatred to blind people to truth and advances an entire community toward the abyss of destruction. "Kolvillàg: la culmination du fanatisme, de la bêtise. *Le châtiment ultime*" (SK, 55); "Kolvillàg: the culmination of fanaticism, of stupidity. *The ultimate chastisement*" (O, 55) [my emphasis]. Good contends with Evil throughout the book in rather conventional apocalyptic fashion. We discover an undercurrent in the text that is supportive of the position of Good and stresses the urgency of its ultimate victory. Yet, ironically, in Kolvillàg Evil and Death triumph in utter reversal of the apocalyptic tradition.

Despite this reversal, however, Good and the forces of life are not permanently stilled. For the better part of the century, the apocalyptic destruction of Kolvillàg and the fate of its inhabitants has remained unknown, the sole survivor, Azriel, bound to silence. The narrative paradoxically relates a tale that should never have been disclosed; the vow of silence is broken, the hidden truths escape. Azriel's silence, which had evolved into a wall isolating him from life, is destroyed, and this effects his return to life and into human action. Azriel opts for life and not the silence of death.

"Now choose life, so that you and your children may live" (Deuteronomy 30: 19) is echoed in Azriel's eventual decision to recount the destruction of Kolvillàg, for in speaking, he believes he will save the life of an anonymous young man, the child of survivors of the *anus mundi,* who wishes to commit suicide. As Wiesel has stated: "Words can bring man closer to himself, to God and to others" (Cargas, 1976, 6). The power of Good rises from the victory of Death and Evil that was Kolvillàg as Azriel breaks his silence and brings the nameless young man back to life.

This novel and its tale of Apocalypse emerge from the tension between life and death, good and evil, tradition and revolt. Moreover, the novel firmly rests on the conflict between language and silence and the fundamentally paradoxical premise of silence being expounded through speech. Silence in all its degrees and significations stands at the epicenter of the story initially reflecting the negativity of death and destruction, then the hope of resurrection and life. But the silences that dominate extend beyond this basic level of significance and point to a prophetic statement. As Azriel describes the orgy of death that consumes Kolvillàg, he remarks: "Et soudain je compris avec toutes les fibres de mon être pourquoi je frémissais à cette vision d'épouvante: je venais d'entrevoir l'avenir" (SK, 254); "And suddenly I understood with every fiber of my being why I was shuddering at this vision of horror: I had just glimpsed the future" (O, 281). Wiesel's apocalyptic vision—his prophecy—operates on two distinctive levels. First of all, it reflects with obvious hindsight the fact that mindless hatred, such as is demonstrated in Wiesel's allegorical "everytown" would lead to Auschwitz. Secondly, and more importantly, Wiesel's vision also projects the universal horror that evolves from Auschwitz. For Wiesel, Auschwitz finds its origins in the Kolvillàg allegory; Hiroshima proceeds from Auschwitz.[4] The gruesome future that Azriel witnesses represents Wiesel's profoundest fears concerning the possibility of a universal nuclear holocaust, a point to be developed more fully later.

The primary importance accorded to silence in this text imparts to it a driving force that directs the story. Central to the other characters, and representing a necessary force for the formulation of the tale, silence stands as the center of a wheel directing its force to the outer parts. Once called into being by Moshe during the *herem** prior to the onslaught of the climactic *Totentanz* that annihilates Kolvillàg, silence manifests in turn its various aspects. Like a wall, it metaphorically separates Azriel from humanity and forces him to become a mute wanderer. The imposed silence rendered him a *navenadnik*, a wanderer without a home or human contact, a man as much dead as alive. But this power of silence to exile Azriel also possesses the positive force of regeneration.

Wiesel has postulated that there are many shades of silence. In *La Ville de la chance* Michael recognizes it is only when he is silent that he actually lives; he is defined by and in silence. Wiesel's art lies in his poetic restraint and verbal sobriety that enable him to layer language and evoke the various shades and degrees of silence sensed by his protagonists. Despite the painfully wearisome burden imposed on him by silence, Azriel benefits from his exile. His wanderings enrich him as he touches others. He recognizes the fundamental importance of assisting others, even momentarily. His role as *navenadnik* permits him to unite the scattered elements of creation, thus participating in the process of re-creation and redemption.

The silence that has pressed Azriel into this unwanted role is linked to another silence: that of the Pinkas.[5] This text recounts the history of the Jewish community of Kolvillàg, and thus represents another silent witness to the past. In a negative manner, as a closed unread document, it symbolizes the silent power hidden in destruction and evil. But the Pinkas also symbolizes the hope for dialogue that might yet be established. The muted tale concealed within its pages, the story condemned to silence, is eventually recounted. The silence of Kolvillàg is paradoxically exposed by speech. By telling the tale, Azriel ensures the modification of the negative powers of silence, or as Max Picard notes: "Silence . . . is more than the mere negative renunciation of language. . . . It is rather an independent whole, subsisting in and through itself. It is creative, as language is creative" (15). It is this creative power of silence that Azriel releases in breaking his vow. The emerging word and imminent dialogue that humanity constructs with it will serve to unite all beings to God, Who is silently drawn into the affair. Azriel's decision leads him from negative silence into language before *l'énonciation* dissolves back into a modified form of silence, which reflects God. One silence is destructive, the other creative. The catalytic element deemed necessary to effect such an ontological metamorphosis of silence is humanity. Language and silence remain static, stagnating without the human factor. Language, when used in the context of

---

*herem: most commonly it refers to excommunication through a solemn religious ceremony. This ritual can similarly declare a curse, or exhort a sacred oath.

human relationships, becomes a means for establishing dialogue and positive silence, thereby joining man to God.

These ideas establish the basis for the remainder of my current argument as well as the means for linking it once more to Wiesel's particular apocalyptic vision. Negative silence contains those elements which, when placed in association with viable personal dialogue, modify and realize the word. Once established, however, language directs one back to its true source: God. God stands as a silent partner in true dialogue. People represent the means for moving from human stasis (negative silence) to human action (the word) that contains the existence of the divine (positive silence). Just as the word of God brought about *bereshit,* the beginning of creation, so can humanity reestablish its bond with the silent Creator through such an ontological modification of silence.

The negative silence that shrouds Kolvillàg is shattered by Azriel, as only thus can he prevent the nameless young man from committing suicide. Engaging the youth in the story of the dead town will transform him; he will become a partner in keeping the memory and message of Kolvillàg alive. Again, the biblical injunction "now choose life" underlies Azriel's choice. Continued silence would represent not choosing, remaining indifferent, and indifference threatens life.

Herman Melville wrote: "And death be busy with all who strive—/ Death with silent negative" (7). This point is taken up by Azriel at the onset of the novel. Death is negative and meaningless, he reasons with the suicidal youth. Death is not a response to life's traumas. A sense of urgent frustration haunts the early pages of the text. A deadly, negative silence hovers over the two characters. Azriel's experience permits him to recognize the threat posed by such silences. Yet, ironically, Azriel himself is bound to his silence. He is prevented from acting freely and speaking openly. He remains chained to death, to the silence that has been his raison d'etre. And yet, the closed book and the silence of the dead town have condemned Azriel to life, a sentencing that likewise signifies freedom. He is alive; death and silence have granted him life. In return, he can now choose to cast off the murderous silences of the past and bestow life.

Wiesel espouses the following Hasidic concept: "Chaque être est au center de la Création, chaque être justifie la Création" (CM-CH, 200); "Every person is the center of creation—every person is called upon to justify creation" (SM, 190). Creation is life. Azriel's experience has demonstrated the meaningless nature of death. And still death, with all its horrors, can produce life. Azriel has been condemned to survive; he can now rupture his sterile silence and offer life. He must speak; he must justify his life as a survivor as well as the lives and deaths of those whom he carried with him and who are hidden by the silent text of the Pinkas. "L'important," Wiesel believes, "c'est de combattre le silence par la parole ou par une autre forme de silence" (PE, 14); "What matters is to struggle against silence with words, or through another form of silence" (K, 21).

As demonstrated earlier, imposed death such as that which Wiesel witnessed in the *anus mundi* results in oppressingly negative silence that stifles the voice and life. To an extent, this is also true of this novel, though Wiesel has radically departed from his earlier usage. Here, the doomed victims willingly impose silence upon themselves before the tragedy. Their decision represents a positive act of rebellion against God and humanity. The community comprehends the gravity of its situation. The libelous myth of ritual murder threateningly spreads, and its malefic power ferments further hatred. Gradually the people of the town gravitate into three distinct groups: The silent Jews, the plotting non-Jews, and those who remain indifferent. Active dialogue that had once united Kolvillàg is muted or utterly silenced, and an atmosphere of distrust descends. The evil inherent in the accusation of ritual murder constructs a silent, murderous wall between neighboring communities. Thus, without dialogue and further encumbered by mounting hatred, hope is lost.

Even the underlying belief in humanism and universal brotherhood, which should offer hope to modern society, represents nothing more than an inhuman chimera. On the very eve of the pogrom, some Jews still cling tendentiously to these false hopes: "Notre ère est dominée par l'humanisme, le libéralisme. On ne tue plus son semblable au nom de légendes démodées et absurdes" (SK, 196); "Ours [our era] is dominated by humanism, liberalism. We no longer kill our fellow-man in the name of obsolete and absurd legends" (O, 213). In contradiction to these hollow, articulated presumptions stands the silent specter of destruction: "On préparait à un festin de sang, à une célébration de la mort" (SK, 164); "A bloodbath was in the making, a celebration of death" (O, 178). As if to accentuate the utter solitude and helplessness of Kolvillàg, Wiesel erects a wall of silence between the town and the outside world.

Into this silent abyss is introduced the character of Moshe. The biblical Moses achieves the physical and spiritual freedom of the enslaved Israelites and leads them to Sinai for the revelation in silence and words.[6] Wiesel's Moshe stands as the antithesis to his biblical namesake. His actions represent the epitome of revolt against the absurdity of the Jewish condition, of the ancient covenant and of God's own culpability. He is considered a madman precisely because of this lucidity and his sense of revolt. Nevertheless, Moshe is among those madmen who, as Wiesel has stated, "are pure and beautiful, madmen who try to save the world and not to destroy it, to help, not to hurt" (Edelman, 1978, 15).

Moshe's revolt is twofold. First, foreseeing the destruction of the community, he devises a scheme to save them by offering himself as scapegoat and confessing to the murder of a missing Christian child. His noble act of self-sacrifice seemingly contradicts Jewish law, and Moshe is admonished by the rabbi for considering it. It is in the rabbi's final statement: "Qui renonce à sa vie, rejette la vie, rejette celui qui donne la vie" (SK, 135); "Whoever renounces his life, rejects life, rejects Him who gives life" (O, 144), that we uncover the essence of this first phase of Moshe's revolt. By rejecting life, he repudiates the Creator of life. Moshe's action questions the validity of God's creation and furthermore proposes the first of several challenges.

Moshe's attitude suggests various significant perceptions. First, he reminds the rabbi and the leaders of the community that the Jews and the Torah, God's law, are uniquely bound. The Torah is considered by the Jew to be a source of joy, freedom, goodness, and life. Though projecting a universal message, the Torah would possess no value without the Jew and be rendered a meaningless text. Moshe must exercise his human freedom in order to protect humanity and to preserve the Torah, hence ensuring life. Secondly, Moshe appears to believe the Hasidic concept that: "Chaque homme doit voir en autrui un *Sefer-Torah*. . . . Chaque être est sacré. Chaque personne mérite le respect" (CM-CH, 203); "Every person. . . must see in the other a *Sefer Torah*—a Holy Scroll. Every human being is sacred; every creature deserves respect. (SM, 193). Each member of the community is a Torah, an idea that further heightens Moshe's responsibility to save the people. Finally, offering his life to safeguard the Jewish community and the Torah symbolizes a fundamental revolt against God, Who has allowed such a dangerous and absurd situation to arise. Yet Moshe's revolt also affirms life as his actions should protect the Jews, the Torah, and therefore life itself. By transgressing the law, Moshe aspires to protect it. In offering his life, he will hope to preserve the lives of others.

Moshe's audacious plan for survival is not an act of silent, passive submission, but one that speaks of courageous determination to preserve life. When this attempt fails, however, he enters into the second phase of his revolt. He concludes that the doomed Jews must rebel against their destiny, God, and history in yet another manner. At a solemn religious ceremony, the *herem*, Moshe leads the Jewish community into voluntary silence. Earlier in the novel he had suggested that people have demonstrated their capacity for perverting and cheapening language to obtain their own ends. Silence alone appears to have escaped their grasp. In Moshe's view, silence retains its purity. It must be noted here that Moshe demonstrates a dangerous degree of naiveté as he chooses to ignore the negative and destructive elements silence can entail.

Moshe's design in convincing the Jews of Kolvillàg to impose silence voluntarily represents a fundamental rebellion against Jewish attitudes to bearing witness.[7] As he explains to the assembled community, no matter what tragedies have befallen the Jewish people, they have been meticulously recorded by someone who had miraculously survived. He believes the time has come for this posture to be radically modified:

> Mémoire et coeur de l'humanité depuis trop longtemps, et depuis trop longtemps la risée des nations que nos histoires amusent ou agacent, nous allons adopter une loi nouvelle: celle du silence.
> (SK, 217)

> We have been mankind's memory and heart too long. Too long we have been other nations' laughingstock. Our stories have either amused or annoyed them. Now we shall adopt a new way: silence.[8]
> (O, 238–39)

Moshe continues: "Nous allons lancer le défi absolu non par le langage mais par l'absence du langage, non par la parole mais par l'abdication de la parole" (SK, 218); "We are going to impose the ultimate challenge, not by language but by absence of language, not by word but by the abdication of the word" (O, 239). The divine injunction to bear witness is to be rejected, a move calculated to force God to speak. If testimony is required by the Creator, He must become its ultimate source. The Jew as universal moral conscience will remain mute.

Moshe's revolt does not halt at this unabashed challenge to God. He similarly rebels against humanity and history. The goal is straightforward: Suffering and the history of such suffering are intrinsically linked. If Moshe can delete one side of the equation for universal suffering, the other would cease to possess any validity. Moshe and the Jews of Kolvillàg would thus usher in the messianic age.

Michael Berenbaum has expressed opposition to Moshe's theory, believing "the intrinsic link between suffering and the history of suffering is not explained or developed" (98), and his point is well-taken, coming as it does from a theological and philosophical bias. Yet he has overlooked the fact that Moshe as a character in a novel is merely responding to a desperate situation when he offers his wildly revolutionary direction to the Jews of Kolvillàg. Berenbaum correctly states that advocating such a stance would place Wiesel "perilously close to positions he has strenuously rejected" (98). Moshe's extreme solution does not honestly reflect Wiesel's own philosophy, though that near-Jobian sense of revolt against God and humanity fundamentally accords with certain aspects of his writings. If anything, Wiesel's ideas appear more in harmony with

Azriel's and with the latter's decision to break his vow of silence in order to save a life in the ensuing dialogue. Beyond the purely philosophical question, I would presume that Wiesel could support the idea of revolt against God, but not its corollary of silence proposed by Moshe. For him to endorse Moshe's silent rebellion in totality would indeed signify the author's acceptance of negative silence and death, a course of action clearly not deemed expedient in the first part of the novel, nor in the light of the general evolution of the theme of silence in his works. Moshe's action, though bold and binding within the context of the story, represents an option doomed to failure.

The seeds of this failure readily manifest themselves in the character of Shmuel, Azriel's father and the chronicler of the Pinkas. Shortly after the *herem,* Shmuel summarily breaks the oath as he records the ultimate, definitive events of the tragedy of Kolvillàg. Shmuel's rebellion opts in favor of the word, of the transmission of testimony until the last possible moment, even though the deadly silence threatening Kolvillàg invades the text itself. Shmuel's revolt achieves its climax when, having completed the text, he has Azriel read what has been written. The message, however brutal, ungodly or cruel, must be transmitted despite the recently sworn vow and despite the silence of God.

Azriel, however, ignores his father's ultimate lesson and opts to maintain the *herem's* silence, the silence of death and destruction. Moshe's envisaged "age without suffering" never arises; Azriel remains locked in silence. His years of wandering and isolation have produced no positive results until that evening in Paris when he encounters the nameless youth. Suddenly, he is faced with the possibility of sharing in creation by saving a life.

Azriel's tale brings us full cycle in this analysis, for the story of Kolvillàg does not merely present Wiesel's debate for and against silence, but it also permits the reader to perceive his vision of the approaching Apocalypse. It was the approach of this vision that urged Moshe to convene the *herem* and impose silence. This vow of silence eventually erected a metaphorical wall between Azriel and the world, a wall that initially appeared indifferent to the fate of the youth. "Le mal est dans l'indifférence" (PE, 106); "Evil resides in indifference" [my translation], and it must be defeated.

All critics of Wiesel's works see this novel as another possible evolutionary step away from the Holocaust. They believe the use of Kolvillàg allows him to utilize allegory to reflect upon that event. The evidence amassed is formidable: Blind hatred leading to senseless, absurd carnage; the silence of God; the indifference of humanity; the tension between maintaining silence about tragedy, and the pressing responsibility to bear witness. Each of these elements reflects aspects of Holocaust literature and of Wiesel's earlier works. Such a reading of the text allows Wiesel's fiction to remain firmly entrenched in a particular mold. Wiesel's oeuvre, however, has gradually evolved from the stark geography of the *anus mundi* to a more universal stance. As a Jew, Wiesel's task is quite simply as follows: "Un Juif qui oeuvre pour son peuple, loin de se retrancher de l'humanité, oeuvre aussi pour elle" (EDS, 179); "By working for his own people a Jew does not renounce his loyalty to mankind; on the contrary, he thereby makes his most valuable contribution" (OGA, 173), and "Sa mission [celle du juif] n'a jamais été de judaïser le monde, mais de l'humaniser" (UJA, 24); "His [the Jew's] mission was never to make the world Jewish, but rather, to make it more human" (JT, 13). Given his concept of the Jew's role in creation, Wiesel's intention in presenting this vision of apocalypse clarifies the reader's perception of his view of the Holocaust by the use of allegorical hindsight, and offers prophetic insights into the universal holocaust which may await humanity.

This hypothesis is based on one sentence in the text: "Pitié pour cette génération qui voit tout et ne comprend rien" (SK, 58); "Woe to this generation which sees everything and understands nothing" (O, 58). This phrase, stated in almost biblical fashion, is articulated by Azriel at the beginning of the novel when the vow of silence is still in effect. Azriel's guarded secret remains shrouded in the imposed silence of the *herem,* and thus it cannot be that which the present generation can view but cannot comprehend. To what then does he allude? Azriel refers to the Holocaust, that which finds its basis in the evil of allegorical Kolvillàg. The nameless youth, the child of Holocaust survivors, suffers not only because of what his parents endured in the *univers concentrationnaire,* but also because their experience remains concealed from him. He can, to an extent, appreciate a degree of their torment, as can all humanity. But some element is hidden; some mystery lies concealed. As George Steiner suggests: "It [the Holocaust and other mass murders, 1933–45] was no mere secular, socio-economic phenomenon. It enacted a suicidal impulse in Western civilization" (*Bluebeard,* 42). Wiesel himself warns: "Sans Auschwitz, il n'y aurait pas eu d'Hiroshima. . . . C'est à Auschwitz que l'avenir a été mutilé et joué" (EDS, 176); "Without Auschwitz, there would have been no Hiroshima. . . . It was at Auschwitz that men mutilated and gambled with the future" (OGA, 171). More precisely, humanity refuses to understand the evil that was unleashed at, and is symbolized, by Auschwitz. Such evil would imply to the Hasidim so close to Wiesel's heart that: "Le monde court à sa perte, l'homme à sa chute" (CH, 165); "The world [is] doomed, mankind rushing to its fall" (SF, 158).

The general attitude of critics perceives Kolvillàg as an allegorical depiction of Auschwitz, as the "dress rehearsal" for it. In the light of additional information culled from Wiesel's writings and thought, Kolvillàg, in a purely allegorical sense, engendered Auschwitz that in turn produced Hiroshima. As

Wiesel has pointed out: "L'extermination d'un peuple mène inévitablement à celle de l'humanité" (UJA, 51); "The annihilation of a people leads inevitably to the annihilation of mankind" (JT, 36). Allegory emphasizes facts that might easily represent humanity's future.

In the collections of essays and portraits that preceded the publication of the novel in question, Wiesel demonstrates a lucidity and concern about the mounting hatred and intolerance in the world. His compelling considerations recall the prophetic statements of Rabbi Israel of Rizhin:

> Dans un monde déshumanisé, desséché, fermé au désir et au salut, le désordre sera cosmique, la culpabilité aussi. A l'approche de la fin des temps, le bien et le mal se côtoieront, deviendront un. . . . l'igno-rance régnera. Les gens médiocres se sentiront à l'aise sur la terre et dans le monde spirituel, tandis que l'homme avec une âme, l'homme de conscience, aliéné partout, ne se maintiendra nulle part. (CH, 165)

> In a dehumanized, arid universe, robbed of desire and salvation, dis-order would be on a cosmic scale and so would guilt. With the dawning of the end of time, good and evil would go hand in hand, would become one. . . . ignorance will reign. Mediocre men will feel at ease on earth and above, while men of spirit and conscience will be alienated. (SF, 159)

Thus in this novel, those regularized patterns that had characterized and even sanctified life in Kolvillàg alter. People metamorphose. Lies and hatred typify human thoughts. The fear and panic that the situation in Kolvillàg tragically promises hastens even the religious in their prayers. The world one had known in Kolvillàg has been transformed owing to the presence of living Evil.

In his essay, *"Une Génération après,"* Wiesel sounds warning notes similar to those expressed in this novel. Mankind has lived through the hell of Auschwitz with all its dire warnings and has mastered nothing. "On n'a rien appris. Auschwitz n'a même servi d'avertissement. Pour de plus amples informations consultez votre quotidien habituel" (EDS, 248); "Nothing has been learned; Auschwitz has not even served as a warning. For more detailed information consult your daily newspaper" (OGA, 9). The same can be said of Kolvillàg. Though the town has suffered tragedies over the centuries, no one appears to have learned anything from violence and senseless death. The blood libel now serves as the dangerous pretext for mass murder, despite its being the twen-tieth century. This fact alone would offer ample proof of humanity's sad inabil-ity to learn from its past. According to Wiesel: "Aujourd'hui plus qu'hier et, à cause d'hier, l'impossible [un holocauste nucléaire] devient vite possible" (PE, 104); "Today more than yesterday, and because of yesterday, the impossible [nuclear holocaust] is rapidly becoming possible" [my translation]. The image Wiesel paints of contemporary civilization could effortlessly be his allegorical Kolvillàg on the eve of its destruction. "Trop de haines s'accumulent dans trop d'endroits" (PE, 104); "Too many hatreds are accumulating in too many places." [my translation] When hatred and evil are given free rein, death will win.

> La meute, abrutie de violence, refusa de croire. Son besoin de tuer, d'avilir l'humain en l'homme, de l'offrir en pâture aux bêtes de la nuit n'était pas encore assouvi. Ivre de puissance, de cruauté, elle réclamait davantage de sang, de triomphes, de victimes. (SK, 251)

> The frenzied mob refused to believe, refused to listen. Its need to kill, to debase man, to offer him as fodder to the beast of night, was not yet assuaged. Drunk with power, with cruelty, it demanded more blood, more triumphs, more victims. (O, 277)

The death of Kolvillàg represents, therefore, Wiesel's silent vision of a possible apocalyptic scenario. As stated earlier, his idea of apocalypse differs from traditional approaches in that he believes that the horrors that he has witnessed can be averted by positive human action. The perfect example of this within the text is Azriel's act of compassion in saving the nameless youth. This individual action must continually be repeated in order to expel the threat of indifference, and to render the world more human and more humane. Our failure to deal justly and lovingly with our fellow human beings could produce the same deathly results as at Kolvillàg, where human hatred allowed Death and Evil to achieve victory. "Soudain un brasier rouge, jaillissant des entrailles de la terre et de la nuit, s'élança vers le ciel. Les flammes, irrésistibles, balayaient les espaces" (SK, 251); "Suddenly a red blaze, spinning from the entrails of the earth and night, soared skyward, irresistibly sweeping space" (O, 278). Once unleashed, the dread fireball spares nothing.

> Par son intensité, le feu assuma un rôle divin; gigantesque, imprévisible, sa seule vue rendait fou. La ville basculait dans l'irréel. Marchands et commis, ouvriers et patrons, filles et garçons, tous entremêlés . . . bourreaux et victimes . . . fuyaient dans tous les sens, emportés par le carrousel des flammes. (SK, 252)

> By its immensity, the fire assumed a divine role-gigantic, unpredictable, its very sight maddening. The town was toppling into illusion. Merchants and clerks, laborers and employers, girls and boys, all intermingled . . . murderers and victims . . . fleeing in every direction, carried by the carrousel in flames. (O, 278)

Wiesel presents a scene of absolute destruction. "Le sol se fend en mille endroits et les maisons s'effondrent" (SK, 253); "The earth splits in a thousand places and the houses tumble down" (O, 280). Above the noises of the burning town and the cries of the dying, one element alone begins to reign supreme: "Le silence. . . tout est dans le silence" (SK, 254); "Silence. . . everything is in silence" (O, 280–81) For the first and, to date, only time in Wiesel's fiction, the author does not silence horrific details of holocaust, but rather stresses them as if to impress the memory into our minds and force us to consider the consequences of hatred: "Calcinées, les demeures; carbonisés, les cadavres. Dissipés, les rêves et les prières et les chants. Toute histoire a une fin comme toute fin a une histoire" (SK, 254); "Charred dwellings. Charred corpses. Charred dreams and prayers and songs. Every story has an end, just as every end has a story" (O, 281).

Wiesel has stated: "C'est en songeant au passé que nous aspirons à sauver notre avenir commun" (PE, 104); "It is in considering our past that we aspire to save our common future" [my translation]. Such sentiments reflect Azriel's reaction to the young boy and his decision to break the oath. Assuming responsibility for yourself and for others deprives death of its silent victory at Kolvillàg, for the tale—allegorical or factual—will live, and its warning will be transmitted; death will also be deprived of another victim.

The novel poses a more serious question: Was Moshe's vow of silence the proper course and response? That question may be extended beyond the purely contextual framework of the novel: Is silence ever an answer? Wiesel stresses that silence has many shades of significance. Positive silence must be used in tandem with the word as the generative matrix that leads human beings into dialogic relationships with others and with God. It is the silence that frames the response *hinenni*. Negative silence, however, represents the antithesis of this notion, and approximates to death and indifference. Negative silence introduces evil into the world.

Wiesel's apocalyptic vision is one that escapes from silence and bluntly reminds humankind what may await it. Wiesel's persistent preoccupation with silence in this text, as well as in the rest of his literary works, highlights the desire to demonstrate the urgent necessity to speak out, to use words and actions in order to combat the mounting destructive forces that threaten the human race. "Mais notre société préfère n'en rien savoir. Silence partout" (UJA, 47); "But our society chooses not to take notice. Silence everywhere" (JT, 32). People and governments tragically continue to endorse indifference rather than action. Genocide exists; wholesale slaughter and violence are commonplace. "Ne dites pas, ne dites plus que vous ne saviez pas. Lorsqu'un peuple se meurt, aujourd'hui, en plein XXe siècle, cela se sait" (PE, 31); "Don't say any longer that you didn't know. When a people is exterminated today, in the latter part of the twentieth century, it is known" [my translation]. Wiesel's apocalyptic vision that issued forth from the Pandora's box allegorically named Kolvillàg silently menaces humankind. Yet in the guise of action, positive silence from which arise the words for dialogue, hope is extended. "Is silence the answer?" Wiesel asks. "It never was. And that is why we try to tell the tale" (D, 19).

CHAPTER **7**

The Mute Son, The Missing One

Le Testament (1980) and *Le Cinquième fils* (1983)

> *You left me my lips, and they shape words,*
> *even in silence.*
>
> O. MANDELSTAM

> *Les morts ne font partie de la Haggadah.*
>
> E. WIESEL

The Passover Haggadah* recounts the story of four sons. "With reference to four sons doth the Torah speak: one wise, one wicked, one simple, and one who does not know how to ask" (4). These sons are the legacy of Jewish faith. Moreover, they represent the divergent possible paradigms of Jewish self-identity into which any generation might evolve. Wiesel's two novels, *Le Testament d'un poète juif assassiné (The Testament)* (1980) and *Le Cinquième fils (The Fifth Son)* (1983), represent his views of two such futures. He has chosen two distinctly different young men in order to develop his thoughts: Grisha, the son of a Jewish poet whom Stalin had liquidated in August 1952, and a nameless young American, the child of Holocaust survivors. More important, through Wiesel's art we become privy to the relationships that exist between fathers and sons and the manner in which tradition is transmitted and

---

*Haggadah: the special book that relates the story of the Exodus from Egypt and that is used in retelling this moment of Jewish history at the seder, the Passover meal. The Haggadah contains history, stories, *midrash,* and popular songs. The word stems from the Hebrew verb *hagid,* to tell.

identity nourished. Despite their different national origins, the two sons in question are uniquely linked by a common element: Silence.

Wiesel's use of silence in these two novels operates through the relationships of fathers and sons. The haggadah repeats the biblical injunction "And thou shalt tell thy children on that day" (17). The Jewish parent has a moral and religious duty to relate all aspects of Jewish history to the child, as well as transmitting the universal message of Jewish life with its links to God and to humanity. This parental responsibility is distinctly neglected in the novels in question. In *Le Testament,* Paltiel Kossover cannot discharge his obligations simply because his life and work have been silenced by death. Though he had never truly known his son, his testament symbolizes his desire to fulfill that parental duty. It also becomes his means for confessing his failures to his son.

In *Le Cinquième fils,* the nameless protagonist faces the frightening silence of his father, Reuven Tamiroff. Reuven's silence represents the explicit impact of the *shoah* upon his life and its continuing impact manifested by his sense of guilt for simply having survived the *univers concentrationnaire.* The son is surrounded by signs and silences that infect his soul and cause him to hunger for the truth concerning his father and those experiences that divide the two generations. In very different fashions, Grisha Kossover and the nameless Tamiroff youth symbolize the traumas of the Second Generation, the children of the post-Holocaust world.[1]

LE TESTAMENT

Silence in *Le Testament* evolves both as theme and technique. The son must attempt to surmount the almost insuperable wall of silence separating him from his father. Grisha Kossover's case represents near impossibility, since his father is dead. Moreover, in his attempt to preserve his father's memory from those who would take it from him, he consciously renders himself mute by biting off his tongue. According to Freud, such an action deliberately taken to ensure mutism represents a death wish, a desire to exchange life for the silence of death (Vol. 8: 32, 52–54, 58, 72–73, 87, 163 *et al.*). And yet, Grisha's mutism leads not to death but ironically to the realization of his own responsibility to transmit his father's testament. The mute boy becomes the silent receptacle for the father's story, one which the Soviet officials had intended to relegate to silence, and to which Grisha must give voice. Besides using silence to typify the relationship of father and son, Wiesel also utilizes it to represent the product of tension between imposed silence (historical manipulation, the dissemination of propaganda, or revisionist history), and the necessity to bear witness. Silence evolves as the means by which one achieves success in a rebellion that aims to overcome the powers of negation.

Wiesel's mission as witness to the Holocaust has led him to bear testimony to other causes. One of the most urgent of his recurring themes has dealt with the plight of Soviet Jewry. *Le Testament* marks his return to that world. He attempts to present the struggle of Soviet Jews for survival as a religion and a "nationality" within the Soviet state. He also examines the betrayed hopes of those Jews who had placed their faith in the socialist ideals of the Russian Revolution.

Wiesel's creation, Paltiel Kossover, is one such Jew. The scope of his life represents a broad image of the young idealistic Jewish radicals whose yearnings for social justice and equality catapulted them into the revolutionary movements that raged across Europe from 1900 until the Second World War. More than a revolutionary, Paltiel is also represented as a Yiddish poet whose works found considerable favor in the USSR after the war. Wiesel erects in this fictional characterization a symbol of those twenty-four Jewish poets and intellectuals who were executed by the NKVD on Stalin's orders on the night of August 12, 1952. Yet more than a mere symbol of the murdered poets, Paltiel represents the difficulty for any Soviet Jew to maintain an authentic Jewish identity in a state that seeks, at best, to minimize one's existence. Paltiel's struggle is transmitted in his testament, a unique confession that is destined for eyes other than those of the NKVD.

Paltiel's testament was written for his son Grisha. The document is the father's method of conveying the essence of his life's failure to his son. Though soon to be murdered, Paltiel hopes his words might mysteriously reach Grisha so that the boy might learn from his father's mistakes and misunderstandings, and perhaps undertake to combat those forces that condemned Paltiel to the silence of death.

The manuscript of Paltiel's testament is saved from destruction by a featureless prison stenographer, Zupanev. Zupanev represents one of those unique Wieselian characters whose actions guide the course of events. He ensures the survival of Paltiel's words and serves as messenger to deliver them to Grisha. And yet, a fundamental question arises from his actions: Why should Zupanev wish to betray the Soviet system and assist the survival and transmission of Paltiel Kossover's confession and poetry? The text reveals that Zupanev is a Jew, who by virtue of his contact with Paltiel has recognized his responsibilities to act in the face of evil. His revolt projects him into life and into protecting the words of the executed poet. He will act as a resurrecting force and will temporarily speak for the murdered poet, serving as guide and teacher so that in time Grisha might assume his father's voice. Zupanev's act of rebellion would, however, appear to conclude on a note of bitter irony, as the words he had snatched from certain death are transmitted to a mute. Nevertheless, Grisha Kossover is "a living mute [who] will cause the words of a dead man to reverberate" (Franck, 1980, 16) [my translation]. Grisha's self-imposed affliction will not impede his willingness, nor his ability, to comprehend his father's words. His actions will ensure their transmission, and with them the story of Paltiel's existential struggle for identity. In his unique manner, Grisha will wrench his father's tale from the silence of death and give it the necessary voice to promote the truths manifested within.

Grisha's preoccupation with his unknown father dates from an early period in his childhood when he chanced upon two vestiges of the man: A faded photograph and a volume of Paltiel's poetry. Fear initially restrains his mother, but eventually she tells him the man's identity. His response to this, though demonstrating a childlike naiveté and simplicity, likewise possesses a unique sense of communion and silent communication bonding father and son: "Mon papa est une photo. . . mon papa est un livre. . . . Son père s'adressait à lui dans une langue qu'il ne comprenait pas. Peu lui importait; il posait les doigts sur ces lignes, sur ces mots—et cela le rendait heureux" (TP, 25); "My father is a picture. . . . My father is a book. . . . Then his father would speak to him in a language he did not understand. He didn't care: he moved his fingers over the lines, over the words, and that made him happy" (T, 37). Like a blind person, the young Grisha communicates with his father by touching the silent, printed words in his father's books. The ensuing joyous dialogue with this unknown being resurrects the father. "Mon père n'est pas mort. Mon père est un livre et les livres ne meurent pas" (TP, 27); "My father is not dead. My father is a book, and books do not die" (T, 39).

Wiesel's introduction of the volume of poetry and the photograph not only permit Grisha to know his father in a uniquely spiritual sense, they also emphasize the centrality of the role played by silence in this text, as well as its elemental position in general communication. The silent dialogue Grisha establishes with his father through these tangible symbols reflects the myriad of critical ideas espoused by a variety of modern literary theorists who stress the fundamental significance of the dialogic bond between text and reader achieved in the art of active reading.[2] Though Grisha's first reaction to his father and to his father's writings appears childlike, it does reflect his profound future relationship with both, as well as his own particular quest for truth.

Not only does Grisha communicate with his father by means of the text but also by a message without a code: The silent image of his father's photograph. Max Picard states: "Images are silent, but they speak in silence. They are a silent language"[3] (91). Thus, at an early age, the boy has established a firm though silent relationship with Paltiel. Ironically, the preservation of that bond becomes the central factor in the boy's becoming mute.

Zupanev bears the testament of the dead father into the boy's silence. He is the essential link between father and son, ensuring the continuance and evolution of their earlier dialogue. As father and son communicate in silence, so too does Zupanev encourage his own silent dialogue with the boy. These three central characters commence their silent voicings of a story that must be recounted. And years later, when Grisha has obtained permission to emigrate to Israel, he silently carries the story of his father's life and death with him. To Soviet officialdom, mute Grisha poses no threat. But within him lies the story of a man whom that same officialdom tortured and then silenced. Much like the Bratslaver Hasidim who before the Holocaust smuggled out the chair of Rebbe Nachman from the Soviet Union piece by piece, and then reassembled it in Jerusalem in the midst of their new community in Mea Shearim, Grisha steals his father's story out of Russia to Jerusalem where the testament is written down. This act of transmission becomes Grisha's first task upon arriving in Israel. His father and his father's story are with him, and necessitate Grisha's giving them a voice, or as Ossip Mandelstam wrote: "You left me my lips, and they shape words, even in silence" (108). Grisha becomes his father's lips; the written words become his father's voice.

Paltiel and his story do not merely present us with the engrossing saga of the development of one man's character, but also with Wiesel's ideas concerning the problematic task of the honest Jew to maintain an authentic identity. Moreover, Paltiel's struggle is symbolic of Soviet Jewry and of its silent struggle against an oppressive system that sought to crush Jewish identity.

Paltiel's revolt springs from his desire to regain authenticity and truth in his life. As Camus proposes in *L'Homme révolté*: "Rebellion cannot exist without the sentiment that, somewhere and somehow, one is right" (423) [my translation]. The Communist ideology Paltiel had freely chosen to espouse does not fulfill his idealistic expectations. The course of his life as a Communist has led to frustrating meaninglessness.

> Malgré tout ce que j'ai pu apprendre, et j'ai appris beaucoup, je ne connais pas les réponses qu'il faudrait apporter aux questions graves, essentielles qui concernent l'être humain. L'Individu, face à l'avenir, face à l'autrui, n'a aucune chance de survivre. (TP, 77)

> In spite of everything I was able to learn—and I've learned a lot—I don't know the answers that will have to be given to the grave, fundamental questions that concern human beings. The individual facing the future, facing his fellow man, has no chance whatsoever of survival. (T, 20)

Again, compare Camus's description of the rebel at the moment of revolt:

> Up to this point he has at least remained silent and has abandoned himself to the form of despair in which a condition is accepted even though it is considered unjust. To remain silent is to give the impression that one has no opinions, that one wants nothing, and in certain cases it really amounts to wanting nothing. . . . But from the moment he speaks, even though he says nothing but "no," he begins to desire and to judge. (423-24) [my translation]

The attacks of Camus's rebel resemble Paltiel's situation, whose rebellion demands judgement for his actions and his life. It is his son, Grisha, who will sit in judgement of him.

Paltiel's confession, in which lies his rebellion, evolves from the tension created between his Jewish identity and the Communist affiliations that it spawned. The struggle between secular values and Jewish identity eventually led to the silencing of the latter. The origins of that silencing lay in his early life when he had witnessed hatred of the Jew and evidence of Jewish passivity. As a result, Paltiel felt that traditional Jewish ways must be rejected in favor of the Communist approach, which ironically had a firm basis in prophetic Judaism, replete with its messianic aspirations. For Paltiel and his Communist friends, humanity's task becomes that of associate with God and eventually, within the Communist framework, the usurper of God's position and influence.

Paltiel's testament allows him the unique opportunity to review his past. In this *descente aux enfers,* he comes to realize that by truly being a Jew, he was also a Communist. The first proof for this occurs when Paltiel recalls his father's advice as Paltiel left his home in Liyanov. The paternal message is firmly anchored in the teachings of prophetic and rabbinic Judaism: "en secourant les pauvres, en regardant, en écoutant ceux qui ont besoin de nous, nous avons simplement le privilège de vivre notre vie, de la vivre pleinement" (TP, 73); "in helping the poor, in looking after and listening to those who need us, we are but exercising our privilege of living our life, of living it to the fullest" (T, 96). His father then places this into the context of Paltiel's Communistic beliefs.

> Tes amis communistes . . . je ne les connais pas. Je sais seulement qu'ils aspirent à diminuer le malheur dans le monde. Cela compte, cela seul compte. . . . L'essentiel c'est qu'ils se battent pour ceux qui n'ont ni la force ni les moyens de se battre. L'essentiel, c'est que tu sois sensible à la souffrance d'autrui. . . . Le vrai danger, mon fils, se nomme indifférence. (TP, 74)

> I don't know your Communist friends. . . . I only know that their aim
> is to diminish unhappiness in the world. That is what counts, that
> is all that counts. . . . What matters is that they are fighting those who
> have neither the strength nor the means to fight. The essential thing
> for you is to be sensitive to the suffering of others. . . . The real dan-
> ger, my son, is indifference. (T, 97)

The final aspect of his father's testament is an exhortation to remain Jewish: "Tu es juif, juif avant tout; c'est comme juif que tu aideras l'humanité. Si tu t'occupes des autres au détriment de tes frères, tu finiras par les renier tous" (TP, 74); "You're a Jew, a Jew first and foremost; it is as a Jew that you will be helping mankind. If you care for others to the detriment of your brothers, you will eventually deny everyone" (T, 97).

In his fashion, Paltiel does reject his Jewishness, and in turn is himself repudiated and condemned by the very Communist movement in which he had placed such hope for the Jew and humanity. Paltiel's quest for truth and justice has caused him to recognize that communism demands lies, half-truths, and disinformation. Paltiel, however, demands truth; he expects it of his comrades and of the party itself. For him, Lenin's fellow Bolsheviks had been heroes, founders of the first socialist state. When, however, he and his friends are informed that the old guard were to be viewed as traitors to the Revolution, they are stunned. Such calumnies eventually transform into the horrors of the Stalinist purges. As fellow revolutionaries disappear, the messianic dream is savagely mutilated, and lost in the politics of a movement more concerned with power and self-preservation than with ideals and principles. Such attitudes confuse Paltiel, especially upon his return to the USSR when he attempts to comprehend the party line concerning conciliation with the Nazis. Paltiel's inability to understand is indicative of the silent internal struggle between the Jew and the Communist, between someone seeking truth and someone now forced to disseminate lies.

Wiesel heightens this struggle by the symbolic use of Paltiel's *tefillin*.[4] As Paltiel travels about Europe and engages in a host of activities, he carries with him these silent reminders of his Jewishness and his father's advice: "Promets-moi de mettre tes phylactères tous les matins" (TP, 74); "Promise to put on your phylacteries every morning" (T, 97). During the early stages of his wanderings, Paltiel remains faithful to his promise, despite the erosion of other vestiges of his Jewish identity. But, in turn, the *tefillin* are eventually placed aside in a corner of his existence. Yet despite their disuse, Paltiel refuses to be separated from them. They form a silent, tangible link with his father, his Jewish past and his own silenced Jewish identity. When asked to lend his *tefillin* to a mysterious *navenadnik,* Paltiel refuses. His firm refusal to be separated from these ritual objects symbolizes a silent challenge against his adopted Communist image. The mere possession of the *tefillin* marks a bond with the Jewish people, tenuous though it may be. Despite his various "transgressions," there remains this single outward sign to remind him continually of his heritage. And when his European saga has ended and he returns to Soviet Russia, the *tefillin* are among those fragments in a suitcase that comprise his life.

The union between father and son through the symbol of the *tefillin* is eventually broken. Paltiel's link with his father exists only so long as they are among his possessions. When they mysteriously disappear, the resulting rupture is rendered absolute, for it is only then that the Holocaust and its enormity of evil manifest themselves. The *tefillin,* symbol of vibrant Jewish life and profundity of belief, are lost prior to the Soviet Army's liberation of Paltiel's native town, Liyanov. Entering the town, Paltiel discovers the Jewish world of his childhood has vanished. Standing before the mass grave of the Liyanov Jewish community, Paltiel seeks to reunite himself with his murdered family. His failure to do so reinforces his sense of utter isolation and of the meaningless nature of his present existence. Yet, he does hear his father's voice: "Vivant ou mort, la place d'un Juif est au milieu des siens" (TP, 244); "Dead or alive, a Jew's place is with his people" (T, 292). Paltiel has exiled himself from his Jewish identity and, in Wiesel's thought, from his rightful place in humanity. By denying his authentic image, he has condemned himself to live and die a lie.

The introduction of the Holocaust serves another significant purpose. As in earlier novels, the *shoah* represents the specter of destruction and the silence of death. In this text, its inclusion symbolizes a creative presence. Throughout the protagonist's odyssey, he has written mediocre poetry extolling Communist ideals. Once, however, he has witnessed the devastation of the *anus mundi,* he is metamorphosed. It is the solitary silence of the millions of dead and the rapidly fading memory of their world that seize him. The direct contact between Paltiel and the effects of the Holocaust give him a new voice, the tangible result being the collection of poems, *J'ai vu mon père en songe.* This slim volume stands as a memorial to that lost world, to Paltiel's father, and to Paltiel himself.

The Holocaust serves as another impetus. From the moment he had left his family, Paltiel has struggled with the dual nature of his character: the Jew and the Communist. His Communist inclinations led him to abandon the daily ritual of putting on his *tefillin,* though indeed he continued to carry them with him. This act of refusal epitomizes his "breaking" with elements of his past, his people and his God, though God remains an integral part of his consciousness. But after visiting Maidanek, Paltiel rebels against God in classical Jewish fashion. He rejects that image of a loving, compassionate God, as it no longer conforms to his own impression of the Creator. God, no longer a source of life, becomes a grave digger.

While standing at Maidanek, a mysterious voice asks Paltiel what it is he wants. His terse, antagonistic response: Redemption. "So do I. . . . So do I," replies the other, urgently adding: "And so does He" (T, 316). This mystical experience has a profound effect upon the protagonist. If indeed God is a grave digger, if as Paltiel believes humanity becomes responsible for ultimate redemption, then he must seek to do what he deems necessary to banish God and expedite salvation. For him, the redemption of the survivors was accomplished by the Red Army. Despite communism's negative face, the ideology has come to symbolize redemption, life, and hope. Thus it is that Paltiel Kossover decides to join the Communist Party.

That action would appear to indicate the ultimate suppression of Jewish identity. Yet earlier in the story, when he had been fighting with Communist forces in the Spanish Civil War, Paltiel had stumbled upon near-forgotten ancient Jewish cemeteries. The tombstones with their weathered inscriptions were silent memorials to a people whose message and memory form the essence of Paltiel's own character. The Jew within Paltiel cannot be erased or easily sublimated. Though Paltiel's authentic Jewish image may be momentarily quashed, it cannot be permanently silenced. Thus, despite his decision to become a member of the party, this Jewish essence persists and silently continues to influence him, as evidenced in the memorial to his father's world, *J'ai vu mon père en songe*.

That volume of poetry provides another example of Paltiel's continuing silent struggle. Though the poems do resurrect aspects of the lost Jewish world of Central and Eastern Europe, none evoke the memory of his father. The collection's original structure had included an opening poem lyrically and surreally depicting Paltiel's father leading a silent funeral procession. That particular poem was to have served as a striking metaphor for the annihilated civilization of which Paltiel had once been a part. At the last moment, however, the poet opts to delete those verses for fear of upsetting or annoying the Communist reader. And yet, how many Communists would have been capable of reading Yiddish? What reason might therefore have induced this rather cowardly form of self-censorship? I would propose that the protagonist consciously omits this particular poem out of a profound sense of guilt for his having abandoned his Jewishness, for having broken his promise to his father, and for the subsequent disappearance of the *tefillin*. Thus, in this bout of the struggle between the Jew and the Communist, the latter would seem to have gained an advantage. But, as Paltiel learns, Soviet communism will tolerate no degree of Jewish identity. New pogroms erupt, striking at a primary source for maintaining Jewish identity: Words. Jewish presses are closed; books are seized, writers imprisoned.

It is at this tense moment that Grisha Kossover is born. The child serves as a catalyst to stimulate the revival of the father's authentic Jewish image and to permit him to perform the parental duty forming part of the creed and cycle of Jewish life: "Impress them [commandments for a good life] on your children. Talk about them when you sit at home and when you walk the road . . ." (Deuteronomy 6:7), words ironically encased within the *tefillin.* Grisha becomes the means of terminating the painful existential struggle Paltiel has endured. The son will assist the father in rehabilitating the father's silenced image.

An important feature of Jewish life is the transmission of names. During the Spanish Civil War, Paltiel had experienced a unique event: "Un matin, dans les ruines d'un cimetière . . . je vis une pierre tombale dont l'inscription me fit frémir: Paltiel, fils de Gershon . . ." (TP, 182); "One morning, among the ruins of a cemetery . . . I came upon a tombstone whose inscription made me shiver: Paltiel son of Gershon" (T, 219). His precise name had died centuries before, only to be reborn again in him. The chain of Jewish life had been maintained, despite the often cruel vicissitudes of Jewish history. The effect of that experience later manifests itself in Paltiel's decision to name his son after his father, thereby reviving a name in the community of Israel. Not only will that name be retrieved from the silence of death, but Paltiel consciously decides to revoice it in the ritual of *brit mila,* the ceremony of circumcision when a male Jewish child is introduced into Israel's ancient covenant with God.

Paltiel's regeneration as a Jew achieves more complete realizations with the resurrection of the symbol of the *tefillin:*

> Je retrouvai mes phylactères, un jour, dans un tiroir et, à leur contact, je tressaillis. L'instant d'après, sans savoir ce que je faisais ni pourquoi, je les sortis de leur sac, les embrassai et les mis sur mon bras gauche et sur mon front . . . (TP, 278)

> I found my phylacteries one day at the bottom of a drawer, and touching them I trembled. If they could only speak, I thought. The next second, without knowing what I was doing or why, I took them out of their bag, kissed them and put them on my left arm and forehead. (T, 332)

This act propounds several significant implications. First, it represents Paltiel's silent means for Grisha to observe the use of an important symbol of his faith. Secondly, the silent bond that Paltiel and Grisha establish through the straps of the *tefillin* will be more fully developed later when Grisha discovers his father's photograph, his poetry, and finally the testament itself.

In the testament Paltiel had hidden a letter to his son in which he stresses the importance of being true to one's heritage and to one's image: "Mon père, dont tu portes le nom, le savait, lui. Mais il est mort. C'est pourquoi je ne peux que te dire: souviens-toi qu'il savait, lui, ce que son fils ignore" (TP, 77); "My father, whose name you bear, knew. But he is dead. That is why I can only say to you—remember that he knew what his son does not" (T, 20). The testament becomes a dual confession: The one desired by Soviet officials to "prove" Paltiel Kossover's guilt, and a religious confession, the *viddui,** recited by a believing Jew on his deathbed. Paltiel has recognized his mistakes and advises his son against them, an action that transforms the document into a traditional Jewish will (צוואה), which is primarily an ethical dissertation. I would suggest that the passionate lucidity it expresses stems from Paltiel's revolt against communism and the nation-state it had created. As Camus suggests in *L'Homme révolté:* "Awareness, no matter how confused it may be, develops from every act of rebellion: The sudden, dazzling perception that there is something in man with which he can identify himself, even if only for a moment" (424) [my translation]. Grisha's birth provided the *point de départ* for Paltiel's rebellion. The struggle Paltiel has endured all his life finally explodes in the revolt contained within the testament. Even the ultimate sentence penned moments before his ignominious execution sounds the call to continued resistance and rebellion. And in that rebellion, Paltiel finally assumes his role as father, teacher, and guide.

At the beginning of this chapter, I stressed my belief that the novels under discussion deal with the development of the identity of the post-Holocaust generation and the specific relationships between fathers and sons. Grisha's relationship with his father transpires in meaningful silence. But, despite the message imparted to him in the testament, Grisha would remain a stranger in the USSR, a fact emphasized by his Hebrew name, *Gershon,* "a stranger in a strange land." Moreover, his being an outsider has been rendered visible by his having been circumcised, a difference that would always separate him from non-Jewish men in Soviet society. His mother states: "Il souffrira, il souffrira, c'est inévitable, mais il saura pourquoi" (TP, 277); "He will suffer, he'll suffer, it's inevitable, but he'll know why" (T, 330–31). Furthermore, the contents of his father's testament will render Grisha a metaphysical outcast. Therefore, it is fitting that Grisha should leave for the land of his ancestors where his father's silenced voice can become Grisha's method of speaking: Not as his father, but in place of his father. Gershon the son of Paltiel will no longer be

---

*viddui: the personal confession (though written in plural terms) that an individual makes to God. Repeatedly recited on Yom Kippur, it also serves as an individual's final confession on the deathbed.

a stranger; his father's testament will no longer be silent. Together, father and son will create hope for the future.

LE CINQUIEME FILS

At the World Gathering of Jewish Holocaust Survivors held at Jerusalem in June 1981, Elie Wiesel noted that survivors and their children have been divided by an event that touches both, though in radically different ways. This idea forms the core of the action of Wiesel's 1983 novel, *Le Cinquième fils*. The story concerns a survivor and the sense of alienation and guilt that the Holocaust evokes and the specter it continues to cast.

As Wiesel indicates in *Signes d'exode* (153–161), survivors and their children face two distinct possibilities. The least painful scenario for parents would be silence when they cannot find the words to express the realities of the *anus mundi*. In such cases, the survivors choose to abrogate parental responsibility, which is to transmit the lesson of their experience to their children. The second possibility lies in recounting as much as the parents are indeed capable of telling. The novel in question deals with such choices, specifically with Reuven Tamiroff's decision to opt for silence, and the effect this has upon his son.

The title of the novel, *Le Cinquième fils,* links its metaphysical core with the symbolism of Passover, the Jewish festival of freedom and redemption. The Haggadah speaks of four sons; however, Wiesel's novel seeks out a fifth son, a silent, missing one: "Bien sûr, il y a aussi un cinquième fils, mais il ne figure pas dans le récit, car il n'est plus. Or, le devoir du père juif est envers les vivants. . . . les morts ne font pas partie de la Haggadah" (CF, 33); "There is, of course, a fifth son, but he does not appear in the tale because he is gone. Thus, the duty of a Jewish father is to the living. . . . the dead are not part of the Haggadah" (FS, 35). Yet the identity of this fifth son remains enigmatically wrapped in silences as shifting and oppressive as those evoked in Wiesel's trilogy. Moreover, despite the symbols of Passover upon which Wiesel has constructed the novel, neither Reuven nor his son is free. Both are imprisoned by the almost ineffable nature of the Holocaust experience.

Le Cinquième fils represents a continuation of Wiesel's first novel, *La Nuit*. Both works evolve directly from the *anus mundi*. The characters in *Le Cinquième fils,* like those of the trilogy, are psychologically broken individuals desirous of evading the past by relegating it to silence. Their lives are dominated by the deafening silences of Auschwitz, negative silences that victoriously predominate in a text for the first time since the first novels. The generation that endured the *univers concentrationnaire* has been affected by its destructive power. Reuven Tamiroff is a man characterized by silence. And, the father's silences painfully estrange the son, who is obliged to accept it as part of his patrimony. The narrative presses this seal of silence on both characters, forcing each into exile: The father separated from his son and thereby from the future; the son distanced from his father and thereby from his rightful knowledge of the past. Together, they silently and ironically cry for release and redemption. Even when Reuven finally begins to relate the past so long silenced and guarded from his son, the initial result is that of the stifling, paralytic silence of Auschwitz.

The novel's structure is likewise reflective of the characters. Just as they are stunted, broken figures, so is the novel fragmented by the introduction of textual silence and shifting narrative forms. The use of *le grand silence typographique-respiratoire* approximates a metonymy for stuttering, as the narrative flow of the original French text is repeatedly broken by such textual interruptions 95 times in 230 pages. As earlier noted, this technique symbolizes the victory of negative silence over the word, and of language's apparent impotence in the face of Auschwitz. As in earlier novels, these applications of textual silence occasionally dissolve into *la page blanche* (a total of eleven times), especially when the narrator appears obliged to pause and collect his thoughts, if not his sanity.

These are not the only elements that fragment the text. The primary method of narrating the story is through the rather traditional personal point of view, in this case that of the nameless son. However, unknown elements from the past are advanced into the text by means of epistolary narrative in letters addressed by Reuven Tamiroff to his son, and by additional letters written by the nameless son and narrator to the enigmatic "fifth son," Ariel. Finally, near the novel's conclusion, the story is told by means of a diary entitled *Journal d'Ariel* written by the anonymous son who has assumed the identity of the "fifth son," now known to be his dead brother. The combination of these techniques and variations of narrative style creates a text that progresses haltingly while imparting a sense of frustration, anger, and guilt. The silent gaps in the text likewise symbolize tension. These moments of mutism are negative and debilitating, with words themselves becoming synonymous with separation and isolation. The continuity of life has been shattered, and man seems impotent to restore it. This sense of rupture manifests itself not merely by the disjointed text, but also by the weighty silences that are evoked by it. These silences project a particular burden of guilt that intensifies the reality of open rupture and separation, which nothing appears capable of bridging. For Reuven, the omnipresent silences of the *anus mundi* isolate and condemn him to a lifeless environment from which he addresses the missing and silenced "fifth son," while his living son must exist in the void of his father's silences.

Wiesel's use of the fragmented text and its accompanying silence imparts a sense of the torment experienced by survivors and their children. As the narrator relates: "les enfants des survivants sont traumatisés presque autant que les survivants eux-mêmes" (CF, 197); "The children of survivors are almost as traumatized as the survivors themselves" (FS, 192). The psychology of survivors, and their relations with their children within a "survivor family" unit, emerge from the predominating silences of this text as central themes. In *Le Jour,* the anonymous protagonist stated that in each survivor there were time-bombs waiting to explode. Each survivor's timebomb will affect him or her in its own particular way. In the case of Reuven Tamiroff and his son, this destructive internal device produces a silent void that separates father and son, depriving both of full lives, and denying the son his rightful heritage as the child of a survivor. Furthermore, this silence is the destructive silence of Auschwitz and not the more regenerative silence that had gradually evolved in the novels of the trilogy. In this text, the silence that is encountered represents death, absence, rupture, exile, and betrayal. And yet, as in the earlier novels, this same silence does provide a creative matrix that will promote the formation of questions.

The most common trauma faced by any survivor is guilt for having survived. As Leo Eitinger of the University of Haifa stresses, the most common question posed by the survivors of the camps is "why did I survive?" (76). The survivor's tendency is to incorporate within himself images of the dead, a process described as "identification guilt" by Robert Jay Lifton. Though Lifton's ideas derive from his studies of the survivors of the atomic blast at Hiroshima, they are in perfect accord with the voluminous findings on Holocaust survivors made by doctors, psychologists, and scholars. Each survivor of such manmade tragedies sees himself or herself as an amalgamation of all the corpses; the survivor becomes the corpse and condemns himself for not having died. Wiesel concludes *La Nuit* on just such a bitter note. The corpse sees itself as being responsible for the rupture that exists between itself and the dead who constitute an integral part of that being. "In identifying so strongly with the dead . . . the survivor seeks both to atone for his participation in that breakdown, and to reconstitute a form of order around that atonement" (Lifton, 1967, 497).

One common trait exhibited by many survivors is the need to disappear, to avoid the dangers of *auffallen,* or drawing attention to oneself. There were several methods for accomplishing this, the most common being to fade into the general decor one chooses for building a life after having survived. In the case of Reuven Tamiroff, his son's description of him would appear to exemplify this: "Il [Reuven] n'attire l'attention ni par sa manière de parler ni par sa façon de se taire. Il recherche l'anonymat. Pour le remarquer, il faut l'observer de près" (CF, 16); "Neither his way of speaking nor his manner of keeping silent attracts attention. He seeks anonymity. One must see him at close range to take notice" (FS, 16). This desire to become anonymous would definitely provide the basis for Reuven's choice of setting for his post-Holocaust existence: America. One's chance of achieving absolute anonymity is enhanced in the "great melting pot" that allows people like Reuven to disappear into the social tapestry. Moreover, Reuven's need to escape, to hide, and to wallow in his own guilt is most easily achieved in New York City, "une cité faite pour les misanthropes" (CF, 57); "the city is made to order for misanthropes" (FS, 59). Reuven would therefore appear to have made a conscious choice to disappear into the faceless, homogenous mass that is America.

Silence extends to Reuven's work as well, for he is a librarian. And in the silence of the library, he proceeds with an almost obsessive task of compiling information about his favorite author, Paritus-le-borgne, One-Eyed Paritus. Despite Reuven's insistence that Paritus's *Méditations obliques* profoundly influenced the religious and antireligious thought of numerous other philosophers, this particular philosopher's name receives no mention in any source about religion or philosophy. Wiesel presents an enigmatic figure whose existence is doubtful, a technique he has frequently employed in other novels. And, as in those previous texts, this mythical, mystical character lies behind all primary action. I would suggest, therefore, that an attempt must be made to uncover his actual identity.

If one attempts to establish some degree of truth by an etymological search, the results offer rather intriguing evidence. The name Paritus suggests a Latin base, the closest root being *paro,* which itself generates several other forms, such as *parito* and *pario.* The root *paro* and its most closely related form *parito* mean to prepare, to get ready, to be about to do a thing. It is obvious from Wiesel's textual evidence that Reuven is preparing something through his "research," though both intention and consequence are not divulged. Like Reuven's son, the reader remains trapped in a silent void of ignorance. Continuing this investigation, the Latin *pario* means to bring forth (as children). More interestingly, this form not only possesses distinct etymological links with *paro* but similarly with the Hebrew verb *porah* (פרה), to bear fruit, a morpheme that when transformed (פרייה) can likewise refer to having children.

In the full name of this mysterious philosopher, One-Eyed Paritus, the determining *le-Borgne* (One-Eyed) indicates the loss of an eye or the serious obstruction of vision. I believe Wiesel has used this term with reference to Reuven Tamiroff, as he has indeed lost sight of the world in which he lives. His suffocating sentiments of guilt have driven him into a silent universe that distorts and deforms the reality around him. If, as I believe, the name Paritus has been used by the author as a synonym for father, then Reuven's "research" is about himself and his relationship to the "fifth son," his son, Ariel, who died during the Holocaust. His vision has become oblique, his energies channelled into letters written to that dead son. This is perhaps the origin of Paritus's *Méditations obliques,* a proposition that receives authoritative support when the narrator, wishing to read his father's investigations into the life and writings of Paritus, discovers those letters in his father's notebooks. The significance of this discovery will be treated later. For the moment, however, one can observe in this incident the degree to which Reuven has indeed been blinded *(le-borgne)* to his parental responsibilities to his living son, a boy who becomes a nameless entity in the face of the wall of silence erected by his father.

Moshè Garbarz confided to his son that the actual heritage of Auschwitz is not transmittable (7), yet together with his son he sets down his testimony of daily existence in the *anus mundi*. Though the difficulty of transmitting that nearly ineffable experience presses Moshè Garbarz toward silence, he recognizes his urgent and unique responsibility to speak as a survivor, and especially as a parent who happens to be a survivor. Speaking becomes a particular mode of survival. It is precisely this logic that Reuven rejects. He refuses to speak, abdicates his responsibilities as parent and as a human being, and merely stagnates in his silent contemplations of the horrors of the past. Within the Wieselian universe, every human being must attempt to establish dialogue with fellow souls. True human contact is vital and assists the individual in an attachment to life. Moreover, within the framework of parental responsibilities, dialogic exchange aids the evolution of a child's character and identity.

Reuven's determination to remain silent confuses his son. Mysteries are evoked that have no apparent resolution. Even when Reuven's friends attempt to bridge the gap between father and son, past and present, they are aware that certain secrets can only by divulged by Reuven himself. His son struggles to understand those things that his father ought to tell him, but which have remained silenced. The son's failure to force his father to speak and thus enable him to uncover some degree of truth leads to a sense of mounting frustration and anger.

The narrator finally forces his father to speak when he announces the chance discovery of his father's correspondence with the dead "fifth son," Ariel. The effect of Reuven's story on his living son is stunning, implanting within the boy seeds of guilt for being alive. The nameless narrator views himself as the source of malefic silence that has dominated the home and had eventually driven his mother into catatonic madness. In his estimation, his very existence is the cause for the personal and domestic suffering he has witnessed all his life.

Reuven's silences seem to have stemmed from his own guilt at having "brought forth," (*porah*), Ariel during the war and having been unable to preserve his life. These guilty silences rise out of his psyche to deform his living son's identity. This anonymous son suffers greatly, for he has been obliged to formulate questions that might offer some responses in the face of his father's silence. The youth desperately examines himself, not to establish who he actually happens to be, but rather to understand his father. Reuven's silences and the enigma of his personality hold the key to unlocking his living son's identity. The boy becomes entangled in a complex web of searching for an identity comprised of three souls: Reuven, Ariel, and the narrator himself. The narrator vainly seeks to fuse the three into one. His guilt at having usurped his brother's position in his father's life further complicates his own natural development. Confused and driven to distraction, the narrator urgently seeks to construct bridges between himself, his father, and his dead brother. These bridges consist of words in his own letters to Ariel.

Through his letters and meditations, the narrator gradually assumes the identity of his dead brother. This act of *dédoublement,* or doubling, in which the *moi-mort,* the dead "fifth son," and the *moi-vivant/ -survivant,* the living youth, are projected together, momentarily provides a name for the anonymous son. Robert Jay Lifton postulates that "doubling is an active psychological process, a means of adaptation to extremity" (*Doctors,* 422), an adaptation that requires the dissolution of the psychic glue that had assumed the solidity of the original self. In Wiesel's novel, the nameless narrator has never possessed a stable psychological self as a result of his father's silences. Thus, when faced with the shock of truth, the original self, which has deemed itself "guilty" and even destructive, rapidly adopts the identity of the dead brother. Moreover, the nameless protagonist feels this action of resurrecting a lost, silenced name from the oblivion of the Holocaust will forge a link between father and son, and offer him some reason for living—but at what a price. He becomes a living dead man, deprived of his own authentic identity, eaten alive by "the Lion of God," Ariel.

In his quest for an identity that has led him to this moment of *dédoublement,* the narrator has seemingly also decided to accomplish that which his father had attempted and failed to do after the war. As the "fifth son," the narrator similarly assumes the responsibility of achieving one particular goal: The death of the Angel, the SS commander who had liquidated the ghetto of Davarowsk and had been directly or indirectly guilty of Ariel's death. The "sons" of Reuven Tamiroff link together, aspiring to avenge the past, and perhaps thereby to exorcise the ghosts that control and silence Reuven. With their union, Wiesel effects an ironic realization that the Jewish God of life and justice has temporarily been usurped by a sadistic Nazi-like god of death. In seeking to execute righteous vengeance, the narrator betrays the primary Jewish ethos in general, as well as that particular code adopted by the majority of Jewish survivors not to become executioners in a vain attempt to extract a degree of revenge.

The novel's conclusion remains highly enigmatic. It is revealed that the events narrated in the course of the story were not contemporary, but had occurred ten and twenty years before. Despite the passage of time and the events that had transpired, there has been no resolution to the crisis of identity. The protagonist remains anonymous, fragmented, hovering between life and death. He would like to understand all that has transpired, but a foreboding ignorance sadly shrouds him. One curious notion is advanced, however, concerning his relationship with his father: "Certes, nous avons eu nos différends, nos querelles, nos conflits; mais les distances se sont muées en liens renouvelés" (CF, 230); "Surely we have had our differences, our quarrels, our conflits; but the differences have been transformed into renewed ties" (FS, 219). How was this transition achieved? Were these new links established when Reuven broke his silence in order to reveal the identity of the "fifth son"; or, did they evolve following the narrator's attempt to avenge Ariel's death? The responses to these questions and others are hidden in the silences and ambiguities that abound in this text, and which have come to symbolize the relationship between father and son. Or perhaps, for the moment, our inability to respond clearly to such mysteries indicates a pressing need for the arrival of the Messiah, who will resolve such insoluble problems, an attitude that seems to correspond to that of the anonymous narrator: "Le Messie risque d'arriver trop tard. . . . Tant pis: j'attendrai tout de même" (CF, 229); "The Messiah may well come too late. . . . Never mind, I shall wait nonetheless" (FS, 219). And, in expressing that thought, the narrator places himself firmly within Jewish tradition as expounded by the medieval sage Maimonides in the penultimate statement of his Thirteen Articles of Faith: "I believe with perfect faith in the coming of the Messiah, and even though he may delay, nevertheless I anticipate every day that he will come," a belief fervently cherished by hundreds of Jews incarcerated in the ghettos of European cities during the war and chanted by pious Jews as they entered the gas chambers. Meanwhile, in the silent interim between the present and the Messiah's advent, one can merely pose questions, for as the Haggadah says of the youngest son who does not know how to ask, one has the moral obligation to teach him to do so.

CONCLUSION

In these two novels, we become privy to the pains associated with the creation of identity. In the first, Wiesel traces the lengthy means by which the identity of Paltiel Kossover was wrenched from the silence of death. Conversely, *Le Cinquième fils* considers the painful process of having one's living identity plunged into the abyss of silence. Both novels demonstrate Wiesel's abiding belief in the importance of dialogic relationships between parents and children, a vital element for establishing an authentic image of oneself and, in Wiesel's view, for creating an honest Jewish identity. For Wiesel, Jewish identity projects one into life and entails a moral responsibility to preserve and protect it.

These novels do not lightly suggest this notion of a challenge; they demonstrate how humanity must often struggle and, if need be, rebel against those forces that would destroy or silence aspects of its true nature. More precisely, these texts present Wiesel's vision of the Jew as an everyman, a being who suffers for whatever reasons and must eventually defend his or her rights and beliefs, as well as those of all people. Each individual must participate in life, become a part of history. It is only in that manner that the truth of history can be safeguarded from menacing silence, and that positive, creative silence can be properly integrated into history.

CHAPTER **8**

Madness and Memory
LE CRÉPUSCULE, AU LOIN (1987) AND *L'OUBLIÉ* (1989)

La vérité de Dieu est dans le silence.
E. JABÈS

A man who does not exist,
A man who is but a dream. . . .
W. B. YEATS

The evolving phenomenological nature of silence in Wiesel's novels has simultaneously pressed protagonists and readers toward the realization that from the nihilistic ashes of Auschwitz a renewed and radically transformed dialogue has begun to emerge. In *Otherwise Than Being; or Beyond Essence*, Emmanuel Lévinas states that "saying [speaking] is already a sign made to another, a sign of this giving of signs, that is, of this non-indifference, a sign of this impossibility of slipping away and being replaced, of this identity, this uniqueness: here I am" (145). The refound voice that initiates dialogue assumes a sense of responsibility to and for the "other," and aspires to reestablish a sense of moral equilibrium in the universe. Moreover, the emerging dialogue that provides the impetus for the rebirth of Wieselian protagonists similarly engages each reader, necessitating a profound exploration of the self. The authorial assertion "here I am" transmutes into an urgent, primordial question for the reader: "Where are you?" or as Wiesel states elsewhere: "I write to explore my own self as much as I write in order to help you explore yourself" (AS 3:230).

As has previously been demonstrated in this study, the rediscovered voice and the ensuing revitalized dialogue have frequently been threatened by the encroachment of abiding negative silences. Wieselian protagonists and, by extension, readers of Wiesel's literary universe, are subjoined in the persevering struggle against those silences. Though occasionally a bitter conflict, reader/narratee recognize the profound implication of their engagement. From those silences rise other propositions illustrating further Wieselian themes: Madness and memory, two notions I consider fundamentally associated for the author. Wiesel notes, "I am in love with madmen" (AS, 3:231), and, indeed, madmen litter the Wieselian literary landscape from *La Nuit* to his most recent novels, *Le Crépuscule, au loin (Twilight)* (1987) and *L'Oublié (The Forgotten)* (1989). As these "mad" characters grapple with that which they had experienced, their volatile memories simultaneously propel them toward mystical madness. "I am for mystical madness," Wiesel writes, "a madness that has only one obsession—redemption, only one concern—one's fellow man" (AS, 3:253).

Wiesel's *mise-en-discours* and finely constructed textual structures in these novels guide the reader into intensely holy spaces. In each work, Wiesel's language establishes a precise space in which the narratives transpire, a space whose parameters are profoundly personal, and where the reader similarly detects the hovering presence of a transcendent spirit. Throughout the early novels, authorial intention had gradually limited physical space, thereby facilitating the transition from freedom into exile, slavery, and death.[1] This constriction of physical space served the fundamental catalytic function of pressing all action to a metaphysical level where a normal diachronic sense of events had become fragmented, thrusting narrators and readers into an indeterminate, dreamlike realm. In the two novels currently under consideration, one such domain is represented by the Mountain Clinic, an asylum for the mentally ill; the other, a most private arena, focuses upon one man's failing mind and his son's quest to salvage some fragments of that memory. I would subsequently suggest that these novels and their chosen decors represent intensely religious spaces where silence and language fuse into a single, mystical phenomenon requiring reverent attention. Both texts correspondingly emerge as powerful psychodramas in which the protagonists confront those challenges posed by the dichotomous reality of madness, and the fragile nature of memory.

LE CREPUSCULE, AU LOIN

"Pedro. Est-ce toi, Dieu?" (VC, 134); "Pedro, are you God?" (TBW, 115). This simplistic query resounds across the second half of *La Ville de la chance* and echoes yet again in Wiesel's tenth novel, *Le Crépuscule, au loin.* Pedro, the mysterious alter-ego of *La Ville's* narrator, Michael, is "resurrected" in *Le Crépuscule, au loin,* which represents a unique phenomenon in Wiesel fiction as, with the single exception of the name Moshe, no other has to date been reemployed. As suggested in Chapter Three, the question cited above proffers several significant clues as to the identity of Pedro. There, I had suggested Pedro served a symbolic and metonymic function, namely the transformation of the divine manifestation from the silent *Shaddai* to the communicative form, *Tzur.* Wiesel's choice to incorporate Pedro into the opaque text of *Le Crépuscule* would appear a priori to signal a reintroduction of the mystical, dialogic and restorative qualities of *Tzur* hitherto elicited in *La Ville de la chance.* And yet, as with those biblical tales integrated into his novels, so now does Wiesel provide a host of reversals and contradictions centering upon the reintroduced Pedro. These inconsistencies merit attention.

If Wiesel wishes the reader to identify the Pedro of *La Ville de la chance* with the absent presence of the Pedro of *Le Crépuscule, au loin,* one must wonder precisely why the protagonists themselves are different: Michael in *La Ville de la chance,* Raphael in *Le Crépuscule.* Might such an onomastic alteration merely reflect another ludic aspect common to Wiesel's fiction? As Michael had emerged as a paradigm for humanity soon after the *shoah,* so Raphael represents a similar, significant development. Raphael's name, based upon the Hebrew root *rafa* (רפא) meaning healing/healer, would intimate that fifty years after the nightmare of the Holocaust a movement toward a "healing" of humankind, of the divinity, and of the relationship between them, had commenced.

The reversals in this novel extend beyond the obvious transmutation of narrators' names. In *La Ville de la chance,* Michael had been apprehended and imprisoned. There, he suffered the unique torments of the "prayer," hoping to save Pedro's life. The situation recounted in *Le Crépuscule,* though somewhat analogous to that in *La Ville,* presents notable contrasts. Pedro, who had slipped behind the Iron Curtain in order to locate Raphael's brother, Yoël, has disappeared, conceivably imprisoned. Thus, Pedro has assumed the role of prisoner previously exercised by Michael in *La Ville.* Moreover, in *Le Crépuscule,* Raphael, prompted by an anonymous caller, determines he must enter a mental asylum in order to divine the truth concerning Pedro. Raphael, in becoming a willful prisoner, initiates an action that closes the symbolic circle of reversals propounded in the two texts. Michael, the incarcerated narrator of *La Ville,* becomes Pedro, the mysterious, imprisoned character of *Le Crépuscule;* Raphael, the narrator of *La Crépuscule,* passes from freedom to voluntary confinement in order to discover Pedro, or some trace of his friend. Reversal concludes in a significant intertextual union: God's greatness (Michael: *Who is like unto the Lord*) fuses with divine healing (Raphael: *Healing of God*).

Each manifestation is linked to the other by the absent presence: Pedro. The affiliation of these two narrators, each an orphan whose father had been murdered during the *shoah,* similarly licenses them to inaugurate a penetratingly private quest for the missing father, symbolically represented by Pedro.

This metonymic allusion emphasizes the exegetical meditation that unfolds throughout *Le Crépuscule.* A penetrating silent bond relates these two texts and their narrators, each measuring his particular distance from Pedro, and consequently discovering meaning in life. Michael rediscovers the potent significance of his own name, and recognizes his explicit obligation to reintroduce that power into the shattered, post-Auschwitz world. At *la Clinique de la montagne,* Raphael enters a sort of "holy of holies" where the silent omnipresence of Pedro, his specific mystagogue, conducts the narrator through a chronometry of suffering analogous to the circles of Dante's Inferno. The sundry personalities Raphael encounters, both individually and collectively, evoke excruciating mysteries that have driven them into their derangement. And, at the core of this madness lies the inexplicable silent contradiction between the sense of a just and loving deity, and the evil manifested during the *shoah.*

David Paterson has suggested that one must approach the survivor-author and the fiction she or he creates in the light of Mikhail Bakhtin's theories concerning the narrator-author (22–28). Bakhtine proposes an intimate link between the two, the author's voice frequently becoming that of the narrator. Accordingly, one must accept the notion that Wiesel's voice and the psychology/spirit establishing it become Raphael's. The narrator, his fears, doubts, and faith earnestly reflect those of the author. Entering the asylum represents a corresponding uniquely disturbing means for author-narrator to confront the invisibly silent presence of Pedro. Pedro-*Tzur* possess the key to resolve the apparent discrepancy between God "the consuming fire" (Deuteronomy 4:24), and God, whose fire does not consume (Exodus 3:2), but rather represents mystical communion that announces healing, liberty, and entirety in the divine-human dialogue. Furthermore, *Le Crépuscule's* narrative obliges the reader to penetrate to the crux of the real objective of Wiesel's literature: To represent in words the essence that such representations miss, which is to say, to depict via *l'énonciation* and *la parole* a "presence" that effectively remains unnameable yet simultaneously pursued.

I believe that the primary intent of echoing *La Ville de la chance* in *Le Crépuscule* seeks to extend the emerging dialogue, to draw *Tzur* more comprehensively into this world. But in considering the text, one cannot ignore certain typographical and narrative features that establish parallels with yet another Wieselian novel: *Le Serment de Kolvillàg.* That text is occasionally punctuated by italicized passages signifying the nameless protagonist's interior monologue in which the young man evokes memories of old Azriel who had imparted to the narrator the nonitalicized text that is the tale of Kolvillàg's apocalyptic death. Through these soliloquies, Azriel gains visible and added dimension. They similarly stress the dialogic nature bonding the two first-person narrators: Azriel (roman typography) and the nameless youth (italicized typography). In *Le Crépuscule,* a similar typographical device permits Raphael to invoke and evoke Pedro concurrently[2]. The narrator conveys traces of the enigmatic Pedro, who emerges as a sort of touchstone for the narrator. "Je vais devenir fou, Pedro. Je le sens, je le sais. Plongé dans la folie comme dans la mer, je vais couler, me noyer" (CAL, 11); "I am going mad, Pedro. I feel it. I know it. I have plunged into madness as into the sea. And I am about to sink to its depths" (TW, 11). As the text evolves, these passages, themselves visible representations of a silent dialogue with Pedro's nonpresence, unfold into prayer. Raphael's silent thoughts, this prayer, also allows the narrative itself to be punctuated in a positive fashion.

One visible exercise of silence in Wieselian narrative has been his recourse to *le grand silence typographique-respiratoire.* Wiesel employs this particular device whenever his narratives reach a juncture beyond which language would lose all representational values. That which the author should desire to transmit via the word remains practically ineffable. To press language to such a task would distort it beyond recognition; mimesis would miscarry, the text itself forfeiting its communicative significance. Hence, Wiesel resorts to the typographical pause, a breathing space for author-narrator, as well as for reader-narratee.

As in his other novels, this device appears frequently throughout *Le Crépuscule.* And yet, here Wiesel occasionally uses these white fissures in order to emit the italicized soliloquies, a silent sub-text that escapes from a visible textual wound. Though the primary narrative appears to have reached a point beyond which meaningful communication becomes infeasible, or even absurd, and silence would logically represent the most efficacious response, Wiesel elicits Raphael's "prayer." Like Mallarmé's entrapped swan, this non-gratuitous white hiatus produces a text, itself symbolizing the narrator's silent soliloquy cum prayer. Wiesel similarly demonstrates the creative power inherent in such silence and the purpose it can propound, for these italicized passages do not represent confused mental ramblings, nor verbal nonsense. Through them, the narrator acknowledges and address "the other": Pedro. As such, dialogue is implied, even if "the other's" response remains unperceived. Thus, structurally, *Le Crépuscule* demonstrates a further evolution of silence: The subtle evocation of prayer, a feature again relating this test with its spiritual antecedent, *La Ville de la chance.* In *Man's Quest for God,* Abraham Joshua

Heschel notes: "Prayer may not save us, but prayer makes us worth saving," then further defines prayer as "an invitation to God to intervene in our lives" (15). The formerly blank spaces of *le grand silence typographique-respiratoire* now surge with language, words that consolidate and then soar in these messages to Pedro, a prayer petitioning for strength, guidance, and healing.

Entering the Mountain Clinic, Raphael recalls that " la rédemption divine dépendait de celle des hommes" (CAL, 124); "divine redemption depends upon human redemption" (TW, 100). His extended "prayer" signifies his profound yearning to heal and to be healed. Driven to despair and distraction by the incessant, anonymous midnight caller who has defamed Pedro as "un personnage amoral, immoral. Il m'a fait souffrir" (CAL, 225); "totally amoral. A sadist. He made me suffer." (TW, 179), a being who "mouchardait" (CAL, 238); "was a rat" (TW, 191) and "serait devenu un collaborateur du pouvoir soviétique. Pire: un agent provocateur" (CAL, 247); "[became] a Soviet collaborator. Worse, he was an *agent provocateur*" (TW, 198). Raphael signals his determination to enter the Mountain Clinic in order to ascertain the truth about his friend. In a manner of speaking, Raphael tacitly responds to a silent cry from Pedro whom Raphael senses to be in danger: "Pedro, tu es en danger. Plus qu'avant, plus que jamais. C'est de ma faute. J'ai mal fait en évoquant ton image dans un de mes récits. Tu es devenu visible, donc vulnérable. Tu es devenu une cible" (CAL, 250); "Pedro, you are in danger. More than ever before. And it's all my fault. My portrait of you made you visible. Therefore, vulnerable. You became a target" (TW, 200). Raphael's reaction to this situation signifies the affirmation: *Hinenni,* "Here I am," an existential statement confirming the existence of a vital I-Thou relationship and the recognition of a bond of friendship. As Pedro had previously saved Raphael from the threat of despair, so now does Raphael descend into the depths of incipient madness to rescue his friend.

In *La Ville de la chance,* Pedro assisted Michael in his precarious *descente aux enfers* where the protagonist probed the depths of his psyche for that inner power that would prove to be his salvation. Raphael must similarly descend into an abyss of madness in order to redeem Pedro. Martin Buber recounts the following parable concerning the Hasidic master, Rabbi Shlomo, in his *Tales of the Hasidim: The Early Masters:*

> Rabbi Shlomo said: "If you want to raise a man from mud and filth, do not think it is enough to keep standing on top and reaching down to him a helping hand. You must go all the way down yourself, down into mud and filth. Then take hold of him with strong hands and pull him and yourself out into the light. (277)

Definitive action is required to assist and to heal another. By choosing to penetrate into the poetic madness and silence of the Mountain Clinic, Raphael actively engages reality and simultaneously reflects a significant talmudic citation: the boldfaced go to hell, the shamefaced to paradise. That is to say that those who boldly demonstrate their holiness and adherence to just principles should rightfully descend into the pit in order to save others, to raise up that which has become base. Raphael's endeavors also demonstrate the courage required to attain that level of spiritual healing that Martin Buber labels "inclusion," or that desire to experience the other side of a given relationship. Wishing to discover the truth about his friend, and hoping perhaps to find Pedro at the clinic, Raphael's descent into the kingdom of madness symbolizes the protagonist's efforts to reach that Buberian state of inclusion that can subsequently render his healing efforts more effective.

At the asylum, Raphael encounters eleven madmen, characters whose names and stories suggest the panoply of human history and of the tragic state of the human race. Adam, Cain, the Silent Prophet, Abraham, the Man in the Flames, the Dead Man, the Scapegoat, Joseph, Zelig, the Messiah, and the man who believes he is God. With the exception of Zelig, each inmate represents a biblical incarnation and, as such, represents a shard of the vision of the absurd in the Wieselian literary universe. Each similarly inculcates one of Wiesel's own accusations against God. Raphael similarly recognizes Pedro's direct links to each patient: "Tout ce que je sais, Pedro, c'est que mystérieusement tu es lié à ce malade et à tous les autres" (CAL, 91); "All I know, Pedro, it that in some mysterious way, you are linked to this patient and to all the others"[3] (my translation).

Though the stories recounted by the inmates represent reversals of the biblical tales upon which their names are predicated,[4] though the totality of their collective tale might conceivably be read as a lachrymose vision of Israel's tragic history and of the perplexing nature of theodicy, one must search silence's function elsewhere. Its role in this novel resides in the enigmatic character, Pedro, in his relationship to Raphael, and in the latter's efforts to heal and to reconcile. Above I cited Raphael's recollection that "la rédemption divine dépendait de celle des hommes" (CAL, 124); "divine redemption depends upon human redemption" (TW, 100). Raphael himself recognizes the vital bond between the divine and the human dimensions, and appears to espouse the cabalistic and Hasidic principle that *tikkun olam,* or universal redemption, can only be achieved by humans searching out the hidden elements of the creator, and meaningfully reuniting them.

At the beginning of this chapter, I quoted Wiesel's support for "mystical madness." It would be beneficial at this moment to cite a specific portion of his definition where Wiesel stresses that mystical madness "has only one obsession—*redemption,* only one concern—*one's fellow man*" (AS, 3:253) [my emphasis]. Given the precise context of *Le Crépuscule,* Raphael's decision to enter the Mountain Clinic indicates his willingness to descend into the silent chasm of madness itself: "Je vais devenir fou, Pedro" (CAL, 11); "I am going mad, Pedro"[5] (TW, 11) in order to expose the truth about Pedro's disappearance and his activities in Soviet Russia. Raphael's intended action emphasizes his anxiety for his friend, a fellow human being, and his longing to redeem Pedro. Such an act of redemption should be read as an act of healing. Raphael's engagement in it must similarly be viewed in the light of one soul practicing "inclusion," imagining Pedro's particular reality in a superhuman effort to save him. And yet, perhaps the situation described here might represent the reverse. For example, might the mysterious midnight informant be Pedro himself?

Buber presents a series of Hasidic tales in which the soul to be healed is drawn into a specific circumstance where it learns to become self-sufficient and thereby to emerge whole. As in *La Ville de la chance, Le Crépusucle* hints that Pedro possesses the mystical puissance to decipher the machinations of Raphael's mind. Raphael's inner monologue would then represent a definitive response to that still-small voice perceived by him alone. His decisions and actions, like those of Abraham, Moses, and Samuel, portray reactions to a particular stimulus. His unique manner of answering *Hinenni* to Pedro's silent voice must correspondingly be read as the *where are you?*, a question that constructs a dialogic bridge uniting two human souls. This implied silent dialogue and Raphael's metaphorical query *where are you,* exemplify the narrator's pursuit for God, in this case Pedro-*Tzur,* the communicative essence of the divine that also maintains the power to enlighten Raphael, and to resolve the bitter contradictions surrounding the character and nature of Pedro. More significantly, the narrator's quest clearly and directly becomes associated with the author, the proof lying in Raphael's surname, Lipkin.

This study of silence and the multifaceted roles the phenomenon exercises at a variety of levels in Wiesel's narratives has heretofore underscored the literary and religious connotations reflected in the onomastic element. Though primary attention has focused upon first names, this novel requires an analysis of the protagonist's surname. When European Jews were obliged to adopt "standardized" family names for the purpose of taxation, census, etc., rather than adopting existing surnames, or those that European governments would force upon Jewish families, many Jews reverted to the adaptation of a *kinnui,* defined by Benzion Kaganoff as

> a noun that first appears in the Talmud. It means "surname," "byname," or "substitute name." It derives from the Biblical verb mean-

ing "to give an epithet." In the Middle Ages, Jews made a distinction
between a Hebrew or sacred name *(shem hakodesh)* and a secular
name that related to it in some way. The secular first name is called
the *kinnui*. (126)

The *kinnui* could then easily be accommodated to the vernacular, and hence
into an authentic Jewish surname.

The family name, Lipkin, emerged from a *kinnui* of Eliezer, Wiesel's own first
name, which the author curiously evokes at the conclusion of *La Ville de la
chance,* where it is that of the catatonic youth whom Michael heals, and draws
again into a life of dialogue and meaning. It is highly significant, therefore, that
Wiesel embraces this silent means to link *Le Crépuscule* to *La Ville,* setting them
as complementary texts probing the same mysteries of creation and demanding definitive responses to pressing moral and religious questions.

In his essay "From *Night* to *Twilight:* A Philosopher's Reading of Elie Wiesel,"
John K. Roth proposes the notion that "*Twilight* complements, not to say completes, a quest begun with *Night . . .*" (Cargas, 1993, 73). Though not disputing
his assertion, I would recommend that *Le Crépuscule* complements, or even per-
fects *La Ville de la chance,* both standing as a single and persistent pursuit that
was initially announced in *La Nuit (Night).* Both actively aspire to engage the
creator in meaningful dialogue. *Le Crépuscule* also illustrates the author-narrator's
intense obsession to affect the healing process via the word: "le conteur: il ne
cerche guère à enseigner ni à convaincre, mais à *rapprocher, à créer de nouveaux
liens*" (CH, 11); "the storyteller does not really seek to teach nor to persuade,
but rather *to reconcile, to create new links*"[6] (my translation and emphasis).

Raphael's decision to seek out traces of Pedro at the Mountain Clinic emphasizes the authorial intention to uncover God, and thereby to re-create authentic post-Auschwitz bonds with the creator. In order to achieve that goal, the
author-narrator plunges into the asylum, where the curious parade of individuals initiate Wiesel-Raphael into their private and collective delirium.
Author-narrator participate in the madmen's seemingly unintelligible dialogues with God; and yet, through each encounter, author-narrator gradually
resurrect Pedro's most consequential teaching: "on doit aimer les hommes, on
doit célébrer leur humanité" (CAL, 253); "[Pedro taught me] to love mankind
and to celebrate its humanity" (TW, 201). In the French text alone, author-
narrator states: "J'ai donné ma main à un homme au milieu de l'univers; vous
[informateur] ne réussirez pas à me la faire retirer" (CAL, 253); "I gave my
hand to a man at the center of creation; you [informer] will never succeed in
forcing me to withdraw it" (my translation). The union established through the
word and dialogue, here metaphorically illustrated by the extended hand, will
not be broken, even in the light of that evidence imparted by the mystically

mad inmates of the clinic. Their testimony appears ironically to have reinforced the author-narrator's determination to stand with humanity and with God.

"Et si c'était Dieu qui était fou?" (CAL, 271); "What if it is God who is mad?" (TW, 213). This formidable and disquieting quest is put to Raphael during his ultimate encounter with the man who believes he is God. This tormenting proposition catapults Raphael into a state of tense mutism followed by the imposition of *le grand silence typographique-respiratoire,* silences that initially invite, then draw the reader into the essence of the madman's query. This silence possesses the sort of power reputedly attributed to black holes. Matter, in this instance the vitality of the text together with judgements and beliefs it has instituted with the reader, is swallowed into what appears to be a meaningless void. And yet, the narrative does resume, and in the presence of the inmate who believes himself to be God, author-narrator engage upon a formal and profound exploration of God's necessity of humanity, and humankind's responsibility toward itself, again an analogous situation to that which had concluded *La Ville de la chance.*

"Si Dieu est fou, que nous reste-t-il à espérer?" (CAL, 271); "If God is mad, what hope if there for man?" (TW, 213). The words and silence Raphael has heard while at the clinic would certainly point toward the fatuousness of the assumption that a just, loving deity had initiated creation and brought into being the human race. How could an omniscient, *sane* creator, knowing the barbarity and horror that humanity would perpetrate, have set human history into motion? Or, had the Almighty foreseen such possibilities and had, thereby, been driven mad? Considering such plausible notions, Raphael simultaneously experiences fear and hope. "Tu crois encore en ma bonté, en ma justice? Tu es fou, mon pauvre, eh oui, tu es fou . . ." (CAL, 271); "You still believe in my kindness, my justice? My poor man, you are mad . . ." (TW, 212). One must indeed be insane to maintain belief in God, the creator who remained silent at Auschwitz and, for many, abides in remaining silent while humanity destroys His work.

And yet, the silent subtext that has repeatedly risen to the surface throughout the novel now emerges to become a wholly visible message of hope. The man who believes himself to be God states "il s'agit de ne pas crier pour vous-même. Mais pour autrui. Et *pour moi* aussi" (CAL, 272); "What matters is not to cry for yourself. Cry for others. And *for me* too" (TW, 213) [my emphasis]. Each human is responsible for every other being, for the world in which all live, and exhibiting such a sense of moral obligation will clearly do the will of the Almighty, and will assist in the reunion of the dispersed elements of the divine in creation. Such human enterprise assists in healing creator and His work; it reestablishes the fundamental integrity of creation.

Sitting beside this old madman, Raphael experiences the proximity of the living presence of Pedro, a spirit that signified word, dialogue, and communion. "Comme Adam, je suis interpellé par Dieu" «Où es-tu?» " (CAL, 276); "He feels like Adam, who was asked by God: *Where are you?*" (TW, 215) [my emphasis]. Two diverse, yet intelligible paths silently materialize for Raphael: Like the mad Adam encountered at the clinic, he can beseech God to destroy His creation, eradicating His error; or, like the first Adam, he can strive to renew and to perfect creation.[7]

And the encroaching twilight that brings another night? Like that at the conclusion of Albert Camus's *L'Etranger,* this moment is manifestly charged with signs of transcendency and symbols intimating dialogue and hope. "C'est la nuit. Et le silence. Et la solitude qui . . . n'est pas la vraie solitude" (CAL, 278); "Night. And silence. And this solitude that . . . is not actual solitude"[8] (my translation). In *La Ville de la chance,* Pedro had instructed Michael that silence does not represent a void, but rather embodies the mute presence of God. Such silences are replete with purpose; such silences positively enjoin each individual into the struggle against the "night." So, too, in the concluding paragraphs of *Le Crépuscule,* the evoked silence teams with messianic hope: "De très loin, de très haut, une étoile arrive suivie de tant d'autres" (CAL, 278); "From far away, a star appears [followed by so many others]" (TW, 217) [my addition].

During these instants of epiphany, Raphael unanticipatedly recognizes an acute resemblance between the face of his silent companion and that of another old madman, whom as a child in Europe he would visit every Sabbath in order to "offrir un étincelle de paix" (CAL, 279); "offer a spark of peace" (my translation). Though Wiesel employs the French word *paix* (peace), I hypothesize the Hebrew word *shalom* (שׁלום) underlies his choice, since that term stems from the root *shalem* (שׁלם), meaning *whole.* Moreover, in the present context, I would suggest that *whole* should be read as *healed* or *healthy,* as such a reading permits Raphael's tale itself to become complete. As a child, Raphael's visits to the old man cast him in the role of a healer. That very man to whom Raphael had brought succor had subsequently healed the narrator when he fell ill with typhus. "[Raphael] dut son salut à quelqu'un d'autre" (CAL, 27); "[Raphael] owed his salvation to someone else" (TW, 24). In the evening's emerging silence, Raphael discovers himself at the center of the universe, where he again possesses the power to heal, to repair the rent fabric of dialogue, and conceivably to usher the peace and wholeness, which is the ultimate promise of the messianic era, into creation.

L'OUBLIE

"En hébreu, *Massora*—tradition—provient du verbe *Limsor*—transmettre: être juif, c'est s'insérer dans la tradition pour la transmettre" (CH, 11); "In Hebrew *massora*—tradition— comes from the verb *limsor*—to transmit; being a Jew means putting oneself into the tradition in order to transmit it"[9] (my translation). In many ways, this uncomplicated statement, a sort of injunction, echoes across the pages of Wiesel's 1989 novel, *L'Oublié (The Forgotten)*, as Elhanan, the elder protagonist, senses the onset of Alzheimer's disease. While his memory and mind are imperceptibly silenced, Malkiel assumes the responsibility to gather together the traces and shards of that fading memory in order to incorporate them into his personal and communal tradition. Malkiel must become the keeper of said tradition, and thereby strengthen the weakened chain of memory, transmitting it to future generations.

In the novel's opening passage, "Prière d'Elhanan," the father sounds a primordial Jewish cry: "Dieu de vérité, rappelle-Toi que sans la mémoire la vérité devient mensonge car elle ne prend que le masque de la vérité. Rappelle-toi que c'est par la mémoire que l'homme est capable de revenir aux sources de sa nostaglie pour Ta présence" (OU, 10); "God of truth, remember that without memory, truth becomes only the mask of truth. Remember that only memory leads man back to the source of his longing for You" (F, 12). The silent oblivion into which a patient with Alzheimer's disease descends is indeed the cruelest hell, as she or he no longer recalls the most basic facts: Identity, human relationships somber in a meaningless limbo. One's origins, deeds, triumphs, and failures pass into the *kaf-hakela*, "cet abime où toute vie, toute espérance et toute lumière sont recouvertes d'oubli" (OU, 11); "the chasm where all life, hope and light are extinguished by oblivion" (F, 12). Thus, in one sense, silence exercises a most nefarious and threatening role as it manoeuvers throughout the text to enfold Elhanan in the straitjacket of forgetfulness. Silence correspondingly provides the necessary stimulus for Malkiel to engage upon his profoundly personal crusade to salvage the past, and thereby his own history, before he looses it to the encroaching silence of his father's disease. That quest metamorphoses into a voyage back to his own roots, to that village in the Carpathian mountains where his father had been born, where the grandfather whose name he possesses was buried. Throughout the course of this moving saga, these two men, linked by the evident genetic bond, draw near to one another and validate a unique spiritual bond formed of their common legacy. Wiesel's narrative relates the tales of two parallel lives that slowly draw together, the narrators metaphorically fusing, joining their energies until they become virtually indistinguishable from the other.

This process commences not without difficulty, nor without resistance. Malkiel represents the Second Generation that has attained its maturity in a free and open society. His identity, though rooted in a sense of Jewishness, more fully reflects his American birthright and the rebellious heritage of the youth culture of the late-1960s and 1970s. Silence subtly, metonymically announces the plight of America Jewry and its preference to associate passively with the Jewish experience, rather than engaging it more thoroughly than had previous generations. "C'était tellement simple d'attirer le bonheur; il leur suffisait de faire abstraction du passé, de tourner la page" (OU, 91); "It was so simple to attract happiness; all they had to do was set aside the past, turn the page" (F, 72). For Malkiel, this translated into forgetting his father and the individual and collective history Elhanan symbolized. Yet, once Malkiel acknowledges his obligation to his father as well as to the past, a metaphoric couple—Malkiel/Elhanan—emerges, and permits a transfusion of memory that will only cease when Elhanan's mind enters the definitive chasm of silent oblivion.

By embracing the charge to preserve what he might of his father's memory, Malkiel not only places himself within the Jewish tradition of recording and transmitting, already shown to be of paramount importance for Wiesel and for the Jewish people, but he concurrently projects himself upon his distinctive pilgrimage into his father's world, an existence destroyed by the Holocaust, and yet which remains vital in his father's faltering recollections. By eliciting Malkiel's promise to return to his native Romanian village, Elhanan ensures an additional bond between three generations: his father's, his own, and his son's. For Malkiel, however, the reasons underlying his father's desire for him to return to Europe appear vague, almost inexplicably morbid. Upon his arrival, the Jewish cemetery mutely stands as the sole witness to a once vibrant, productive Jewish community. His ramblings through the tombstones, his encounter with the only surviving Jew, Heshl, the half-crazed drunkard who had been the communal grave digger, frustratingly lead Malkiel on a search for that which can no longer be found. Heshl leads Malkiel to his grandfather's grave and reveals to the youth that his grandfather's funeral had been the ultimate burial in the town, since the entire Jewish community had soon thereafter been deported en masse, never to return. What, therefore, had proved so imperative for Elhanan to entreat his son to return? As a child of a survivor, Malkiel comprehends the immensity of the Jewish tragedy during the *shoah*. Some further rational buried in the dim recesses of his father's failing memory exhorted the promise to discover that which has been lost, that which Elhanan senses had occurred but has subsequently been forgotten.

I believe one must pause at this juncture in order to consider the enigma represented by Wiesel's choice of title for the original French edition: *L'Oublié*. The novel, treating as it does the fragile nature of memory and its humiliating and ruthless disappearance, might have been entitled *l'oubli*. This French noun translates as *forgetting, forgetfulness,* or *oblivion.* Moreover, when dealing with knowledge of any sort—be they by nature factual or merely the daily recognition of persons, places, and events—the word signifies a lapse or failure of memory. Yet Wiesel has opted to employ the past participle of the verb *oublier* (to forget): *oublié* (forgotten). Whether one chooses to view this participle as either masculine or neuter, the verbal form imposes upon the reader certain semantic inferences. First, as Elhanan forgets, he too is forgotten, tragically and ironically erased from his own memory until he will cease to exist for himself. A second reading, more importantly, would refer to something or to some episode that has been forgotten, or that has been transformed into an unmentionable event that strenuously resists all efforts of voluntary memory to bring it to the conscious surface. A French synonym, *innommable,* is defined in *Le Petit Robert* as "that which cannot be named. . . . [something] too vile, too ignoble to be referred to" (my translation). This semantic linkage of *oublié* and *innommable* becomes essential in understanding the novel's title and its action.

Wiesel's intention as represented in the novel's title would thus appear to refer to a particular event whose ontological and phenomenological natures have pressed it into the darkest hollows of Elhanan's mind, where its traces linger in a near-ineffable state. That silent essence, however, does menace Elhanan, who wishes to exteriorize the repressed memory:

> Je suis coupable . . . Voilà pourquoi je suis puni . . . Comme le fils hérétique d'Abouya, j'ai regardé là où il ne fallait pas . . . J'ai vu un péché s'accomplir . . . un crime . . . J'aurais pu, j'aurais dû agir, crier, hurler frapper . . . J'ai oublié nos préceptes et nos lois qui imposent à l'individu de combattre le mal dès qu'il apparaît . . . J'ai oublié qu'on ne doit jamais rester spectateur. . . . (OU, 52)

> I am a guilty man. That is why I am being punished. Like Abuya's heretical son, I gazed when I should not have gazed and turned my eyes away when I should not have. I saw a sin committed . . . a crime . . . I could have, I should have, done something, called out, shouted, struck a blow. I forgot our precepts, our laws, that require an individual to struggle against evil whenever it appears. I forgot that we can never simply remain spectators. . . . (F, 43)

Elhanan expresses a more sinister realization: "Oui, il y avait pire, il y a pire: c'est oublier qu'on a oublié " (OU, 52); "Yes, there was worse, there is worse: to forget that one has forgotten" (F, 43). Do such passages reflect Elhanan's advancing dementia, or do they represent the old man's desperate efforts to rupture the increasingly opaque silence at the core of his being? I opt for the latter, a choice I believe manifests dual intention: first, to effect a priori a comprehensive confession before the collapse of his mental faculties, thereby rendering Elhanan another mute statistic on some register of Alzheimer's victims; second, an urgent bid to transmit to his son the entire truth of his life, replete with his self-professed "crime."

Should such an assertion be condoned, the reader together with Malkiel must query the precise cause for Elhanan's alleged sense of culpability. One plausible explanation could focus on the sensitive proposition of Jewish passivity in the face of the Nazis' murderous racial theories and their extermination policies. Such considerations have merited scholarly attention in a variety of studies. In *La Ville de la chance,* Wiesel himself similarly recounted and, through the voice of his narrator, decried apparent Jewish acquiescence. Such a potentiality, however, could not rationalize Elhanan's onerous remorse, since he had fought with a group of Jewish partisans against the Nazis and their fascist Romanian pawns. He and his fighting comrades ranked among those forces who assisted the Red Army in liberating his native town. Moreover, his partisan brigade had even exacted its own justice by executing the sadistic anti-Semitic leader of the fascist *Niylas.*

Such evidence would ostensibly absolve Elhanan from any degree of blame founded upon Jewish nonresistance. Exploring for plausible textual evidence to justify Elhanan's outbursts, the author has ironically provided a subtle marker. The clue provided resides in the name of another character: Tamar. As has repeated been demonstrated in the course of this investigation of silence, names furnish silent signs, recurrently facilitating a comprehension of, and appreciation for, Wieselian narrative, and various considerations arising from it. In this case, however, the significance does not lie in the name's own translation, but in the metonymic allusion it establishes.

Tamar happens to be Malkiel's fiancée, though he has determined marriage to be unsuitable until he has completed his pilgrimage to Eastern Europe and divined those things forgotten by his father. The explicit context in which Wiesel introduces Tamar resounds with sexual overtones. Malkiel, who is in Romania, considers a sexual liaison with Lidia, his local guide. "Ai-je le droit de m'amuser avec une inconnue?" (OU, 23); "Have I the right to amuse myself with an unknown woman?" (F, 21). His query focuses on the possibility that such a relationship would betray his bond with Tamar. The manner in which this passage conjoins Tamar to sexual desire and a sense of betrayal elicits the radical significance in the choice of the name. The allusion indicates a bond with a biblical tale to which the name is linked and which similarly renders the key to unlocking Elhanan's "forgotten transgression."

The name Tamar emerges in three separate biblical episodes, two of which merit current attention. In the first (Genesis 38:6, 11), Tamar is the wife of Judah's elder sons, Er and Onan, who died prior to her conceiving children. When Judah refused her a third son in marriage, Tamar disguised herself as a prostitute in order to entice her father-in-law to sleep with her, a union that produces twin sons, Perez and Zerah. The second tale (2 Samuel 13, repeated in 1 Chronicles 3:9) relates the rape of King David's daughter, Tamar, by her half-brother, Amnon, and Amnon's consequent murder—the revenge of Tamar's brother, Absalom. Both narratives frankly treat sexual matters; but, it is the second, the rape of Tamar, that imparts the key required to fathom Elhanan's guilt.

While in Romania, Malkiel ascertains his father, while fighting with the Jewish partisans, had witnessed the violent rape of the wife of the chief of the *Niylas,* though she happened to be free of any blame. Her victimization merely represented another barbaric consequence of war. This event and his own reaction to it, both so repugnant to Elhanan's moral sensibilities, have suppressed the rape. Moreover, his silence surrounding it has transformed into a lie. That rape, in French a masculine noun, *viol,* must be viewed as the fundamental element determining the form of the novel's title, namely, the masculine past participial form: *oublié.* Extending this view, by forgetting the event—ironically another masculine noun in French: *événement*—and through an imposed, selective amnesia, Elhanan had ventured to abrogate his own supposed culpability. By endeavoring to forget, he now presumes his punishment lies in absolute oblivion in which he will also be *oublié,* forgotten.

Wiesel has not attempted to establish here so simplistic and almost infantile a construct of "reward and punishment." It is, however, that in exploring the nature of memory and forgetting that the author does sound an alarm against the temptation to forget. The narrative metaphysically announces a weighty injunction incumbent on all humanity to preserve as comprehensive a record as possible of human events despite any logic to the contrary, for human salvation resides in our being able to contemplate that chronicle, and to assimilate that which might serve humankind in avoiding the tragedies of the past. Moreover, for the Jew, for whom the loss of memory represents a principal tragedy, this concept emerges as a religious obligation. Each successive generation bears the solemn duty to transmit intact the message, the biblical rape of Tamar being as representative of a people's history and its underlying ethos as are the prophetic pronouncements or the articulation of the law.

In *L'Aube,* Wiesel's second novel, Elisha faces the prospect of murdering the British officer, John Dawson, to avenge the hanging of several Jewish terrorists. Accepting that role not only establishes the narrator as a murderer but similarly inculpates those women and men who represent the foundations of

Elisha's character. As he becomes a murderer, so are they transformed. Malkiel, learning of his father's "crime," embraces its particular onus. And yet, to achieve a more perfect perception of his father and of the rape itself, Malkiel feels the necessity to encounter the victim, now an old woman.

That confrontation provides Malkiel with another astounding mystery of memory: The profound longing of certain persons to forget. Madame Calinescu emphasizes: "Dieu, dans Sa bonté, m'a aidée à les [les souvenirs de la guerre] effacer de ma mémoire. Vous êtes encore jeune, monsieur. Vous ne pouvez pas comprendre les vertus de l'oubli" (OU, 290); "God in His mercy has helped me erase them [traces of her wartime experiences] from my memory. You're still young, sir. You can't understand the virtues of forgetfulness" (F, 217). This woman represents the antithetical pole of Elhanan, as she has willed herself to forget, whereas Elhanan cannot remember. Malkiel forces her to recall liberation day, and through it, her repressed memories of the rape itself. It is Malkiel who restructures and relates the possible course of events, obliging the woman to relive her humiliation. "De quel droit venez-vous rouvrir mes blessures? . . . Qui vous autorise à forcer ma mémoire? Pourquoi tenez-vous à ce que je me revoie souillée, meurtrie, répudiée dans ma chair comme dans mon âme?" (OU, 298); "By what right do you reopen my wounds? . . . Who authorized you to rifle my memory? Why do you force me to see myself again soiled, bruised, dishonored in my flesh as in my soul?" (F, 222).

This climactic scene casts Malkiel in the ironical and bizarre role of mental archeologist and verbal rapist. He willfully thrusts himself upon the former rape victim in his private obsession to exhume this episode, so critical to his own comprehension of his father, from the sepulchral silence to which it had been consigned by both the victim and Elhanan's advancing disease. Madame Calinescu maintains her mutism with regard to the rape, and that frightening silence obliges Malkiel to construct his own scenario of events through a series of questions. Steadily, through the ensuing silent dialogue that bonds the former victim to Elhanan's son, Malkiel recognizes that his father had been unsuccessful in thwarting his comrade from raping Madame Calinescu, and that he had exhibited compassion toward the woman after the rape. "Grace à lui [Elhanan], il m'arrive de croire que tous les hommes ne sont pas mauvais. Je suis persuadée qu'il était honnête et charitable" (OU, 298); "Thanks to him I believe from time to time that not all men are evil. I believe that he was honest and a man of charity" (F, 223). Had Elhanan sought to obstruct the rape, or had he stood impotent in the face of act and before the victim? Had he abdicated his moral responsibility for others, or had he genuinely acted justly? Action or indifference? The ultimate truth is not revealed but remains forever imprisoned in the silence engulfing Elhanan's mind. And yet, through Madame Calinescu's remark, "he was . . . a man of charity," assuages Malkiel's own sense of guilt, and would appear to justify the physical and metaphysical journey upon which he had embarked.

Might this scene also be construed as a paradigmatic parable focusing upon the necessity and, indeed, upon the moral obligation to remember? I believe such an interpretation not only possible, but similarly marks a probable metonymic reading of the entire narrative. This powerful episode undeniably serves to remind the reader of that particular lesson, as well as to expound upon the mystery of the Holocaust and of life. "Grace à vous [Madame Calinescu], j'ai appris quelque chose d'utile et peut-être d'essentiel: l'oubli aussi fait partie du mystère. Vous avez besoin d'oublier, et je vous comprends; moi, je dois combattre l'oubli, essayez de me comprendre aussi" (OU, 299); "Thanks to you, I've learned something useful and perhaps essential: forgetting is also part of the mystery. You need to forget, and I understand. I must resist forgetting, so try to understand me, too" (F, 223).

This episode eventually dissolves into the stark mutism of *la page blanche,* that silence being broken by Malkiel's recollection of Tamar and of one cause for tension in their relationship, an article authored by Tamar that had been critical of Israeli policies in the occupied territories. Attempting to provide a balanced view of Israel—its need for vigilant self-defense in order to maintain its security and to protect the lives of its citizens, compared with Israel's more aggressive nature toward Palestinians on the West Bank—Tamar's image had articulated certain possibilities, if not a reality that many would have preferred to have remained in silence. Now, however, rather than harboring a sense of disappointment in Tamar's action, Malkiel comprehends its more profound significance.

Before departing for America, Malkiel visits his grandfather's grave. While silently beseeching his grandfather's assistance, Malkiel simultaneously pledges himself to his tradition and heritage according to Elhanan's wishes: "Sa volonté, grand-père Malkiel, moi, Malkiel, ton petit-fils, je l'accomplirai, je te le promets. Ce qu'il a enfui en lui-même, ce qu'il a confié à sa mémoire éteinte, je la révélerai. Je témoignerai à sa place, je parlerai pour lui" (OU, 310); "Grandfather Malkiel: I, Malkiel, your grandson, will fulfill his wishes, I promise you. What he has buried within himself, what he has entrusted to his extinguished memory, I will disclose" (F, 232).

CONCLUSION

"Where wast thou when I laid the foundations of the earth?" (Job 38:4). Thus begins the troubling conclusion of the bewildering Book of Job. Following Job's questions and the lengthy discourse concerning the nature of God and of His justice, the Almighty responds and Job becomes mute: "I am of small account; what shall I answer Thee? I lay my hand upon my mouth" (Job 40:4). The realization that evil may indeed represent a possible manifestation of God encourages two possible human responses: madness or silence. Job opted to become mute before the inexplicable mystery that is the divine.

Le Crépuscule, au loin and L'Oublié are as troubling as the biblical story of Job. Their respective explorations of madness and memory draw the narrators and reader through a veritable mine field of realities that represent the direct heritage of the *shoah,* as well as highlighting the frustrating and frequently tragic inconsistencies inherent in the human condition. Edmond Jabès notes that "l'homme n'existe pas. Dieu n'existe pas. Seul existe le monde à travers Dieu et l'homme dans le livre ouvert" (100); "Man does not exist. God does not exist. Only the world exists through God and Man in the open book" (my translation). Jabès's statement parallels Wiesel's belief that God and humanity acknowledge one another through unique dialogic movement, perhaps the most fundamental aspect of that communication being the question. In the two texts analyzed in this chapter, the narrators like Job challenged chaotic, nihilistic silences by the imposition of their questions, their ultimate purpose being to effect a radical evolution of silence, and thereby to reestablish a cosmos of dialogue.

The Hebrew word for *question* is *she'ela* (שאלה), a noun at whose center stands אל, *El,* one of the names of God. By posing onerous, demanding questions, the narrators of Le Crépuscule and L'Oublié have sought to draw humanity and God into the emerging dialogue. Each narrative in its particular context emphasizes the notion that Wiesel does not simply seek to establish an existence of precarious relevance founded on renewed dialogue wrenched from silence, but signifies a life of messianic significance.

CHAPTER 9

Conclusion

Can you describe this?
A. AKHMATOVA

*How is life with God still possible in
a time in which there is an Auschwitz?*
M. BUBER

braham, Moses, and Samuel perceived the call of the divine and responded *Hinenni*, "here I am." Theirs was not merely a timid response, but a bold affirmation of the mysterious though perceivable presence of "the other," as well as a confirmation of their own existence. Their reply signifies dialogue emerging from previously meaningless silence. Viktor Frankl has professed the following: "Man should not ask what the meaning of life is, but rather he must recognize that it is *he* who is asked" (111). From the silent, murderous chaos of Auschwitz, Elie Wiesel's novels call out to each reader, imploring her or him to answer. The resulting engagement is frequently profoundly disturbing as these texts inexorably draw the active reader into the emerging dialogue, sanctioning life, and establishing an irrevocable sense of moral responsibility.

Penetrating into the literary universe of Elie Wiesel is akin to entering a monastery or to proceeding into the bleak solitude of a desert where one hopes to gain purification by silence. A mystical silence forms the substance of every word he has penned. Silence is its seal; it marks each reader, imprinting its message upon individual minds. The silence of humanity stands in anticipated conflict with the silence of God. But in these silences, Wiesel has sought to derive meaning from nothingness, truth through questions, and hope for the future, in much the same way as the rabbinic sages of antiquity when they compiled the Talmud.

According to Simone Weil, "when literature becomes totally indifferent to the struggle between good and evil, it betrays its essential function and cannot aspire to excellence and greatness" (428) [my translation]. Wiesel's oeuvre seeks to take a position for humanity against evil—and, if need be, against God. He witnessed the Nazi death machine as it silenced the lives of six million Jewish men, women, and children, together with countless other innocent victims. Such malevolent silences can never be expunged from his mind or writings. Yet from that negative, riotous silence have evolved other silences that proved to be regenerative. In breaking that silence, language realizes all that silence would like to achieve but cannot. Thus, language emerges, and from it reverberates a voice arguing for sanity and good.

The Nazis' actions represented the ultimate rebellion of nihilism against all moral emotion and ethical values. In this, silence stands as a negative cancer that sought to extinguish forever the Jewish voice and its ethos. Wiesel's language is anchored in, and nourished by, the silence from which it emerged. The refound voice, tenuous symbol of life, frequently is stifled by the realities of horror and death of the *univers concentrationnaire* that are held at bay by authorial silences. This voice perseveres in its attempt to fashion some way of being heard while preserving silence as an integral part of its message.

The silence of evil that represents humanity's heritage from the *anus mundi* has led Wiesel to formulate his particular challenge and quest. With belief in the ancient traditions of Judaism, he has attempted to discover that path that might lead to universal redemption. Assuming that humankind has been created in the image of God, he then professed his belief that humanity alone in creation possesses moral freedom and will and is uniquely capable of spiritual communication with fellow beings and God. Humanity's moral duty is to decrease suffering through understanding, not to increase it by hatred. Wiesel's ethos endeavors to achieve this primary goal.

The oppressive silences of the *anus mundi* that annihilated the image of humankind and of God are the ones initially encountered in Wiesel's novels. They choke the souls of the protagonists and inhibit their return to a full life. Living in painful exile, these early protagonists longed for death and as solitary, moribund individuals existed as specters on the fringes of life.

Gradually, Wiesel has uncovered meaning in the silences shrouding such characters. Life-giving elements abound, though often hidden from view. Silence provided the positive materials for advancing the Wieselian quest. Each novel unveiled another possibility for reconstructing life after the Holocaust. Wiesel insists on approaching the post-Holocaust human condition from a Jewish perspective. The authentic Jew represents a contemporary everyman, an existentially engaged being whose fate and that of humanity lie in her or his hands. Thus, Wieselian protagonists have undertaken to unveil and revoice those hidden keys, then to offer them as affirmations of life by silently presenting to their fellow beings the gift of friendship.

Dialogue emerges as central to Wiesel's quest for meaning after the Holocaust. As Martin Buber stresses: "Fully mature dialogue is a real bridge of the gap between man and man so that each partner can see the meeting and its situation not only from his own side but from the other's as well" (*Between Man*, 97–98). The potentiality for dialogue lies hidden in all aspects of silence in Wiesel's novels. The protagonists strove to wrench meaning and truth from it. Dialogue extends hope in the expectation of reestablishing a semblance of validity in a world gone mad. It will allow human beings to rise above the barbaric degradation of the *anus mundi* and inch toward God, even challenging Him, if need be. In dialogue, each individual becomes a complete person, a living being possessing unique characteristics, and a vital force that is then ushered into the world. This represents one of the most pressing evolutions of silence in Wiesel's work.

Dialogue itself is frequently threatened by the resurrection of hatred, bigotry, and death, or even by a world that would prefer to forget the truth and remain deaf to the refound voice. Such factors must be combatted, and Wiesel's oeuvre has done that. Silence became a tool or a weapon for fighting indifference and forgetfulness. For Wiesel, humanity must seek out the silenced facets of Good and the deformed image of God and the truth behind them: "not by the love of God . . . but out of his own love for God" (Szklarczyk, 1978, 145) [my translation]. To find the hidden, silent God of Auschwitz, Wiesel postulates that one must first save one's fellow beings. But how is salvation possible when "all is mystery on 'Planet Auschwitz'?" (SE, 121) [my translation]. The questions that may eventually lead to redemption are born from the degrees of silence found in Wiesel's texts. As the events are wrenched from the abyss and truth voiced to warn humanity, one can view Wiesel's oeuvre and the accompanying theme of silence on which it is constructed as an act of faith: Faith in humanity's perfectibility despite Auschwitz; faith in God despite His silence.

APPENDIX A

Cultural Anti-Semitism

According to Bernard-Henri Lévy: "L'antisémitisme est consubstantiel à la culture française;" "Anti-Semitism is consubstantial to French culture" (*Le Monde*, "Dossiers et documents: L'Antisémitisme," 103: juillet, 1983: 4) [my translation]. His view may appear unduly harsh, but the evidence collected over the centuries overwhelmingly supports his thesis, and indeed extends it, for anti-Semitism is an element of all European cultures. Thus, Wiesel's depiction of violent anti-Semitism may be seen as reflecting the European milieu in which he lived, and in which the majority of his novels are set.

Though the term anti-Semitism was only coined in 1879 by Wilhelm Marr, its origins extend beyond the medieval period into the years directly following Jesus's mission in Judea. The Jewish Wars (66–74 C.E.) and the Bar Kochba Revolt (132–35 C.E.) resulted in anti-Jewish policies being implemented in the Roman Empire, especially during the reign of Hadrian. These anti-Jewish attitudes were adopted by the early Church, so that by 321 with Constantine's acceptance of Christianity as the empire's official religion, these prejudices, concepts, and claims of the early Church fathers were instituted and practiced as state policies. Jews were excluded from high office, from the military, and in certain areas of the Roman world were even prohibited from owning real property. The Church came to view itself as *Verus Israel*, the true Israel, and the continued existence of the Jewish people constituted a contradiction to the Church and the Roman world.

From the sixth to the tenth centuries, the Church moved to separate Jewish and Christian communities, a notion interpreted more violently from the beginning of the eleventh century, when Jews were physically persecuted and eventually expelled from various kingdoms in Christendom. With the First Crusade in 1096, Christian policy was transformed into one of vengeful violence as Crusaders massacred whole Jewish communities en route to the Holy Land.

The Fourth Lateran Council of 1215, while establishing the doctrine of transubstantiation, aided in the evolution of two new myths of the guilt of the Jews: First, the existence of Jewish plots to desecrate the Host; and second, the blood libel. The Church professed its dogmatic belief in a universal Jewish conspiracy against Christ and all Christians. Eventually, it obliged Jews to wear a "Jewish badge," thus rendering them physically obvious, a move that evolved into the popular belief that Jews were anatomically different. This notion further evolved into a doctrine of *foetor judaicus,* "the Jewish smell," which was the converse of the Christian "odor of sanctity."

These Church doctrines persisted and became the basis for numerous popular stereotypical images of the Jew. Luther's strong anti-Semitic sentiments found fertile ground in Germany, eventually spreading to many other areas of Protestant Central Europe. By the sixteenth century, a statement by Erasmus, himself a Roman Catholic and contemporary of Luther, demonstrates the severe anti-Jewish emotions he discovered in European society: "If it is incumbent upon a good Christian to detest the Jews, then we are all good Christians."

The age of enlightenment heard appeals for Jewish emancipation, notably in France from Montesquieu and Rousseau. Other philosophers, such as Diderot, D'Holbach, and Voltaire, continued to propose anti-Semitic beliefs. Voltaire especially held the view of the Jew's intellectual inferiority and inability to reason or to formulate logical thought. Many of his ideas became fundamental to modern anti-Semitic notions of the Jew's alien nature and unwillingness to coexist with non-Jews in society.

The nineteenth century further refined the former stereotype of the Jew as alien. Theodor Herzl, the founder of modern Zionism, considered European anti-Semitism a form of xenophobia that the Church initially had introduced and encouraged. The growing nineteenth-century nationalist movements had no role for the alien Jew, even in societies where Jews had been emancipated. Full assimilation was encouraged, yet even when the Jew opted for this, he was still viewed as a stranger and a source of defilement, a bearer of those elements that threatened society. The socialists perceived the Jew as the progenitor of capitalism, while the capitalists saw him as the originator of socialism.

The nineteenth century and the early years of the twentieth century witnessed a proliferation of "scientific" and scholarly studies that postulated several major anti-Semitic innovations—the conspiratorial nature of the Jewish people and of their religion, the racial inferiority of the Jew, and the innate Jewish desire to enslave the world. Many of these texts were written in France, the most virulently anti-Semitic being Arthur de Gobineau's

L'Essai sur l'inégalité des races (1853–55), Edouard Drumont's *La France juive* (1886), and Louis-Ferdinand Céline's *Bagatelle pour un massacre* (1937), among some of the more infamous. But France was not alone, as H. Steward Chamberlain's *Die Grundlagen des neunzehnten Jahrhunderts* (1899) and the anonymously written *Protocols of the Elders of Zion* (*ca.* 1895) reflect similar social attitudes across Europe.

Culturally transmitted prejudices represent a fact of life, and examples range from attitudes concerning women to those of a religio-racial nature. Wiesel's depiction of the howling anti-Semitic mob in *Les Portes de la forêt* is an accurate portrait of this phenomenon. His presentation of two other characters in that novel, Maria and Petruskanu, on the other hand, reflects another aspect of European behavior: The willingness of various individuals to defend Jews' right to life and to civil equality. Similar behavior was demonstrated in France by Emile Zola and other Dreyfusards during the Dreyfus Affair, as well as by scores of men and women in Nazi Europe, the so-called "Righteous Gentiles," who risked life and limb to save Jews. Nevertheless, a culturally determined European Judaeophobia remains an inescapable historical and sociological fact.

APPENDÌX B

The Kaddish

More than most other prayers from the Jewish liturgy mentioned in this study, the kaddish has appeared in a prominent role several times. For the majority of Jews the kaddish exerts a strong emotional power, as it is considered primarily as a prayer for the dead. Its general importance in Jewish religious and social life cannot be disputed, which explains the prayer's repetition in so many of the novels (*e.g., La Nuit, Les Portes de la forêt, Le Serment de Kolvillàg,* and *Le Testament d'un poète juif assassiné*). So that the reader may fully appreciate these references to it, the following translation is offered:

READER:
Magnified and sanctified be His great name in the world which He hath created according to his will. May He establish His Kingdom during your life and during your days, and during the life of all the House of Israel, even speedily and at a near time, and say ye, Amen.

READER AND CONGREGATION:
Let His great name be blessed for ever and to all eternity!

READER:
Blessed, praised and glorified, exalted, extolled and honored, magnified and lauded be the name of the Holy One,

READER AND CONGREGATION:
Blessed be He;

READER:
Though He be high above all the blessings and hymns, praises and consolations, which are uttered in the world; and say ye, Amen.

May the prayers and supplications of all Israel be accepted by their Father who is in heaven; and say ye, Amen.

May there be abundant peace from heaven, and life for us and for all Israel; and say ye, Amen.

He who maketh peace in His high places, may He make peace for us and for all Israel; and say ye, Amen.

It should be noted that each time the reader says "And say ye, Amen," the congregation responds by saying "Amen."

APPENDIX C

Notes on Cabala

Cabala—Jewish mysticism—apprehends God as primarily a transcendent spirit called *AYIN,* Hebrew for *no thing,* as God is beyond our perception of existence. God is absolute nothingness, a parallel to the nothingness to which other mystics allude when relating their experiences with the Godhead. The *AYIN* is the transcendent God whose features evolve into the *AYIN-SOF,* Hebrew for *without end,* the term used for God the immanent, the absolute all. Within a cabalistic/Jewish framework, the paradoxical existence of God the transcendent/God the immanent manifests the act of *zimzum,* or creative contraction, which underlies all aspects of God and His creation.

Zimzum first reputedly manifested itself when God contracted Himself, withdrawing a portion of His light and thus creating a void into which He projected the *KAV,* a beam of creative light that represented the divine will. The *KAV* called our universe into being. The act of *zimzum* represents a seeming contradiction without which there would have been no creative process, no cosmic development. As Gershom Scholem states in *On the Kabbalah and Its Symbolism:* "God's withdrawal into Himself . . . makes possible the existence of something other than God and His pure essence" (111). *Zimzum,* therefore, initiates the cosmic drama, its reality underlining the inherent contradictions in the world. Its existence provides the fertile matrix for continued creation with the contradictory elements reacting in conflict, or in tandem in attempts to regain the harmony that is found in the *AYIN-SOF.*

The task of the cabalist is to harmonize these contradictions of existence in imitation of the *AYIN-SOF,* absolute perfection, which contains no distinctions, no differentiations. The cabalist must seek out the elements of God in creation, or as Scholem notes in his study, *Kabbalah:* "Only through the finite nature of every existing thing, through the actual existence of creation itself, is it possible to deduce the existence of the *Ein-Sof* as the first finite cause" (89).

When the *AYIN-SOF* willed creation and the *KAV* penetrated the void, the divine will manifested itself in ten distinct "tools" or "vessels", the *SEFIROT*. The *SEFIROT* represent the divine attributes, elements of the eternal divinity that exist in creation. Together, the *SEFIROT* create a Tree of Life with the various aspects balancing each other as they descend into the world. The *SEFIROT* are normally considered to zigzag like a lightning flash toward the center of the void, the direction being determined and guided by three unmanifest divine principles, the Hidden Splendors.

The ten *SEFIROT* emanate from the highest to the lowest degree. Each *SEFIRA* (*sing.*) has a distinct meaning and, in descending order, they are:

SEFIROT:	*COMMONLY ACCEPTED MEANING:*
Keter:	Crown
Hohma:	Wisdom
Bina:	Understanding
Hesed:	Mercy
Gevura:	Judgement
Tiferet:	Beauty
Neza:	Eternity
Hod:	Reverberation
Yesod:	Foundation
Malhut:	Kingdom

From *KETER,* which stands at the top, the *SEFIROT* proceed down to the right, then across to the left, back to the right, etc., a flash of lightning that is in perfect balance until it reaches *YESOD,* which then forces the *KAV* directly down to *MALHUT.*

The mystics believed the search for and the contemplation of these *SEFIROT* would result in reunion with God, for as the ancient sages noted in the *Sefer Yezira,* a mystical book about Creation, "ten *sefirot* out of nothing. Ten not nine. Ten not eleven. Understand this in Wisdom and in Wisdom understand. Enquire and ponder through their meaning, so as to return the Creator to His Throne" (10–11) [my translation]. That God is not on His throne would appear to indicate another manifestation of *zimzum* at play in the universe. If God is not on His throne, where is He? The key is found in the notion of exile, for the total scope of cabala deals with the problem of God's and Israel's exiles, of the hope of messianic redemption and of the transfiguration of this world. As Scholem says in *On the Kabbalah:* "At the heart of this reality [Cabala] lay a great image of rebirth, the myth of exile and redemption" (2). According to the cabalists, God exists in exile. The tenth

SEFIRA, MALHUT has been given feminine qualities. This forms a parallel to the notion of the *SHEHINA,* the in-dwelling of God in this world. For the cabalists, the *SHEHINA* evolved into an aspect of God, a semi-autonomous, feminine element of God. Since the destruction of the Second Temple and the beginning of Israel's exile, the *SHEHINA* has remained in exile. The male Godhead and the female *SHEHINA* seek to be reconciled with one another, to join again in a sort of matrimonial harmony. At midnight, God, like pious Jews and students of Cabala, mourns the exile of the *SHEHINA.* At the same moment, the *SHEHINA* in Her exile likewise mourns, though her laments become songs and hymns to Her spouse. Through their actions, the cabalists believed they could help effect a reunion, and thus usher in the messianic age of redemption. In order to hasten and facilitate the reunion of God with the *SHEHINA,* as well as with the nation of Israel, the cabalists of Safed formulated a complex midnight rite: The rite of Rachel (lamenting the exile), and the rite of Leah (hope for redemption). Through these ceremonies, they hoped to encourage reunion.

The in-gathering of all aspects of *ASIYYA,* or spiritual and pure creation, to construct a state of permanent, ecstatic communion between all elements of the universe and God, where demonic powers will remain impotent, lies at the heart of Cabala. This process is called *TIKKUN.* Wiesel poses the following question in *Contre la mélancolie:* "Quel est le sens du *tikkoun,* la réparation mystique?"; "What is the significance of Tikkun, mystical reparation?" —to which the following reply is offered:

> C'est d'être attentif à ce qui arrive autour de vous; c'est en aidant autrui que vous vous aidez vous-même. Vous désirez servir Dieu? Servez ses enfants. Partagez vos trésors, votre mémoire avec eux. La connaissance meurt si elle n'est pas partagée; et la foi aussi. Et tout le reste. (CM–CH, 21)

> It is to be concerned not only with yourself but with everything that goes on around you; help others and you will help yourself. You want to serve God? Start with serving His children. Knowledge is to be shared, as is faith, and everything else.(SM, 21)

TIKKUN represents humanity's responsibility to perfect creation through the performance of small acts of ingathering and redemption. Humankind becomes the keystone of salvation, and its activities must, as Scholem stresses, "struggle with and overcome not only the historic exile of the Jewish people but also the mystic exile of the *Shehinah*" (143).

NOTES

Introduction

1. In the course of my arguments, I shall limit the use of the term Holocaust either because it recalls religious rites and sacrifice or because it decays into contemporary newspeak and cliché (*Cf.*, Alain Finkielkraut, *L'Avenir d'une négation: Réflexion sur la question du génocide*, 79–85). I shall prefer to use the terms *anus mundi, l'univers concentrationnaire, shoah,* or Auschwitz with reference to the Holocaust as they signify the universal absolute evil perpetrated by humanity with God as silent accomplice

2. Heinrich Himmler, Speech of October 4, 1943 in *International Military Tribunal at Nuremburg,* Volume 29, Document PS 1919, 145. *Cf.* the analysis of this particular speech by Saul Friedlander, *Reflets du nazisme,* 103–107. See also its use as *point de départ* for the arguments of Charlotte Wardi in *Le Génocide dans la fiction romanesque,* 5.

3. *La Nuit* first appeared in a more lengthy Yiddish version, *Un di Velt Hot Geshvign* (*And the World Remained Silent*), published in Buenos Aires in 1956 as a memorial to a language and civilization that had been Wiesel's heritage before the Nazi annihilation.

Chapter 1

1. I shall use the term *l'énonciation* as the "something else" placed in opposition to silence in the course of my arguments. I have chosen this particular French term, as it encompasses the fundamental semiological notions of speech (*la parole*), the word (*le mot*) and their inherent linguistic qualities as manifested in a text, as well as how their effective confluence can result in silence.

2. The Greek god was called Harpocrates, the Roman one Angerona.

3. When God addresses humanity, it is commonly in a silence from which a voice is perceived. See also J. Patrick Dobel, "Liturgical Silence," *Commenweal,* 106 (August, 1979): 430–31, 434–35; and Steven S. Schwarzschild, "Speech and Silence Before God," *Judaism* (1961): 195–202 for a Christian and Jewish perspective on this topic. Both articles provide adequate references to additional sources.

4. *Cf.* the 1520 edition of Erasmus's *Adagia* for his views on silence. Many of his ideas had been gleaned from those proposed by Plutarch in the latter's essay, *De garrulitate: Moralia-VI* (Cambridge, MA: Harvard University Press, Loeb Classical Library, 1970), 396–467.

5. The Jewish community has adopted two terms for the Nazi genocide: The Yiddish word *hurban* and the Hebrew, *shoah.* The former has been employed with reference to the destruction of the two Temples at Jerusalem and connotes an impression of the violation of religious and sacrificial life within the Jewish community. The latter term has a biblical antecedent (Job 30:3) and refers to widespread, and even cosmic disaster. Neither term even vaguely suggests sacral associations.

6. Scholem's notion, though demonstrating a universally critical approach to the analysis of any given text, has evolved from a particular Jewish exegetical tradition based primarily on rabbinic interpretation of Exodus 3:15, normally translated as "This is My

Name forever and this is My Memorial for all generations." The Hebrew construct *forever* is spelled with the same radicals as the verb *to be hidden*. The talmudic commentators initially stated that the name of God, the tetragrammaton, is hidden and hence the rabbis developed laws prohibiting the pronunciation of the Name. Their reasoning then proposed that as the word *universe* was the basis for the adverbial construction *forever*, they deduced one had an obligation to seek out God and truth, which were hidden in all existent things in the universe. Human beings, therefore, possessed the unique responsibility to probe all veils that might hide God and thus revoice concealed elements of Creation.

7. The term I employ here, translated as *primary typographical-respiratory silence*, has evolved from certain facets of Ludovic Janvier's arguments about the novels of Samuel Beckett in *Pour Samuel Beckett*.

8. Neher's use of *métaphysique* in his more lengthy arguments appears to conform to Sartre's definition of the term in *Situations, II*, where the latter states: *"la métaphysique n'est pas une discussion stérile sur les notions abstraites qui échappent à l'expérience, c'est un effort vivant pour embrasser du dedans la condition humaine dans sa totalité"* (251).

9. In his study *Elie Wiesel: A Challenge to Theology*, Graham B. Walker, Jr. entitled his first chapter "The Grammar of Silence" where he proposes: "A *grammar* is the formal study of the systems which underlie a language. The language that we are investigating is the language of *silence*. . ." (13). Walker does not then proceed to offer an analysis either of silence or of the systems of silence developed by Wiesel in his oeuvre.

Chapter 2

1. Elie Wiesel, Préface in Ber Mark, *Des Voix, iv*. This preface has been collected and published in *Signes d'exodes*, 116–22. *Cf.*, Jean-Pierre Faye, "La Raturée" in *L'Interdit de la représentation*, 121–28.

2. George L. Mosse extends Frankl's view in *Crisis of German Ideology* where he states: "Once a population had accepted this depiction of the Jew (*i.e.*, a depersonalized abstracted creature without a soul or moral, emotional or ethical content), it was possible to regard him as a cipher, as a figure that aroused no human compassion" (302).

3. The silence of the Allies has long posed a rather demanding question for historians, moralists, and philosophers. Wiesel's own views are clearly delineated in *Le Chant des morts*, 178–89, 201–10. It is ironic that this sort of complicity and incredulity was precisely what Hitler had hoped for. The humanist traditions of European civilization would never allow people to believe in the possibility of systematic, technological mass murder of the Jews or of any other group of so-called "undesirables."

4. *Menuha* was the final divine act of creation. The ancient rabbis puzzled over the paradox provided by the text of Genesis 2: 2–3: "On the seventh day God finished His work". The rabbis recounted: "What was created on the seventh day? Tranquility, serenity, peace and repose" (Genesis Rabbah 10:9). The Hebrew word for these qualities is *menuha*.

5. Similar reactions can be found in Jewish folklore, the most famous example being I. L. Peretz's "The Shabbes Goy." Edward Alexander believes that these sorts of stories "impute to the Jewish people a deep-seated unwillingness to credit the fact that they [Jews] have enemies, and that these enemies are capable of murder; a deep-seated unwillingness, ultimately to credit the existence of evil" (4). Beyond the purely Judaic parameters, consider the following view of Antonin Artaud in *"Van Gogh le suicidé de la société"* where he states: *"Car un aliéné est aussi un homme que la société n'a pas voulu entendre et qu'elle a voulu empêcher d'émettre d'insupportables vérités"* (Tome XIII, 17).

6. Such negative reversals must be seen as the effect of the *anus mundi* upon biblical tale. *Cf.*, Lawrence S. Cunningham, "Elie Wiesel's Anti-Exodus" in *Responses to Elie Wiesel*,

23–28 where Cunningham proposes such a reversal in his discussion of *La Nuit*. He believes the story represents an anti-Exodus, one in which the majority of the biblical elements are negated, reversed, or silenced. Sadly, his brief study does not fully develop the complexities and nuances of this theme.

7. This particular scene has served as a point of departure for numerous examinations of the theological implications for Christians and Jews in Wiesel's first novel.

8. It must be noted that in the greater part of rabbinical literature and commentary, Isaac is not seen as the innocent youngster iconographically depicted throughout the ages, but rather as a fully mature man of thirty-seven who realizes precisely what would transpire and what God expected of him. Jewish commentaries can be found in Genesis Rabbah, Rashi's commentaries, and those of Ibn Ezra.

9. Compare the original French text (NAJ, 135) and its English translation (N, 134). Note that Frances Frenaye's translation offers striking stylistic and morphological variations from the original Wieselian manuscript. This particular example highlights how in the delicate balancing act between sound and sense, which is the art of translation, essential elements of the original are permanently transfigured. Moreover, the elements of silence in this particular passage are more readily visible and sensed in the original than in the translation.

10. The title of Wiesel's third novel is radically altered in English. The title is derived not from its French, *Le Jour* (the day), but from the central action of the story ("the accident") and thus breaks the pattern set by its predecessors, titles that followed the pattern of a day: *Night* and *Dawn*.

11. The Holocaust has created the trauma of survivor guilt par excellence. In the years since the events, psychologists and psychiatrists in Israel, America and Western Europe have carried out extensive research on various groups of survivors. Their results have produced a mass of evidence as to the existence and extent of various degrees of "survivor guilt." The most comprehensive research bibliography in this field has been compiled and edited by Dr. Leo Eitinger, *Psychological and Medical Effects of Concentration Camps* (Haifa: University of Haifa Press, 1981).

Guilt for having survived is not uniquely linked to the Jewish experience during the *shoah*. It is a universal sentiment that received moving expressions in the poetry of the First World War, as well as similar expressions of guilt among survivors of the atomic blasts and among soldiers who had fought in Vietnam.

12. See Brice Parain, *Essai sur la misère humaine*, 158–59, 217–26 where he investigates the origin of the lie, and unfolds additional psychological and linguistic complexities.

13. Wiesel places great weight and ontological significance upon names. In *Le Jour*, Gyula's name stresses the notion of redemption as expressed in Jewish liturgy. גאלה, the Hebrew word, appears in numerous guises. The most quoted biblical passage in which it occurs is Isaiah 59:20: "a redeemer shall come to Zion." The very concept of redemption forms a portion in the daily prayers of Judaism. For example, beginning at the conclusion of the Shema (the Jewish profession of faith) and extending to the words "Blessed art Thou. . .Who has redeemed Israel," the main theme is past and future redemption. On Passover, this notion of redemption is extended and deepened in a series of prayers referred to as *Geulla piyyutim* that are recited in conjunction with the Geulla prayers of the daily liturgy.

14. The biblical foundation for this assertion can be found in Genesis 24:63 with additional rabbinic commentary found in the Talmud, Berakhot 26b–27a, as well as in the commentaries of Rashi and Ibn Ezra.

Chapter 3

1. The noun, *teshuva*, evolved from the Hebrew verb *to return*, which has a high frequency of usage in the prophetic writings (e.g., Hosea 3:5, 6:1, 7:10; Jeremiah 3:7, 12, 14, 22; Amos 4:6, 8-11; Ezekiel 18:23; *et al.*). Erich Fromm in his book *You Shall Be As*

Gods points to the profound significance of *teshuva*: "A man who repents is a man who 'returns.' He returns to God and to himself" (132). The *mahzor** continually reminds the Jew to return as Man is capable of altering a seemingly predestined determination. *Cf.*, Avodah Zarah 17a–b for Talmudic views on *teshuva*.

2. The literary device of the *descente aux enfers* is commonly used to enable a character to know himself or herself through encounters with shades from the past. Past and future meet in a present that produces an elucidation of great importance. Homer and Virgil employed it; even the Old Testament produces its own version in First Samuel 28:3–25. From the Romantic period onward, authors have resorted to this technique as a means for characters to learn more about themselves and their world. It has been given special treatment in French literature: Nerval in *Aurélia*, Balzac in *Le Colonel Chabert*, Proust in *A la recherche du temps perdu* merely being some of those writers who have benefitted from this "learning process." It should be noted that Dante has been conspicuously omitted from this brief listing, as it is my contention that his work is rather a reflection of the medieval religious tradition, and is thus removed from the classical and Romantic traditions in which the *descente aux enfers* serves as a personal learning process.

3. The moment of *teshuva* is not dictated in Judaism since a return can be effected any time one sincerely wishes to undertake such a spiritual journey. But Jewish tradition does set aside a forty-day period of introspection, which begins in the month of Elul (corresponding to the conclusion of the summer season and one month prior to the High Holy Days) and is then followed by the *yomim ne'orim*, the Ten Days of Awe, culminating in Yom Kippur.

4. *Cf.*, the remarks in the Talmud, Ta'anit 16a, which reflect this view. One honors and remembers the dead "in order that the dead should intercede for mercy on your behalf."

5. The *yotzer* prayer is not unique to Yom Kippur. The daily *shaharit* includes the *yotzer* that proclaims God as the creator of lights and luminaries in the universe. The medieval rabbis, notably Rabbi Meshullam ben Kalonymos, "the Great," (tenth century) added the moving *oz b'yom kippur* prayers at this point in the service as a plea for the light of forgiveness, the light of understanding, the light of life.

6. In the month of Elul, congregations commence the blowing of the shofar, thus seeking to wake sinners from their sleep in "evil" ways and to set right their course. *Cf.*, the commentaries of Maimonides in his *Mishneh Torah*, Teshuva 3:4, 5:1–2, 4.

Chapter 4

1. In order to dehumanize people, the Nazis systematically robbed individuals of their names. This was especially true in the case of Jews, a fact that recurs in most accounts of survivors. *Cf.*, Wiesel's remarks at the Thirty-Ninth General Assembly of the Council of Jewish Federations and Welfare Funds when he stated: "Yes, the names are important in Judaism. It is no coincidence . . . that the first thing the Germans did to Jews . . . was to rob them of their names" (*From Holocaust to Rebirth*, 12).

2. *Cf.*, Sartre's remarks about Jews in his essay *Réflexions sur la question juive*, 108–12, where the question of *authenticité* and *inauthenticité* in the Jewish character is discussed.

3. In Hebrew, the word for angel is *malah* (מלאך) which actually signifies a messenger, a role certainly fulfilled by Gavriel. In fact, the entire first episode of *Les Portes de la forêt* reflects certain aspects of a midrashic tale about Abraham. The patriarch's mother, fearing her husband would kill their child, concealed her pregnancy and eventually bore the baby in a cave where she left the infant in the care of the angel

---

*mahzor: literally meaning cycle, the word applies to the prayer book for the Jewish New Year, day of Atonement, and the three pilgrimage festivals as they mark the cycle of the year.

Gabriel. Gabriel nourished and educated the child and came to serve as direct intermediary between God and the future patriarch. In particular ways, Gavriel in this novel serves as God's messenger and a teacher of eternal values.

4. See Appendix A for a detailed note concerning the phenomenon of culturally transmitted anti-Semitism.

5. The proposition that Judas is the paradigm of the Jew cannot be lightly dismissed. The New Testament's doctrinal and historical approach to Judas is one that sets him apart and carefully draws undeniable parallels between the archetypal traitor and the Jewish people. As Hyam Maccoby states: "That it was Judas who was chosen for this role rather than one of the other Apostles cannot be unconnected with the fact that his name functioned as the eponymous characterization of the Jewish people and is derived from the patriarch and the tribe of Judah. The treachery of Judas Iscariot thus symbolized the treachery of the Jews (Judah) as a whole" (127).

Moreover, the various aspects of Judas's character perfectly reflect the Church's teaching about the Jews. Both are children of the devil, Judas being thus identified in John 6:70: "Have I not chosen you, all twelve? Yet one of you is a devil," while the Jewish people are so denoted in John 8:44: "Ye are of your father's desires." In Matthew 26:14–16 and John 12:4–6 and 13–19, Judas is characterized by his avariciousness, a notion extended by the Church to the Jewish people, or as Maccoby notes: "This idea no doubt contributed to the medieval and modern anti-Semitic picture of the Jew as a grasping miser" (130). These identical qualities permit the equating of the character of Judas with that of the Jew. Thus, within the context of the novel, a particular syllogism can be constructed in which Grégor's acceptance of the role of Judas permits him to become the paradigm of the Jew, of the Jew as suffering servant of God, and to recognize this fact and, hence, to struggle to alter this condition.

6. In *Réflexions sur la questions juive*, Sartre says of the Jew who seeks to renounced his Jewishness: "*Mais il ne peut pas choisir de ne pas être Juif. Ou plutôt s'il le choisit, s'il déclare que le Juif n'existe pas, s'il nie violemment, désespérément en lui le caractère juif, c'est précisément en cela qu'il est Juif*" (108). We might therefore view Grégor's present metamorphosis as inevitable and eventually leading him back to his Jewishness.

7. Jewish tradition almost wholly rejects the notion that God could actually have fought Jacob. The Halachic* and Aggadic† traditions propose that the stranger was an angel of the highest order. As Rabbi Dr. David Goldstein states: "A most common midrashic view is that Jacob's opponent was none other than the angel Michael, who was later to become the guardian-angel of Jacob's descendants, the House of Israel. Michael was anxious to return to Heaven before the sun rose so that He could join the angelic ranks as they sang praises to their God" (79). Yet another interpretation points to the opponent's being an evil being, as he is frightened by the light of the approaching dawn. Some Jewish commentators therefore believe him to be Esau's guardian angel, Samael, one of the powers of darkness.

Ellen Fine has argued that in Jewish Aggadic tradition, this figure identified as the "dark antagonist" is the angel Gabriel, a notion that would appear to set well with the novel's story. However, I have found no corroborative evidence in the Midrashic or other Jewish sources to support her thesis. *Cf.*, Fine, 1982, 85. See also Genesis Rabbah 78:1 and the Talmud, Haggigah 14a, which expressly contradict Fine's statements.

Halachah: one of two distinct elements in the Talmud. *Halachah*, literally *walk, way,* or *rule,* is the rabbinic exposition of law that concerns itself with ritual, social, and economic life of both the community and the individual.

†*Aggadah:* the other distinctive talmudic element. The *Aggadah*, literally *narrative*, consists of history, stories, fables, legends, etc. and possesses no coercive power of legal importance.

8. *Cf.*, Ellen Fine, 1982, 88, where she proposes the following hypothesis: "His [Grégor's] long night in the cave recalls Jacob's night wrestling with the angel at Peniel." The fact that Grégor and Gavriel pass more than one night together, and the relative passivity of Grégor as Gavriel unveils the truth about the Holocaust, seem to refute her own statement. I do agree with her that the biblical story, *i.e.*, the struggle at Peniel, underlies the novel as a whole, but Fine overlooks the ultimate moment of conflict when the struggle and "naming" reach their inevitable climax (PF, 216–32; GF, 204–21).

9. *Cf.*, Genesis 33:1: "And Jacob lifted up his eyes. . . ." Though his name has been changed, the former self continues to exist. The events of Peniel altered Jacob's life and his future, but his past cannot be changed, even by an encounter with God.

10. See Appendix B for the text of the kaddish.

Chapter 5

1. The most comprehensive and comprehensible lay study of Cabala is Gershom Scholem's *Kabbalah* (New York: Quadrangle/The New York Times Book Company, 1974). See also Appendix C for a definition of those particular terms and ideas germane to discussions of Cabala in this study.

2. The *even shetiyya* is the massive stone on the Temple Mount in Jerusalem over which the Muslim shrine, the Dome of the Rock, has been constructed. Both Judaic and Islamic legends assert this to be the point from which creation began and view it as the center of the world.

Chapter 6

1. Engel has taken issue with the prevalent view that Kolvillàg does not stem from a particular authorial etymological game predicated upon joining two languages, Hebrew and Hungarian, but rather believes the name ought to be perceived as deriving exclusively from the Hungarian: *Kül villàg*, or the world beyond. (Engel, 1989, 116–17). Such a reading undeniably offers engaging insights and permits Kolvillàg to be linked with its German name, Klausberg. I believe, however, such an approach to be flawed. If Engel's desire is to distinguish in such an intrinsic bond between the German and Hungarian names an evocation of the author's and/or Jews' fears of the world beyond, of the various menaces (anti-Semitism and assimilation) it afforded the Jewish community, one must ignore the evolving universalist nature of Wiesel's message. Engel similarly provides no substantive ties between his Hungarian-German reading of the town's onomastic significance and the name in other languages (e.g., *Virgirsk* in Russian). Moreover, I believe such a proposed understanding would deprive the tale of its allegorical, fairytale atmosphere, evoked as it is by the phrase: "Il était une fois, il y a longtemps . . ." (SK, 9); "Once upon a time, long ago . . ." (O,3), for it is principally in that milieu that the union of the Hebraic and Hungarian (*viz.*, non-Hebraic) world, both fundamental to Wiesel's own past, encounter one another in this apocalyptic narrative.

2. In direct opposition to the fatalistic nature of apocalyptic literature and the writings of the Qumran Essene community, one finds prophetic and rabbinic Judaism emphasizing the notion that cosmic history can be made to respond to human action by means of repentance and good deeds. *Cf.*, Talmud, Baba Batra 164b, Berakot 55a, and Yoma 85b and 86b for discussions of the importance of repentance and its application in both human and divine affairs.

3. The accusation of ritual murder, or the blood libel, is perhaps the most persistent and insidious fabrication leveled against the Jewish people. The myth proposed that Jews would kidnap a young non-Jewish child, fatten him or her, then ritually murder him or her to obtain blood for various Passover rituals and foods. The earliest references to such calumnies are found in Josephus's *Antiquities*. It was, however, under the influence of the Church that the blood libel entered the popular mythology of European thought. The first distinct case occurred in Norwich, England in 1144 when a boy,

William, was alleged to have been tortured and ritually murdered for his blood. The list of places where the blood libel has been leveled against Jews encompasses all of Europe, North Africa, and the Middle East. Such cases have indeed been reported in the twentieth century, and it was a common fable used by the Nazis in their anti-Semitic propaganda, especially in Julius Streicher's newspaper, *Der Stuermer*.

4. *Cf.*, "Entretien," *Tribune juive*, 6–17, as well as Wiesel's own views concerning nuclear peril in *Paroles d'étranger* (102–07) and *Signes d'exode* (188–98).

5. The term *Pinkas* is derived from a Hebrew word for book or notebook. In the Jewish communities of Central and Eastern Europe, such books maintained the records and histories of Jews in a particular town or region.

6. The revelation at Sinai is reputed in the Jewish Aggadic tradition as having been transmitted in silence. *Cf.* Rabbah 29:9.

7. The Jewish preoccupation with setting down the course of history with great exactitude stems from two biblical injunctions concerning the ruthless attack of the Amalekites on the Israelites. In Exodus 17:14 one finds "And the Lord said unto Moses: 'Write it for a memorial in the book;'" and in Deuteronomy 25:19 one reads "Thou shalt not forget." Together, these two verses have served as the impetus for the veritable religious fervor with which Jews have recorded all aspects of their historical and religious experience.

8. E. M. Cioran proposed in *La Tentation d'exister* that because the Jews have effectively been the universal moral conscience for two thousand years it has marked them out for persecution. The Nazis' fury against the Jews, he feels, represented their sense of frustration over this fact. Cioran likewise proposes that the Nazi failure to achieve such universalism as had the Jews merely fuelled their own prejudices and hatreds. (101) Moshe's plan would seek to rescue the Jews from this exact position, an action reminiscent of the belief Freud records in his essays *Moses and Monotheism*, namely that Moses had not been a Hebrew but rather an Egyptian who had imposed a legalistic system on the liberated Israelites. Freud and Moshe would appear to be desirous of absolving the Jews of the responsibility to act as the universal moral conscience.

Chapter 7

1. The term *Second Generation* refers to those children born to Holocaust survivors after the war.

2. *Cf.* Blanchot, *L'Espace littéraire*, 310. This notion of the reader actively engaging in dialogue with a fixed, printed text, a reading that produces something wholly new, has gained significant adherents among contemporary literary critics and scholars.

3. The proposition that the plastic arts are capable of communicating with the viewer is a proposition more completely developed by André Malraux in *Les Voix du silence* and, with particular reference to photography, in two seminal essays by Roland Barthes: "Le Message photographique" in *Communications* 1 (1961): 127–38, and "Rhétorique de l'image" in *Communications* 4 (1964): 40–51. *Cf.*, Wiesel's earlier expression of this idea in "Dodye Feig, un portrait." (UJA, 67–74)

4. *Tefillin* (תפלין), or phylacteries, are two small black wooden boxes with leather straps attached. Inside each are found verses from the Pentateuch: Exodus 13:1–10, 11–16; Deuteronomy 6:4–9; 11:13–21. The *tefillin* are worn by observant Jews during the morning prayers, except on the sabbath and festivals. One is placed on the forehead between the eyes, the other on the left arm by the heart. The wearing of *tefillin* should impose a serious frame of mind and prevent levity during prayer. The complete laws for the wearing of the *tefillin* are found in the Talmud, Menahot 34a–37b and repeated in the *Shulhan Aruh*.

Chapter 8

1. Irving Halperin explores the shrinking limitations of space in Wiesel's first four novels in "From *Night* to *The Gates of the Forest*: The Novels of Elie Wiesel" (45–82) in *Responses to Elie Wiesel*, edited by Harry James Cargas.

2. Significant discrepancies in the use of these italicized passages exist between the French and English texts. Compare, for example, pages 86–87 in the original with pages 71–73 of the translation. Though employed more frequently in the English, the essence is nevertheless preserved in the French by lengthy blocked paragraphs that often begin with the verb *se dire* (to say/tell to oneself).

3. Marion Wiesel's translation of this passage ignores the conclusion of the original: *et à tous les autres*, a remark that extends Pedro's animus and directly joins him to all the inmates.

4. Rosette Lamont has provided a superb analysis of the patients and their tales in her essay, "Elie Wiesel's Poetics of Madness" in *Elie Wiesel: Between Memory and Hope* (130–51), edited by Carol Rittner.

5. The French and English texts, though communicating similar ideas, demonstrate semantic differences. The French verb form *Je vais devenir*, the *futur immédiat/futur proche*, signifies an intention or future direction into madness (*I am going to become/ to go mad*). The English translation does not communicate that intention.

6. The original introduction to *Célébration hasidique* is not provided in the English translation.

7. The introduction of the biblical Adam at this point in the novel draws another interesting parallel with *La Ville de la chance*. See *infra.*, pp. 81–82.

8. Significant and troubling differences exist in the concluding passages between the original French text and its English translation. As in some of his other novels, Wiesel more directly confronts the issue of silence and employs it to advantage in French as opposed to the English translations.

9. See note 6.

BIBLIOGRAPHY

PRIMARY SOURCES

IN FRENCH

Wiesel, Elie. *Célébration biblique: Portraits et légendes.* Paris: Les Editions du Seuil, 1975.
————. *Célébration hassidique: Portraits et légendes.* Paris: Les Editions du Seuil, Collection Points/Sagesses, 1972.
————. *Le Chant des morts.* Paris: Les Editions du Seuil, 1966.
————. *Le Cinquième fils.* Paris: Bernard Grasset, 1983.
————. *Contre la mélancolie: Célébration hassidique, II.* Paris: Les Editions du Seuil, 1981.
————. *Le Crépuscule, au loin.* Paris: Bernard Grasset, 1987.
————. *Entre deux soleils.* Paris: Les Editions du Seuil, 1970.
————. *Un Juif aujourd'hui.* Paris: Les Editions du Seuil, 1978.
————. *Le Mendiant de Jérusalem.* Paris: Les Editions du Seuil, 1968.
————. *La Nuit - L'Aube - Le Jour.* Paris: Les Editions du Seuil, 1969.
————. *L'Oublié.* Paris: Les Editions du Seuil, 1989.
————. *Paroles d'étranger.* Paris: Les Editions du Seuil, 1982.
————. *Les Portes de la forêt.* Paris: Les Editions du Seuil, 1964.
————. *Le Serment de Kolvillàg.* Paris: Les Editions du Seuil, 1973.
————. *Signes d'exode.* Paris: Bernard Grasset, 1985.
————. *Le Testament d'un poète juif assassiné.* Paris: Les Editions du Seuil, 1980.
————. *La Ville de la chance.* Paris: Les Editions du Seuil, 1962.

IN ENGLISH

Wiesel, Elie. *Against Silence: The Voice and Vision of Elie Wiesel.* Edited by Irving Abrahamson. New York: Holocaust Library, 1985.
————. *A Beggar in Jerusalem.* Translated by Lily Edelman and Elie Wiesel. New York: Random House, 1970 [*Le Mendiant de Jérusalem*].
————. *The Fifth Son.* Translated by Marion Wiesel. New York: Summit, 1985 [*Le Cinquième fils*].
————. *Five Biblical Portraits.* Notre Dame, Indiana: Indiana University Press, 1981.
————. *The Forgotten.* Translated by Marion Wiesel. New York: Summit, 1992 [*L'Oublié*].
————. *From the Kingdom of Memory.* Various translators. New York: Summit, 1990.
————. *The Gates of the Forest.* Translated by Frances Frenaye. New York: Holt, Rinehart and Winston, 1968 [*Les Portes de la forêt*].
————. *A Jew Today.* Translated by Marion Wiesel. New York: Random House, 1979 [*Un Juif aujourd'hui*].
————. *Legends of Our Time.* Translated by Steven Donadio. New York: Holt, Rinehart and Winston, 1968 [*Le Chant des morts*].
————. *Messengers of God.* Translated by Marion Wiesel. New York: Random House, 1975 [*Célébration biblique*].

————. *The Night Trilogy: Night, Dawn, The Accident.* Various translators. New York: Hill and Wang, 1985 [*La Nuit - L'Aube - Le Jour*].

————. *The Oath.* Translated by Marion Wiesel. New York: Random House, 1973 [*Le Serment de Kolvillàg*].

————. *One Generation After.* Translated by Lily Edelman and Elie Wiesel. New York: Random House, 1972 [*Entre deux soleils*].

————. *Somewhere A Master.* Translated by Marion Wiesel. New York: Summit, 1982 [*Contre la mélancolie: Célébration hassidique, II*].

————. *Souls on Fire: Portraits and Legends.* Translated by Marion Wiesel. New York: Random House, 1972 [*Célébration hassidique*].

————. *The Testament.* Translated by Marion Wiesel. New York: Summit, 1981 [*Le Testament d'un poète juif assassiné*].

————. *The Town Beyond the Wall.* Translated by Steven Becker. New York: Atheneum, 1964 [*La Ville de la chance*].

————. *Twilight.* Translated by Marion Wiesel. New York: Summit, 1987 [*Le Crépuscule, au loin*].

SECONDARY SOURCES

A. M. G. "Nous sommes tous des mendiants," *La Terre retrouvée*, 15 février 1969, n.p.

Alexander, Edward. *The Resonance of Dust: Essays on the Holocaust and Jewish Faith.* Columbus: Ohio State University Press, 1979.

Alter, Robert. "The Apocalyptic Temper." *Commentary* XLI (1966): 61–66.

Alvarez, A. *Beyond All This Fiddle.* London: Allen Lane, 1968.

Artaud, Antonin. *Oeuvres complètes, Tomes IV et XIII.* Paris: Gallimard, 1964.

Bakhtin, Mikhail. *Esthétique et théorie du roman.* Translated by Daria Olivier. Paris: Gallimard, 1978.

Barthes, R., F. Bovon, F.-J. Leenhardt, R. Martin-Achard, J. Starobinski. *Analyse structurale et exégèse biblique.* Neuchâtel: Delachaux et Niestlé Editeurs, 1971.

Barthes, Roland. *Le Degré zéro de l'écriture, suivi de Nouveaux essais critiques.* Paris: Les Editions du Seuil, 1972.

————. *Essais critiques: Le Bruissement de la langue.* Paris: Les Editions du Seuil, 1985.

————. "Le Message photographique." *Communications* 1 (1961): 127–38.

————. "Rhétorique de l'image." *Communications* 4 (1964): 40–51.

Beauvoir, Simone de. "Littérature et métaphysique." *Les Temps Modernes* (avril 1946): 1154–55.

Berenbaum, Michael. *The Vision of the Void.* Middletown, Connecticut: Wesleyan University Press, 1979.

Bettelheim, Bruno. *The Informed Heart: Autonomy in a Mass Age.* London: Thames and Hudson, 1961.

Blanchot, Maurice. *L'Ecriture du désastre.* Paris: Gallimard, 1980.

————. *L'Espace littéraire.* Paris: Gallimard, 1955.

Buber, Martin. *Between Man and Man.* Translated and introduced by Roland G. Smith. Glasgow: William Collins Sons and Co., 1979.

————. *I and Thou.* Translated and annotated by Walter Kaufmann. New York: Charles Scribner's Sons, 1970.

————. *Tales of the Hasidim: The Early Masters.* Translated by Olga Marx. New York: Schocken, 1961.

Butler, Dom Cuthbert. *Western Mysticism.* London: Constable and Company, 1951.

Camus, Albert. *Essais.* Paris: Gallimard, Bibliothèque de la Pléïade, 1965.

Cargas, Harry James. *Harry James Cargas in Conversation with Elie Wiesel.* New York: The Paulist Press, 1976.

————, editor. *Responses to Elie Wiesel: Critical Essays by Major Jewish and Christian Scholars.* New York: Persea Books, 1978.

————, editor. *Telling the Tale: A Tribute to Elie Wiesel*. St. Louis: Time Being Press, 1993.

Carlyle, Thomas. "The Poet as Hero: Dante; Shakespeare" in *English Critical Essays: The Nineteenth Century*. Selected and edited by Edmund D. Jones. Oxford: Oxford University Press, 1965.

Cioran, E. M.. *La Tentation d'exister*. Paris: Gallimard, 1956.

Daubenhauer, Bernard. *Silence: The Phenomenon and Its Ontological Significance*. Bloomington, Indiana: Indiana University Press, 1980.

Dobel, J. Patrick. "Liturgical Silence." *Commonweal* 106 (August, 1979): 430–35.

Des Pres, Terrence. *The Survivor: An Anatomy of Life in the Death Camps*. New York: Simon and Schuster/ Pocket, 1977.

Eckardt, A. Roy, and Alice L. Echardt. *Long Night's Journey Into Day*. Detroit: Wayne State University Press, 1982.

Edelman, Lily. "A Conversation with Elie Wiesel." In *Responses to Elie Wiesel*. Edited by Harry James Cargas. New York: Persea, 1978.

Eitinger, Leo. *Psychological and Medical Effects of Concentration Camps*. Haifa: University of Haifa Press, 1980.

Engel, Vincent. *Fou de Dieu ou Dieu des fous: L'oeuvre tragique d'Elie Wiesel*. Bruxelles: De Boeck-Wesmael, 1989.

"Entrtien avec Elie Wiesel." *La Tribune juive* 192 (1972): 16–19.

Estess, Ted. *Elie Wiesel*. New York: Frederick Ungar Publishing Company, 1980.

Ezrahi, Sidra DeKoven. *By Words Alone: The Holocaust in Literature*. Chicago: University of Chicago Press, 1980.

Fine, Ellen. *Legacy of Night: The Literary Universe of Elie Wiesel*. Albany: State University of New York Press, 1982.

Franck, Jacques. "Judaisme: Ils ont refait leur âme." *La Libre Belique* (16 avril 1980): 16.

Frankl, Viktor. *Man's Search for Meaning*. London: Hodder and Stoughton, 1964.

Finkielkraut, Alain. *L'Avenir d'une négation: Réflexions sur la question du génocide*. Paris: Les Editions du Seuil, 1982.

Freud, Sigmund. *The Pelican Freud Library*. Volume 8. London: Penguin, 1985.

Friedlander, Saül. *Reflets du nazisme*. Paris: Les Editions du Seuil, 1982.

Friedman, Maurice. *To Deny Our Nothingness: Contemporary Images of Man*. New York: Delacorte Press, 1967.

Fromm, Erich. *You Shall Be As Gods*. New York: Fawcett, 1977.

Garbarz, Elie, and Moshé Garbarz. *Un Survivant*. Paris: Plon, 1984.

Genette, Gérard. *Figures I*. Paris: Les Editions du Seuil, 1966.

Goldstein, Rabbi Dr. David. *Jewish Folklore and Legend*. London: Hamlyn, 1980.

Gracq, Julien. *Liberté grande*. Paris: José Corti, 1946.

Greenberg, Irving, and Alvin Rosenfeld, editors. *Confronting the Holocaust: The Impact of Elie Wiesel*. Bloomington: Indiana University Press, 1978.

Haft, Cynthia. *The Theme of Nazi Concentration Camps in French Literature*. Paris: Mouton, 1973.

Hauer, Chris. "When History Stops: Apocalypticism and Mysticism in Judaism and Christianity." In *The Divine Helmsman: Studies on God's Control of Human Events*, edited by J. L. Crenshaw and Samuel Sandmel. New York: Ktav, 1980.

Heimler, Eugene. "Beyond Survival: An Interview with Elie Wiesel." *European Judaism* 6 (1) (1971–72): 4–10.

Herman, E. *The Meaning and Value of Mysticism*. London: James Clarke and Company, 1916.

Heschel, Abraham J. *Between God and Man: An Interpretation of Judaism*. Selected, edited and introduced by Fritz A. Rothschild. London: Collier Macmillan Publishers, 1959.

————. *God in Search of Man: A Philosophy of Judaism*. New York: Farrar, Straus and Giroux, 1955.

————. *Man's Quest for God: Studies in Prayer and Symbolism*. New York: Charles Scribner's Sons, 1954.

Hoffman, Edward. *The Way of Splendour: Jewish Mysticism and Modern Psychology.* London: Shambhala Press, 1981.

Jabès, Edmond. *Le Retour au livre* Paris: Gallimard, 1965.

James, William. *The Varieties of Religious Experience.* London: Longmans, Green and Co., 1952.

Janvier, Ludovic. *Pour Samuel Beckett.* Paris: Editions de Minuit, 1966.

Kaganoff, Benzion. *A Dictionary of Jewish Names and Their History.* New York: Schocken, 1977.

Knopp, Josephine. "Elie Wiesel: Man, God and the Holocaust." *Midstream* 27 (7) (1981): 45-51.

———. *The Trial of Judaism in Contemporary Jewish Writing.* Urbana, Illinois: University of Illinois Press, 1975.

———. "Wiesel and the Absurd." *Contemporary Literature* 15 (2) (1974): 212–20.

Kronfeld, David Allen. "The Mad Character in Modern Literature." Ph.D. diss., Brown University, 1978.

Lévinas, Emmanuel. *Ethique et infinité.* Paris: Gallimard, 1982.

———. *Humanisme de l'Autre Homme.* Montpellier: Fata Morgana, 1972.

———. *Noms propres.* Montpellier: Fata Morgana, 1976.

———. *Otherwise Than Being; or, Beyond Essence.* Translated by Alphonso Lingis. The Hague: Nijhoff, 1981.

———. *Quatre lectures talmudiques.* Paris: Editions de Minuit, 1968.

Lévy, Bernard-Henri. "Dosiers et documents: L'Antisémitisme," *Le Monde* 103 (juillet, 1983): 4.

Lifton, Robert Jay. *Death in Life: Survivors of Hiroshima.* New York: Vintage, 1967.

———. *The Nazi Doctors: Medical Killing and the Psychology of Genocide.* New York: Basic, 1986.

Maccoby, Hyam. *The Sacred Executioner: Human Sacrifice and the Legacy of Guilt.* London: Thames and Hudson, 1982.

Mallarmé, Stéphane. *Oeuvres complètes.* Paris: Gallimard, Bibliothèque de la Pléiade, 1945.

Maloney, G. A. "Creative Power of Silence." *New Catholic World* 219 (March, 1967): 58–63.

Malraux, André. *Les Voix du silence.* Paris: Gallimard, 1951.

Mandelstam, Ossip. *Selected Poems.* Translated and edited by Clarence Brown and W. S. Merwin. London: Penguin, 1977.

Mauriac, François. *Oeuvres romanesques et théâtrales complètes, Tome II.* Paris: Gallimard Bibliothèque de la Pléiade, 1979.

Melville, Herman. *Collected Poems.* Edited by H. P. Vincent. Chicago: Packard and Company, 1947.

Memmi, Albert. *La Libération du juif.* Paris: Gallimard, 1966.

Merleau-Ponty, Maurice. *Problèmes actuels de la phénoménologie.* Paris: Desclée de Brouwer, 1952.

Mintz, Ruth, editor. *Modern Hebrew Poetry.* Berkeley: University of California Press, 1968.

Mosse, George. *The Crisis of German Ideology.* New York: Grosset and Dunlop, 1964.

Neher, André. *L'Exil de la parole: Du silence biblique au silence d'Auschwitz.* Paris: Les Editions du Seuil, 1970.

———. *Jérusalem, Vécu juif et message.* Monaco: Editions du Rocher, 1984.

———. "*Shaddai:* The God of the Broken Arch (A Theological Approach to the Holocaust)." In *Confronting the Holocaust: The Impact of Elie Wiesel.* Edited by I. Greenberg and A. Rosenfeld. Bloomington, Indiana: Indiana University Press, 1978.

Ortega y Grasset, José. *The Dehumanization of Art and Other Essays on Art, Culture and Literature.* Princeton: Princeton University Press, 1968.

Panikkar, Raimundo. "The Silence of the Word." *Cross Currents* 24 (1974): 154–71.

Parain, Brice. *Essai sur la misère humaine.* Paris: Bernard Grasset, 1934.

————. *Petite métaphysique de la parole*. Paris: Gallimard, 1969.

Parry, M. "The Theme of Silence in the Writings of François Mauriac." *Modern Language Review* 71 (October 1976): 788–800.

Paterson, David. *The Shriek of Silence: A Phenomenology of the Holocaust Novel*. Lexington: University of Kentucky Press, 1992.

Picard, Max. *The World of Silence*. Translated by Stanley Godman. South Bend, Indiana: Regnery/ Gateway, Inc., 1952.

Plutarch. "De garrulitate." In *Moralia, VI*. Cambridge, Massachusetts: Harvard University Press, Loeb Classical Library, 1970.

Preston, John. "The Silence of the Novel." *Modern Language Review* 74 (April, 1979): 257–67.

Rawicz, Piotr. *Le Sang du ciel*. Paris: Gallimard, 1961.

Reischek, Morton. "Elie Wiesel: Out of the Night." *Present Tense* 3 (3) (1976): 41–47.

Rittner, Carol, editor. *Elie Wiesel: Between Memory and Hope*. New York: New York University Press, 1990.

Rousseau, Jean-Jacques. *Essai sur l'origine des langues*. Texte établi et annoté par Charles Porset. Bordeaux: Guy Ducros, Editeur, 1968.

————. *Oeuvres complètes*, Tomes I et III. Paris: Gallimard, Bibliothèque de la Pléïade, 1964.

Rousset, David. *L'Univers concentrationnaire*. Paris: Les Editions de Minuit, 1965.

Rubinstein, Rabbi A. L. *A Companion to the Machzor*. Gateshead: J. Lehmann, 1972.

Sartre, Jean-Paul. *Réflexions sur la question juive*. Paris: Gallimard, 1954.

————. *Situations, I*. Paris: Gallimard, 1947.

————. *Situations, II: Qu'est-ce que la littérature?*. Paris: Gallimard, 1948.

Scholem, Gershom. *Kabbalah*. New York: Quadrangle/The New York Times Book Co., 1974.

————. *The Messianic Idea in Judaism*. New York: Schocken, 1971.

————. *On the Kabbalah and Its Symbolism*. New York: Schocken, 1972.

Schwarzschild, Steven. "Speech and Silence Before God." *Judaism* (1961): 195–202.

Sefer Yezirah. Jerusalem: no publisher indicated, 1889.

Szklarczyk, Lillian. "Le Juif démoli en quête de soi." *Stanford French and Italian Studies*, 10 (1978): 133–46.

Sontag, Susan. "The Asthetics of Silence." In *Styles of Radical Will*. New York: Farrar, Straus and Giroux, 1976.

Steiner, George. *In Bluebeard's Castle: Some Notes Towards the Redefining of Culture*. London: Faber and Faber, 1971.

————. *Language and Silence*. Oxford: Oxford University Press, 1967.

Thibaud, Paul. "La Mémoire d'Auschwitz." *Esprit* 45 (septembre 1980): 3–4.

Triganov, Shmuel. *Le Récit de la disparue: Essai sur l'identité juive*. Paris: Gallimard, 1977.

Trilling, Lionel. *The Liberal Imagination*. New York: Viking, 1950.

Valéry, Paul. *Oeuvres, Tome II*. Paris: Gallimard, Bibliotèque de la Pléïade, 1960.

Walker, Graham. *Elie Wiesel: A Challenge to Theology*. Jefferson, NC: McFarland Inc., 1988.

Wardi, Charlotte. *Le Genocide dans la fiction romanesque*. Paris: Presses Universitaires de France, 1986.

Weil, Simone. "La Responsabilité des écrivains." *Cahiers du Sud* 310 (1951): 426–30.

Wells, Leon, *The Janowska Road*. New York: Macmillan, 1963.

Wiesel, Elie. "Jewish Values in the Post-Holocaust Future: A Symposium." *Judaism* XVI (Summer, 1967): 266–99.

————. "The Fiery Shadow—Jewish Experience Out of the Holocaust." In *Jewish Existence in an Open Society*. Los Angeles: Anderson Ritchie and Simon, 1970.

————. *From Holocaust to Rebirth*. New York: The Council of Jewish Federations and Welfare Funds, 1970.

————. "The Holocaust as Literary Inspiration." In *Dimensions of the Holocaust: Lectures at Northwestern University*. Evanston, Illinois: Northwestern University Press, 1977.

————. "The Jerusalem of David," *The New York Times*, 18 April 1982, 15–16.

Williams, David. "Exile as Uncreator." *Mosaica* 8(3) (1975): 1–4.

Wittgenstein, Ludwig. *Tractatus Logico-Philosophicus*. Translated by D. F. Pears and B. F. McGuinness. London: Routledge and Kegan Paul, 1961.

INDEX

A

Abraham (biblical) 10, 42-44, 81-82, 84, 160, 173
Adam (biblical) 81, 82, 84, 86, 163, 192
adam [אדם] (Hebrew word) 111
Akeda 42-44
Alter, Robert 119
Alzheimer's disease 164, 166, 167
"Angel" 149
anonymous son (*Le Cinquième fils*) 144, 145, 146, 147, 148, 149
anus mundi (see also Auschwitz, Holocaust, *hurban, shoah, univers concentrationnaire*) 1, 5, 23, 25, 33, 37, 38, 42, 45, 46, 50, 53, 65, 76, 84, 94, 95, 99, 105, 106, 108, 111, 116, 123, 127, 144, 145, 148, 174, 175
in *L'Aube* 46
in *Le Jour* 50
in *Le Mendiant de Jérusalem* 106
in *La Nuit* 35-44
in *Les Portes de la forêt* 86, 91, 94
in *Le Serment de Kolvillàg* 123
negative silence of 22-24, 76, 83-84, 94-96
transmission in literature 25
Apocalypse 118
in *Le Serment de Kolvillàg* 120-121, 129-131
apocalyptic literature
traditional 118-119
Wiesel's approach 119
Ariel (character) 145, 148, 149 150
Artaud, Antonin 103, 186
Aube [*The Dawn*] 44-49, 50, 105, 169

auffallen 146
Auschwitz 3, 5, 6, 7, 20, 21, 22, 23, 24, 25, 30-31, 35, 36, 38, 39, 40, 49, 57, 59, 87, 89, 95, 120, 127, 128, 144, 145, 146, 153, 156, 161, 162, 173, 175
in *La Nuit* 35-44
in *Les Portes de la forêt* 88, 94-95
(see also Holocaust, *hurban, shoah, univers concentrationnaire*)
autre/Autre (see also "Other") 66, 78, 79
Autrui 46
Azriel (character) 118, 120-123, 126, 127, 129

B

Bakhtin, Mikhail 156
Barthes, Roland
exegesis of Genesis 32:23-33 97-99
problematics of language 14
temporal nature of silence 17
voice as life 38
Beauvoir, Simone de 5, 24
Becker, Stephen 75
Berenbaum, Michael 54-55, 56, 109, 125-126
beth din 95-96
Bettelheim, Bruno 95, 102
biblical tales 40, 42-44, 72, 73-75, 97-99, 101, 159
Birkenau 27, 35, 37
Blanchot, Maurice 45, 46
impact of Holocaust 20, 46
power of silence 12
blancs (see *grand silence typographique-respiratoire*)

blood libel (ritual murder) 119, 123, 190
Bratslaver Hasidim 137
Buber, Martin 13, 15, 86, 87, 158, 159, 160

C
Cabala 103, 104, 108-111, 114-116, 182-184
Camus, Albert 5, 24, 66, 137-138, 143, 163
Cayrol, Jean 36
Célébration biblique [*Messengers of God*] 42-43, 44, 55-56, 82, 86, 88
Chagall, Marc 103, 115
Cinquième fils [*The Fifth Son*] 132, 133, 144-150, 151
   father-son relationship 145-150
Cioran, E. M. 4, 57, 99, 117, 191
Clara (character) 90, 99, 101
communism/communist party 137-139, 140, 141
Crépusucule, au loin [*Twilight*] 154-164, 171
cultural anti-semitism 177-179

D
David (character) 104, 109, 110, 111-116
Dawson, John (character) 47-48
dédoublement (psychological doubling) 29, 149
descente aux enfers 63, 76, 90, 138, 188
dialogue 7, 29, 73, 83, 84, 86-87, 88, 92-93, 102, 121-122, 130-131, 161-162, 163, 171, 173, 174-175

E
Eitinger, Leo 146
Elhanan (character) 164-170
Eliezer (character)
in *La Nuit* 36, 37-38, 39-44, 49-50, 57, 161
in *La Ville de la chance* 83
Elijah (biblical) 9, 77
Elisha (biblical) 77

Elisha (character) 45, 46, 47-49, 57, 68
Endlösung 1-2
Engel, Vincent 117, 190
énonciation 11-12, 15, 17, 26, 30, 121-122, 156, 185
Erez Yisrael 110
Estess, Ted 32, 43, 96

F
fasting 64
father-son relationships
in *Le Cinquième fils* 133-134, 144-146, 148, 150, 151
in *La Nuit* 42-44,
in *L'Oublié* 164, 165, 169, 170
in *Le Testament d'un poète juif assassiné* 133-134, 135-136, 138-139, 140, 142-144
in *La Ville de la chance* 68-69, 75, 79
"fifth son" (*Cinquième fils*) 145, 148, 149
Fine, Ellen 6, 43, 189
"Four Sons" (Passover ritual; *Cinquième fils*) 133
"Four Questions" (Passover ritual) 48
Frankl, Viktor 33, 49-50, 173
Freud, Sigmund 134, 191

G
Gabriel (angel) 188
Gavriel (character) 86, 88, 89, 90, 91, 94, 95, 97, 99-102
Genette, Gerard 18
gesture 46-47, 51, 52, 114-115
God
appears in silence 9-10, 12
in Auschwitz 33, 37, 38-39, 40-41, 42, 44
in *L'Aube* 46, 49
in *Le Crépuscule, au loin* 155, 156, 160, 161-163
in *Les Portes de la forêt* 87
in *La Ville de la chance* 66, 67, 69, 73-76, 83-84
needs humanity 162
plenitude of 110, 111

Golda (character) 50
Gracq, Julien 11
grand silence respiratoire-typographique (*blancs*)
    defined 16-17
    in *Le Cinquième fils* 145
    in *Le Crépuscule* 157, 162
    in *La Nuit* 33, 38
    in *Les Portes de la forêt* 89-91, 99
    Wiesel's use 23, 28-29
Grégor (character) 86, 87, 88, 89-102
Grisha (Gershon Kossover; character) 133, 134, 135, 142-144
    self-mutilation/mutism 134, 135
Gyula (character) 55-56

H
Haggadah 133, 134, 144
Hasidism
    influence on Wiesel ix, 3, 37, 103, 104
    perception of time 37
    prayer in 61
    silence in 7, 112
    views of evil/hatred 127, 128
    views of man 122, 124
healing 155, 157, 158, 159, 161, 163-164
heder (Hebrew school) 3, 90
Heimler, Eugene 32
hérem 121, 125, 126
Heschel, Abraham Joshua 33, 35, 61, 157-158
hinenni 9-10, 130, 153, 158, 160, 173
Hiroshima 25, 120, 127, 146
Hoffman, Edward 109, 110
Holocaust (see also *anus mundi*, Auschwitz, *hurban*, *shoah*, *univers concentrationnaire*) 1, 2, 6, 10, 20, 21, 22, 24, 25, 32, 45, 46, 49, 71, 82, 90, 91, 111, 126, 127, 140, 148, 149, 155, 165, 185
    etymology of word 14
    giving voice to 140
    impact on literature 20-26
    impossibility to describe 22-23, 32-33

hurban (see also *anus mundi*, Auschwitz, Holocaust, *shoah*, *univers concentrationnaire*) 118, 185

I
"Impatient One" (character) 77, 80, 81
indifference 40, 49, 68-69, 78-79, 126, 130-131
Indinopulas, Thomas 87
interior monologue (see silence and *sous-conversation proustienne*)
Isaac (biblical) 42-43, 44, 55-56
Israel (biblical) 98
Israel (name) 87
Israel (nation) 104, 170; see also Erez Yisrael

J
Jabès, Edmond 171
"J'Accuse" (Emile Zola) 39,
Jacob (biblical) 88, 97-99, 189
J'ai vu mon père en songe 140, 141
Jeremiah (biblical) 37
Jerusalem 104, 105-107, 110, 111, 115
Jew's mission 127, 151
Job (biblical) 25, 56, 171
Jonah (biblical) 73-75, 76, 78
Jour [*The Accident*] 49-56, 105
Journal d'Ariel (*Cinquième fils*) 145
Judas (biblical) 92-93, 189
Jung, Karl 85, 100, 102

K
kaddish 101, 180-181
Kalman (character) 65, 66-67, 83
Kathleen (character) 53, 54, 56
Katriel (character) 109, 110, 111-114, 115
kav 108, 183
kavana 63-64
kdusha (holiness) 35
keter (*sefira*) 109, 110, 111, 112, 183
kinnui 161
Knopp, Josephine 50, 51, 80
Kolvillàg

etymology 117-118, 190
death of 129-131

L

language
debasing of 22
inherent weakness of 12-15, 21, 22, 23, 24-25, 33, 145
Leib, "the Lion" (character) 89-90
Lévinas, Emmanuel 15, 47, 71, 153
Lifton, Robert Jay 146-147
listening 91-92
Liyanov 138, 140
love 114-116
lying 52-53

M

Maccoby, Hyam 189
Madame Calinescu 169-170
Madame Schächter (character) 37
madmen 123, 154
madness 154, 155, 157, 158, 162, 165
mahzor 188
Maidanek 140-141
malhut (sefira) 109-110, 112, 115, 183
Malka (character) 109, 112-116
Malkiel (character) 165-170
Mallarmé, Stéphane 11, 15-16, 157
Malraux, André 5, 24
Mandelstam, Ossip 137
Maria (character) 91, 94, 179
Martha (character) 69
Mauriac, François 5, 20, 39, 45-46
Méditations obliques (see Paritus-le-Borgne)
Meir (character) 69
Melville, Herman 122
Memmi, Albert 88
memory 154, 164, 165, 168
loss of 166-167, 168
Menachem (character) 77, 80, 81
Mendiant de Jérusalem [A Beggar in Jerusalem] 103-117, 117
menuhah 35, 186
messenger 47, 67, 68, 88, 94, 100
Messiah 66, 150

messianic era 163
Michael (character) 60, 61, 62-84, 90, 105, 155, 161, 163
Moché-le-Bédeau (character) 33-34, 37
Moishe-le-Fou (character) 65, 74, 83
Moses (biblical) 10, 109, 160, 173
Moshe (character) 109, 123, 124-125, 126, 191
Mountain Clinic 154, 158, 159, 160
mutism 14, 15, 134, 135
mysticism 107-108, 155

N

Nachman of Bratslav 137
Nagasaki 25
nameless youth (*Serment de Kolvillàg*) 118, 120, 127, 157
names 87
eternal elements in 87
importance for Jews 142, 160 187
importance for Wiesel 70, 71
of God 72, 97-98, 155, 171
revoicing 93, 96-97, 101, 142
significance of *Gershon* 143
significance of *Michael* 70-71
significance of *Paritus-le-Borgne* 147-148
significance of *Pedro* 71,
significance of *Tamar* 167-168
silence of 87, 88, 188
surnames 160-161
navenadnik 78, 118, 121
Neher, André 6, 7, 26, 41, 48, 96, 105, 107
ne'ila ("closing the gates") 62, 80
Niylas 167, 168
nouveuax romanciers 20, 36
nuclear holocaust 127-128
Nuit [Night] 5, 6, 31-44, 91, 100, 103, 146, 161
Akeda in 42-44
elements of silence in 33, 38
family in 34, 41-42
father-son relationship in 42-44
God in 32, 33, 28-29, 40-41, 44

O

Ortega y Gasset, José 19
"other"/ "Other" 68, 78, 79, 157
see also *autre/Autre* and *l'Autrui
Oublié* [*The Forgotten*] 164-170
etymology of French title 166
father-son relationship 164-165,
169, 170

P

page blanche (white page) 14, 15-
16, 90, 100-101, 145, 170
Wiesel's use 23, 28-29
Paltiel (Kossover; character) 134-144
Parain, Brice 12, 13, 57
Paritus-le-Borgne (character) 147-
148
Passover 144
Pedro
in *La Ville de la chance* 70, 71-73,
74-75, 76, 77, 81, 83, 154, 155
in *Le Crépusucule, au loin* 154-164
Peniel (biblical) 88-89, 97-99
Petruskanu (character) 92-94, 179
photographs 136, 142, 191
phylacteries (see *tefillin*)
Picard, Max 17, 57, 107, 121, 136
Pinkas 118, 121, 123, 126, 190
Portes de la forêt [*Gates of the Forest*]
85-102, 179
prayer 61, 62, 83, 157, 158, 164
"prière"/ "prayer" 61, 63, 78, 105
Psalm 150 38-39

Q

Qu'est-ce que la littérature? (J.-P.
Sartre) 5, 21, 24, 25
questions 6, 27, 29, 41, 45, 49, 53,
113, 116, 150, 171

R

rape 168, 169-170
Raphael (character) 155, 156, 157,
158-164
Rawicz, Piotr 20, 21
récit 104
responsibility 60, 116, 134, 162-
163, 170

Reuven (Tamiroff; character) 134,
144-145, 146, 147
revolt against God 96-97, 124-125,
140-141, 159, 162
Roth, John K. 161
Rousset, David 25, 32
Russel, Paul (character) 53, 54

S

Sabbath
in *La Nuit*, desecration of 34-35
sanctity of 35
Samuel (biblical) 10, 160, 173
Sarah (character) 54
Sartre, Jean-Paul
authentic Jewishness 100
existential elements in *Les Portes
de la forêt* 99-100
lying according to 52
role of literature/writer 5, 21, 22,
24
silence 17, 25
Scholem, Gershom 14, 108, 110,
182
Second Generation 134, 144, 146,
148, 165
sefirot (*sefira*, singular) 108, 109-
110, 183-184
Serment de Kolvillàg [*The Oath*] 117-
131, 156
silence in 121-122
sexual union 110, 114
Shaddai 72, 155
Shehina 64, 78, 108, 112, 113-114,
115, 184
Shmuel (character) 126
shoah (see also *anus mundi*,
Auschwitz, Holocaust, *hurban*,
univers concentrationnaire) 21,
53, 75, 118, 134, 140, 155, 156,
165, 171, 185
shteible 100-101
shtetl 3, 4, 32
Sighet 2, 3, 35, 105
in *La Nuit* 32, 34, 35, 37
Signes d'exode 144
silence
as metaphoric character (*Le Serment
de Kolvillàg*) 118, 120, 121

as regenerative force 6, 7, 23
as response to Holocaust 20-26
as response to tragedy 25, 131
as taboo 19
auffallen as 146
biblical 26
death as 49-51, 52, 122, 126-131, 134
definitions (general) 10, 11-13
definitions (Wiesel) 7
divine 12, 27-28, 29, 30, 38-39, 40, 41, 49, 49, 71-72, 84, 125
existential nature of 17
forgetting as 164-165, 166
grand silence typographique-respiratoire 16-17, 23, 28-29, 89-91, 99, 145, 157, 162
in Jerusalem 105, 106
in novel 18-20
listening and 91-92
literary function of 16, 18-20
lying as 52-53, 54
madness as 162
multiplicities of 7, 94, 112, 121, 123
mutism in *Le Testament* 134-136
mystical 107-108, 110, 112, 116
names and 87, 88
negation as 18, 130
negative ontology 12, 13-14, 15, 130, 174
page blanche 14, 15-16, 23, 28-29, 90, 100-101, 145
photographs as 136
positive ontology 11-13, 14, 15-18, 90-91
punctuation and 18, 38
signifying power 12, 173-174
signifying weakness 12-13, 145
sous-conversation proustienne 19, 47, 53, 156, 157
unnameable as 156, 166
unspeakable 25-26, 28, 32, 157, 166
Wiesel's rhetoric of 26-30
"Silent One" (character) 72, 77, 81, 82, 85, 161
Six Day War 104, 106, 109, 114

sous-conversation proustienne 19
Soviet anti-semitism 141, 143
Soviet Jewry 135, 137, 141
Spanish Civil War 141
Steiner, George 13, 21-22, 38, 127
struggling as leitmotiv 88, 89, 97-99
survivor guilt 146, 147, 187
Szklarczyk, Lillian 50, 86, 87, 175

T

Tamar 167-168, 170
tears 51, 56, 80, 81
tefillin 139-144, 151
    significance of 191
teshuva ("return") 60, 90, 187-188
    defined by Wiesel 60, 76
    in *La Ville de la chance* 60-61, 62, 63, 64-65, 76, 84, 87
Testament d'un poète juif assassiné [*The Testament*] 133-144, 151
    father-son relationship in 135-136, 138-139, 140, 142-144
    mutism 134-136
tikkun (tikkun olam) 108, 109, 114, 159, 184
time 33, 34-37
translation ix, 75, 187, 191, 192
Trilling, Lionel 24
"Trilogy" (*La Nuit, L'Aube, Le Jour*) 50, 57, 59
Tzur 72-73, 155, 156, 160

U

univers concentrationnaire (see also *anus mundi*, Auschwitz, Holocaust, *hurban, shoah*) 4, 5, 21, 24, 25, 31-32, 37, 38, 42, 43, 44, 53, 54, 95, 103, 114, 127, 134, 144, 174
    ethos in 43
    language and silence 103
    literary treatment 25

V

Valéry, Paul 21
Varady (character) 65, 74, 83
viddui 143

Ville de la chance [*Town Beyond the Wall*] 59-84, 85, 86, 121, 154, 155, 157, 158, 160, 161, 163, 167
  prayer in 61-62
  "prière"/"Prayer" in 61, 63, 68
  Yom Kippur as metaphor in 66-83

W

Wahl, François 5
"wailing wall" 62
walls 105-106
Weil, Simone 174
Wells, Leon 25
Western Wall (Jerusalem) 106, 109, 112
white page (see *page blanche* and silence)
Wiesel, Elie
  arrival in France 5
  as *navi* 2
  birth 2
  childhood 3-4
  French language 5
  necessity for silence 4-5, 23, 25-26
  novels of (see individual listings)
  rhetoric of silence 26-30
  theme of silence 29-30
  views of universal genocide 127-128
Wittgenstein, Ludwig 21
witnessing 4, 124-125, 131, 135, 137
World Gather of Jewish Holocaust Survivors 144
World War I 22, 25

Y

Yankel (character) 67-68, 74
yeshiva 38, 100
yesod (*sefira*) 109, 110, 115, 116, 183
yizkor 65
Yom Kippur 41, 59
  in *La Ville de la chance* 59, 62, 63, 64-65, 66-83
yomim ne'orim 59, 73

Z

zimzum 182, 183
Zionism 47, 49
Zmirot (Sabbath songs) 34
Zohar 110, 111, 114
Zola, Emile 39, 179
Zupanev (character) 135-137